Mothering in the Third Wave

Edited by
Amber E. Kinser

Mothering in the Third Wave

Edited by
Amber E. Kinser

DEMETER
DEMETER PRESS
TORONTO, CANADA

Published by:
Demeter Press
726 Atkinson College, York University
4700 Keele Street
Toronto, Ontario M3J 1P3
Telephone: (416) 736-2100 x 60366
Email: arm@yorku.ca Web site: www.yorku.ca/arm

Demeter Press logo based on Skulptur "Demeter" by Maria-Luise Bodirsky <www.keramik-atelier.bodirsky.edu>

Cover Art: Barbara Bickel, "But," from the *Women "Enduring Freedom"* series, mixed media on board, 11" by 11", 2001. <www.barbarabickel.com>

Cover Design/Interior Design: Luciana Ricciutelli

Printed and Bound in Canada

Library and Archives Canada Cataloguing in Publication

        Mothering in the third wave / edited by Amber E. Kinser.

ISBN 978-1-55014-485-7

        1. Motherhood. 2. Third-wave feminism. 3. Feminist theory. 4. Mothers.
I. Kinser, Amber E., 1963-

HQ759.M8843 2008   306.874'301   C2008-903913-0

To Chelsea and Isaac for their faith in my mothering.
To Patrick for his faith in my writing.

Table of Contents

Part III: Mothering Contradictions

Part IV: Representing Motherhood

Acknowledgements

I am so very pleased to have had the opportunity to put this collection together. I had the good fortune of being affiliated with several generous and thought-full people. They supported and assisted this project, from the idea that germinated while reading and thinking with my partner Patrick on Surfside Beach, to the final book.

Thanks first to my friends and early graduate assistants, K. C. Gott and Mandy Render, for thinking the book was a good idea and believing I could bring it about. They helped me put together the book proposal and seek out publishers, edit early drafts of the essays, and configure the structure of the book. Thanks to Jamie Collier and Alexandria Mitchell Bradley who stepped in to assist with editing essays, and to Jamie for also doing research on the mama writers. My eternal thanks to my graduate assistant Lahla Deakins, without whose keen eye, meticulous attention to detail, and ability to convert both our editorial thinking to MLA style, I would have been in over my head. Thanks for seeing the book through to publication and for catching all the things I missed.

Much appreciation for my department chair at East Tennessee State University, Charles Roberts, who gave me the freedom to do interdisciplinary work in general, and in Communication and Women's Studies specifically. Thanks to the College of Arts and Sciences at ETSU for encouraging me to present my projects and ideas to the college faculty as the 2006 Jewell Friend Lecturer; and to ETSU for my research leave during which I formulated the book. I am indebted to my colleague and very good friend, Kelly Dorgan, with whom I have been fortunate enough to share working space. She has been a tremendous inspiration to me. Her keen mind and slicing wit have sustained me through much unrest—personal, professional, political.

Thanks to each of the contributors to this book who were so wonderful to work with, and who helped me evolve and shape the work. I appreciate your courageous writing; your openness about revisions, even on short notice; and your excitement about the project. Thanks to hattie gossett, whose essay "who told you anybody wants to hear from you? you ain't nothing but a black woman!" in *This Bridge*

Called My Back, affirmed my "crisis of confidence" feelings, even while giving me hope that I could do a book anyway.

Thanks to Andrea O'Reilly at Demeter Press and the Association for Research on Mothering (ARM) for being ready for this book. When I first approached Andrea with the proposal in my hand, even before I introduced the idea, she told me, "We need to do a book on mothering and third wave." I handed her the proposal and the book took off. I also thank Andrea for trusting my judgment on the essays and for construing "research" more broadly than most academic publishers. Thanks to Renée Knapp at Demeter and ARM for her high energy and peaceful spirit; she has been kind to me and patient with me from the beginning.

My family deserves special mention for their support and encouragement throughout the project, and long before that. Thanks to my mother, Lila Gail, who taught me much of what I know about good mothering; and who has always trusted my ability to do with it what was best for me and for my family. She boasted to relatives via email about the release of the book before it was ever finished. I am grateful to my two tender, bright, and courageous children, who taught me the rest of what I know about good mothering; and who helped make room in our family for my writing. To Chelsea who introduced me to mothering through my first pregnancy; she keeps me focused on third wave thinking as a young, powerful, techno-savvy, and playful feminist in her own right. To Isaac, who embodies the best of the genders; he teaches me to make feminism about boys and masculine culture too. Thank you for announcing proudly, "I am a feminist." I continue to learn from both of my children that my feminism must be limber to be any good. I owe a great deal to my fiercely devoted partner, Patrick, who has believed in me as a thinker more than anyone else. He willingly shared two years of our vacations and weekends with essays and endless conversations about feminist mothering. Thank you for knowing the book would happen, even when all I was working with were emails.

Introduction

Thinking About and Going About Mothering
in the Third Wave

AMBER E. KINSER

This is a book about struggle and complexity. It is a book about women trying to build families out of feminism, ambivalence, and contradictions. Such is the state of mothering in the twenty-first century. Such is the state of mothering in this third wave feminist era.

Mothering in the third wave calls for, among many things, an admission that feminism is messy, and a concession that this isn't something we need to "fix." It means mothering in an *intergenerational space* (borrowing from Jennifer Purvis's work on Kristeva's "Women's Time")—mothering from a site of unusual multiplicity, positionality, opportunity. It means mothering in a time characterized, as Rory Dicker and Alison Piepmeier note, by "global capitalism and information technology, postmodernism and postcolonialism, and environmental degradation" (10). Third wave era mothers are mothering through terrorism, war, and the Patriot Act; through eating disorders and meth epidemics; through hurricane Katrina and other disasters—natural and unnatural. We are fighting marriage bans for some families and marriage promotion campaigns for others; abstinence-only sex "education" and problems of the *No Child Left Behind Act*. We are fighting unprecedented threats to *Roe v. Wade* and to freedoms of speech and religion. We have struggled to reconcile our own perceptions and experiences of the "Mommy Wars" and the "Opt-Out Revolution," with the media hype and sensationalism about these issues.[1] Our families confront pressure to consume, to conform, and to conflate religion with principled action. We explain the atrocities of Abu Ghraib and the importance of sustainable living to our children, while they explain the relationship functions of Facebook and the utility of T9 Word to us (and the techno-savvy among us respond, "Yes, I know"). We mother in tension with the unattainable model of intensive mothering that structures our own thinking in many ways, and that of the people and institutions that populate our lives in many more. These are among the conditions that shape our lives and our families; these are among the conditions to which our mothering practices respond.

While the writers featured here identify as feminist, we have different names for our feminisms: second wave, third wave, libertarian, humanist, and radical;

some prefer Womanist to feminist, or no label at all. Regardless of the location from which we write, the material conditions in which we find ourselves, and the approaches to feminism or mothering we embody, we write as women trying to navigate our way through the sometimes smooth but usually choppy, even treacherous, waters of a third wave era. In this book, we tried to find ways to talk about contemporary feminism and mothering that do not further extend the debates about what gets to count as third wave feminism, though these certainly have been legitimate and useful. Rather, we get to the point of exploring what feminist mothers right now are struggling with and wrestling through. In that exploration, we blur the boundaries between our own mother stories and the empowered mothering vision and imagination of other women writers. We contest the divisions between our experiences and our critical examinations of the institution of motherhood. Recognizing, as have those who have written before us, that the personal is political, we refuse to choose between theory and narrative.

* * *

Dear Jeanin,

When you were in first grade, your school offered the option to be a basketball player or to be a cheerleader. Girls were allowed to play ball but few did; I don't know if boys were allowed to cheer, but none did. Knowing full well my feelings about the girls cheering the team's successes from the sidelines, you, not surprisingly, chose to play basketball, even though you certainly could have opted out of that institution altogether with no dispute from me, a total sports failure, unless you count my own stint with cheerleading which scarcely counted as athletics back in the day, at least not at my ultra conservative school where our skirts were down to our knees on campus (though well up our thighs once we were off campus, situated as we were in the late 1970s).

You hated basketball. I saw myself in you vividly. You held your stomach in pain, or "pain," as you ran in practice; you stayed in the outer margins of the action and out of the fray during the games. You would come over to me mid-game and put your head in my lap and for the life of me I couldn't figure out what was the best parenting move at this point, what would a good feminist mother do here? My gut response, as someone who as a little girl sat in the outfield while playing on a softball team (and I do mean sat—down on the ground), was to say to you, "Who needs this? Screw it. You don't have to put yourself through this; who cares?" But I feared I would only be licking my own old wounds of sports inadequacy that way. Perhaps the best thing was to teach you to be strong and to believe in yourself and to get back out there. Girls can play sports too, you know! YOU GO GIRL! But then I wondered if you would have signed up for basketball in the first place if it weren't for me expecting you to be some kind of first grade feminist icon, here in a nearly rural part of Tennessee, where the principal had two Bibles on his office bookshelf which I thought might shoot lightening at me as someone who left the Baptist church years ago and then had the lapse of reason to return to Baptist country. This is the principal who boasted that

2

they were the only school in the county still using corporal punishment. "How proud you must be," I said, endearing myself to him to be sure.

I wondered how bad cheerleading could be in first grade, the idiocy of offering only basketball and cheerleading as the entire extra-curricular programming at this K-8 school notwithstanding. Besides, what kind of a feminist hypocrite would be a cheerleader herself, and then get all above it when her daughter wants to cheer? Or is it feminist to help your children to learn from your mistakes? Was cheerleading a mistake for me? I remember what Aurora Levins Morales wrote in 1981:

> *Sitting in a kitchen in oh-so-white New Hampshire with old friends, mother and daughter, Ceci says 'It takes three generations. If you resolve your mother you'll both change, and your daughter will have it easier, but her daughter will be raised differently. In the third generation the daughters are free. (93)*

I wonder if you are part of that third generation, or will it be your daughter?

So you dropped out of basketball and joined cheerleading, an enterprise lead by a former homecoming queen about my age (my own position on the homecoming court at one point not at issue here.... Is it?) You were much happier on the squad than on the team and for the most part this felt comfortable to me but I'm still not convinced that I handled that whole thing well. I'm still not convinced I did you justice by playing into the basketball-cheerleading dichotomy and not offering you some other alternative. I wonder, if I weren't such a sports failure, if I could have helped you through that by shooting some hoops (not that I even could) or running some drills (I don't even know if that's what real sports people even say). Maybe I should have offered to help with cheerleading by offering some alternatives to the "Whoopsie" and "Firecracker" cheers,[2] for example. But I really didn't. Since then, and now high school, you've gone out for a couple of teams, sometimes making it, often not, and then started looking at high school cheerleading. I tried hard to mean what I said when I told you I want you to have the power to make your own choices. I reasoned that there are college scholarships for cheerleading, that it's much more athletic than it used to be, that cheerleaders aren't just sex objects anymore.... (Right?) As it turns out, and to my delight (which I tried not to make too obvious), you ended up thriving on the cross country team. But our struggles are far from over.

Will they get you anyway, Jeanin? Will the immense liberation promised by the information technology directing your future deliver immense constraint instead? Are the hours you spend online with (people I hope are) your friends—this significant part of your social life and your necessary separation from me—just that? Or do these hours suggest a potential problem I should be mediating? What are the limits of personal agency? My sense is that you have acted wisely online, but I wonder: will displaying your body and touting your exploits (actual or mythical) on your MySpace page matter more to you later than they do now? If I Google you right now, or a few years from now, what will I find? What will your future job prospects find when they go there (and they will) to learn more about you? What will you find as you surf and scroll for images that help you figure out who you are? Will consumption be your only identity resource? How much will you absorb? How much will you deflect? Do you have the skill to fight the incursion? Remember the struggle captured in Rosario Morales' words:

> *Being female doesn't stop us from being sexist we've had to choose early or late at 7 14 27 56 to think different dress different act different to struggle to organize to picket to argue to change other women's minds to change our own minds to change our feelings ours yours and mine constantly to change and change and change to fight the onslaught on our minds and bodies and feelings. (93)*

And what kind of a freak will that make you, Jeanin?

You want, as I did in my teen years, for the high school guys your age to like you, to be drawn to you. And yet you were not taught a masculine model of womanhood so they don't understand what you are; they weren't taught a framework for understanding your womanness lived freely. They fear the power that rises in you. And though you are not overly concerned about that (something else I envy you for), I know it is troubling to you, and that I am part of that, and I am sorry.

But I continue to muck my way through feminist mothering with you, confident that loving you through feminism constitutes the greatest of affections, and simultaneously secretly terrified that I've done the entire thing wrong. I admire your wit, your confidence and playfulness, and your occasionally problematic (but mostly enviable) sense of entitlement. I love you fiercely.

* * *

Mothering in the third wave means we are living and writing from a climate of increasingly conservative and other problematic US politics that reverberate across the globe and affect us all in profound, though different, ways. We do motherwork in tension with a postfeminist ideology, which asserts that all necessary freedoms for women have been won and that any further work toward emancipation is simply unnecessary—even silly. And all of *this* makes it harder for all of *us* to see the necessity of feminism, and the nuances of feminism. It is harder to feel "the click" of feminist awakening anymore, perhaps a defining characteristic of life in the third wave (Kinser). It means mothering in a time when twines of international warfare, hate, distrust, and danger are tightly interwoven with twines of massive materialism and pressure to consume—into a rope, a noose even, that threatens to strangle the humanity right out of us. But it also means mothering from politics that are relentless in their efforts: to fight what Vivien Labaton and Dawn Lundy Martin refer to as "global hypercapitalism and human exploitation;" to channel our technology so that it emancipates us rather than annihilates us; to challenge insidious and ubiquitous hierarchies of power and oppression (xvii).

Our work here is grounded, not only in our experiences with mothering and confronting the institution of motherhood, but also in the ideas of women who have written before us. Second wave and Womanist writers on mothering, writers on third wave feminism, and still others who have blurred boundaries between printed and electronic forms of mother writing inform our thinking and that of our contemporaries. They all have contributed to current understandings and experiences of feminist mothering in the current era. In the section that follows, I situate our *Mothering in the Third Wave* collection among a larger body of women's writings, both about third wave feminist thinking and about motherhood. My goal for this book is not to make definitive claims about "third wave feminism" or to provide an exhaustive discussion of contemporary motherhood; but rather to interweave considerations of mothering and feminism with third wave sensibilities, and to contribute new voices and tunes and tones to the cacophony.

Writings about Mothering and Feminism in These Times

The body of third wave texts that proliferated in and since the 1990s (including Daisy Hernández and Bushra Rehman; Barbara Findlen; Rebecca Walker; Leslie Heywood and Jennifer Drake; Jennifer Baumgardner and Amy Richards) focused on multiple goals. They worked to articulate what it means to be a third wave feminist; to differentiate second from third wave thought; to justify a rhetoric of "third wave;" and to amplify voice for a new generation of feminists. Such voice focused on younger women's experience and thinking, honored their technological and pop culture savvy, and resisted mightily any narrow definitions of feminism. Later third wave work (Astrid Henry, Rory Dicker and Alison Piepmeier, Vivien Labaton and Dawn Lundy Martin) extended beyond the personal narrative strengths of these texts by focusing more pointedly on theoretical and critical perspectives, and on grounding these in a larger politics of resistance and change. More recent third wave-spirited texts (Melody Berger, Jessica Valenti) continue to evolve feminist work as more accessible for broader young constituencies. Still other texts that inform third wave thinking (even if not identifying with a "third wave" label), such as those by Gloria Anzaldúa; Asian Women United of California; Joy Harjo and Gloria Bird; Daisy Hernández and Bushra Rehman; and Cherríe Moraga and Gloria Anzaldúa, are noted for their emphasis on the experiences and theoretical and aesthetic contributions of women of color. These are typically less focused on "feminist" consciousness than women's consciousness emergent from intersections of race, ethnicity, and culture.

Mothering in the Third Wave follows in the tradition of these texts in its resistance to narrow definitions of feminist living, and in its attention to the particular complexities of feminist life in an era characterized by postfeminist, thank-goodness-the-struggle-is-over ideology. Our book offers considerations of how globalism, technology, and pop-culture shape the form and content of our feminist mothering. It also is similar to these texts in its use of an accessible, narrative style that we hope will appeal to a large constituency of readers, including those who may not self-identify as "feminist" or as academics. *Mothering in the Third Wave* further extends these works in that it moves away from articulating a third wave rhetoric, and toward using "third wave" to describe a current era of feminist living. That is, it conceptualizes third wave as a political moment—a third space (Purvis)—which is not necessarily age- or politics-restrictive. We use "third wave" to characterize intersections of feminism and contemporary life, rather than individuals or specific politics. Our point is not to say that "third wave" can not be about these other things, or "restricted" in these other ways. We simply aim here to think hard about feminist mothering these days; to confess and confront its tensions; to consider the ways we may be uniquely situated; and to write about all of it in ways that "put experiential flesh on these cognitive bones" of ours (Turner and Turner 41).

Third wave work on mothering, though sparse, predominantly is written from the perspective of the daughter, most typically as a way of moving away from traditional family practices and toward more feminist, less prescriptive ones, or as a way of articulating sources and forms of power that are different from that of the mother's (essays in Daisy Hernández and Bushra Rehman's volume are illustrative, as are those in Cherríe Moraga and Gloria Anzaldúa's third wave catalyst, *This Bridge Called My Back*). Other texts include explorations of the interrelationships of ethnicity and motherhood, honoring the motherhood work characterizing various cultures (Patricia Bell-Scott and Beverly Guy-Sheftall et al; Joanna Kadi). Still other, more mainstream, feminist texts (Shari Thurer; Ann Crittenden; Susan Douglas and Meredith Michaels; Miriam Peskowitz; Judith Warner) offer critical perspectives on images and representations of mothers/mothering, and challenge conventional definitions of motherhood.

A proliferation of writing on modern mothering and how women are respond-ing to it emerges in part from the online "momosphere" (Tucker, this volume). Mama writers such as Andrea Buchanan and Amy Hudock; Ayun Halliday; Jennifer James; Camile Peri and Kate Moses; Ariel Gore; Amy Anderson and Sheri Reed; and Bee Lavender—not to mention the plethora of blogs populated by everyday lay writer moms—comprise this authorial community, which also has overlapped online writing with books in print. Highlighting self-defining motherhood identity, these works explore the every day grinds of mothering, unabashedly exposing its darker sides on one hand and its laughable ironies on the other. Frequently feminist in spirit if not in name, such writing extended the reach and widened the audience for thinking about and going about mothering in more self-determined ways.

Mothering in the Third Wave represents an effort to help formulate and amplify a narrative of feminist mothering in contemporary times. Like Cherríe Moraga's work, ours is written from the perspectives of mothers. Our essays offer new insights for interrogating motherhood. They weave together the personal, accessible, and even creative style found in Maureen Reddy, Martha Roth, and Amy Sheldon's volume, with the political and critical examinations of "mothering against" the patriarchal institution of motherhood found in Andrea O'Reilly's work. We strove to extend our reach even further than these texts through: considerations of third wave era social and political concerns, interrogations of feminist confu-sions and contradictions, and a commitment to drawing from women-of-color writers for insight. And yet we recognized as we wrote, as Chrystos did in *Bridge*, that feminism simply does not give us "any answers for correct behavior" in our own lives (68-69).

* * *

Dear Danny,

I found it much more difficult to provide gender-neutral alternatives for you than for your sister. It was nearly impossible to find you clothes that weren't about machinery, sports, or aggressive cultural icons. I probably could have found better selections if we weren't shopping at Wal-Mart, but I was just starting out professionally then and didn't have the financial luxury of boycotting Wal-Mart's practices of class oppression and sexism. Now I have the class privilege of making a "political stance" out of not shopping there (until we needed shin guards for soccer). So, though I placed resistance wherever I could, for the most part you looked like the majority of other boys in your world, wearing the costumes appropriate to performing masculine culture. But you didn't have guns or swords or aggressive action figures. Oh sure, you had Max Steel, but the scuba diving, rock climbing ones, not the ones with weaponry! (That scuba gun was about some sort of fishing I think.) And then somebody bought you a sword and I turned the other way, so somebody bought you another. And you loved them. I stood firm, though, when you wielded them at me! Then your stepbrothers bought you two cap guns with holsters, and you loved them too. I didn't. But I chose to let that go also. I wanted your sister to take karate so that she could learn body confidence, and you to take karate so that you could learn discipline and a set of standards about fighting, since I apparently was not going to forbid it. I admired people I knew who opposed fighting of any kind, feminists who would never let their children have swords or guns…. Maybe their kids didn't invent "shook-a-lizers" like you did, imaginary tools that seemed to function suspiciously like guns but that you assured me were not, as it turned out, guns. Maybe their kids did and they were more steadfast about opposing that kind of play. Maybe they eventually just caved like I did. We did draw some lines; we didn't do G.I. Joes, or buy any toy assault guns, or buy camouflage clothes or army trucks, despite the upsurge in these products and the fervent consumption of them post 9/11. You weren't allowed to aim at real people. I don't know if any of those choices had any useful feminist effect. They felt like they were operating by some kind of feminist standard at the time but they don't look very impressive here in print.

I remember clearly the day your stepdad brought home a Batman costume, complete with six-pack stomach muscles and rippling pecs and arms (a person who was not a sports failure would know the names of these arm muscles…biceps?). You put that costume on and I stood your little body up on the dining room table so that you could see your full form in the mirror. You were consumed by sheer thrill at your reflection, giggling with such delight and staring so intently at this adult-looking body reflected back at you, this powerful, capable, disciplined body claiming to be yours. And I felt my feminism shape-shifting again, reforming to accommodate the legitimacy of a little, powerless child feeling powerfully embodied, re-cognizing that this was no less legitimate for you because you are a boy. This was an unprecedented moment of child empowerment for you; you became convinced that you would, in fact, be "big" someday. I decided that this was a good thing to feel, regardless of sex or gender. I decided in this moment, and not for the first or the last time, that feminist living is messy and complicated and always more complex than it seems. A boy is not simply a passive sponge that inevitably absorbs dominant mainstream messages until he is so saturated that he can't absorb any of the alternative, feminist ones his mother has been teaching him. I don't have to choose between, on one hand, deflecting every dominant message about masculinity, or on the other, giving you over to masculinist forces. I can continue teaching you tools for feminist living that will help you navigate these treacherous waters. But my position here shouldn't be confused with those parents who let their boys purchase toys of aggression willy-nilly, with parents who excuse what un-nerves them in their sons by reciting, "Boys will be boys," with parents who are doing nothing to resist masculinist forces, because our positions really are quite different and really will have different outcomes.... (Won't they?)

Will they get you anyway, Danny? That tenderness in you that buries a baby bird fallen from its nest in winter and whispers a prayer, until the butcher-than-you boy next door mocks you. Will you come to prefer, always, playing with swords to caring for the earth and her creatures? Will the assault of mediated images that seduce you to buy, buy, buy bigger, better, faster commodities of aggression, oppression, accumula-tion tear the gentleness from you? Will you ever be able to see, from your position of privilege, the link between this consumption and the problems it creates worldwide? Will you be able to reconcile loving your Vietnam War vet father with your anti-war stance, and that with your swordplay and self-made Daniel Boone costume? Will your passions for skateboarding and electric guitar send you on journeys into masculine culture from which you may not fully return?

And I wonder now just what my role is relative to your notable affection for video games. Philosophically, I see no difference between the modern combat games and Lord of the Rings games, yet I don't allow the former and do the latter. And most of the time I couldn't care less about your multiple race car games, yet I loathe the Nascar mentality that surrounds us in Tennessee and I don't know how to reconcile the two, or even if I should.

In the end, son, my loyalty is to you first, to my family, and not to feminism. I know I have made you a bit of a freak, and I hope that I have taught you the extra survival strategies you will need for that. I know that my raising you to be socially conscious and sex educated has shoved you out into the margins, and I am sorry. Dress warmly; it's cold out in those margins. I have tried to teach you—I hope I am succeed-ing—that, as Audre Lorde says, "Survival is not an academic skill. It is learning how to stand alone, unpopular and sometimes reviled." It is figuring out, she says, "how to make common cause with those others identified as outside the structures, in order to define and seek a world in which we can all flourish. It is learning how to take our differences and make them strengths. For the master's tools will never dismantle the master's house" (99).

You have challenged and changed my feminist perspectives more than any other person, my son. And yet, I feel most inadequate in mothering you, shaped as you are by masculine culture despite my efforts. Maybe because of them. I admire your tenderness and empathy, your body discipline, your charm. I hope my loving you through feminism had something to do with that. I love you fiercely.

* * *

The women who have contributed to this text come together from a wide variety of backgrounds and locations. We write from Africa, Canada, Japan, Romania, the UK and the US. We write about othermothers, stepmothers, lesbian mothers, allomothers, single mothers, and adoptive mothers. We write as soccer moms, displaced moms, biomoms, moms to our community, moms to our parents, moms to our adult children, moms-to-be, and participants in the momosphere. The mothers, children, and locations we write about are African, African-American, British, Canadian, Chicana, Japanese, mixed-race, Romanian, Swiss, and white. We live very different, multi-voiced, multi-faceted feminisms and motherhoods that we not only articulate and defend, but that we also try to live and practice, even as we question and doubt. We suspected that through our ambivalence, we had some feminist things to say about mothering in these times. In creating this book, we connected with each other about mothering by building bridges across feminisms.

Motherhood Transforming

In Part I of *Mothering in the Third Wave,* writers explore how definitions of mothering and motherhood modify to accommodate the changing cultural landscape of the family. Writers here explore the reciprocally transformative dimensions of mothering, motherhood, mother writings, and the larger political, socio-cultural sphere. In the first chapter, Heather Hewett unfolds her story as a white third wave woman forging a life as a feminist, a writer, and a mother through her readings of fiction and nonfiction by black women writers (such as Cecelie Barry, Toni Morrison, Alice Walker, and Buchi Emecheta) and by alternative online and print autobiographical writers on mothering (such as Ayun Halliday, Andrea Buchanan, Faulkner Fox, and Ariel Gore). Hewett argues that these writers offer her a way to reconceive mothering. Through their imaginative expansions of the multiple meanings of mothering, motherhood, and selfhood, they continue to expose the poverty of public rhetoric about, and images of, motherhood.

Maura Ryan argues that becoming a lesbian mother in the third wave must necessarily incorporate historical precedence, collectivity, and future goals for change. Ryan challenges a biomedical definition of family by exploring the varied other definitions of mothering that lesbian women have embodied before her. Her letter pays tribute to these women for laying the groundwork for her to mother in multiple ways. She also directs her writing toward the future to articulate the necessary challenge facing feminists of attending ever more pointedly to intersections of identity in the struggle to emancipate all people.

Laura Tuley offers two differently compelling texts in her discussion of mothering through post-Hurricane Katrina displacement. In the spirit of Kristeva's *Stabat Mater,* her essay juxtaposes excerpts from the "dispatches" she wrote for mamazine. com about displaced mothering with a more traditional, academic feminist analysis of her displacement as a third wave project. Her essay exemplifies the simultaneous connectedness and disconnectedness that characterize contemporary life, as it crystallizes the struggle to find a sense of place and home.

Lara Lengel, Anca Birzescu, and Jennifer Minda's essay emerges from first-hand experience in locations of global conflicts and terrorist attacks in the Middle East, the UK, and the US. Their chapter explicates the personal narratives of mothers in times of war and the "war on terror." The essay engages in dialogue between third and second wave feminist mothers, yet its tone and spirit come from the heart of mothers of all ages and eras who have lived through moments where they didn't know if their children were alive; and those mothers who have lost their beloved young to the senseless slaughter that results from global conflict.

Mothering Resistance

Part II looks at how mothering can function as a site of resistance—through mothering practices, and to the institution of "motherhood." It looks at how mothering can teach principles of revolution and how everyday resistance and community work can nurture others toward self-liberation. Larissa Mercado-López calls for a reconfiguration of the culturally entrenched tension between mothering and education. The ability of the Chicana mother in school to meet expectations to be the cultural preserver, family backbone, and spiritual adviser are further complicated when the academy demands time away from home and sharing of household responsibilities. Mercado-López argues that her culture regards her absence from the home as neglect, and her inability to perform her domestic 'duties' as incompetence. She proclaims that the Chicana mother must take up the struggle begun by the mothers within the Chicana Movement who practiced motherhood as activism, and who argued that education was imperative to the well-being of the mother, the children, and the Movement.

Marlene Fine's essay explores the implications of living a conventional life in an unconventional way. *What does it mean,* she asks, *when two "out" white lesbians raise two African American sons in a primarily white suburban community?* They are double transgressors, she answers. They transgress the norms of the community in which they live and raise their children by being lesbians, and they transgress the norms of the LGBT community by living a conventional lifestyle. Fine explores ways that cross-cultural lesbian mothering and LGBT community work present multiple sites of struggle, arguing that how her family lives their marginal lives functions as a powerful form of social activism.

Writing about resistance in adoptive mothering in her poetic piece, Andrea Fechner articulates the doubt, love, and anger confronting her as an adoptive mother of biracial, special needs children, particularly in light of her whiteness and privilege. She contests cultural images of motherhood as Utopia through her own stark images of motherhood as struggle, even as she admits that her brutal honesty, and her fear that her children might read the essay some day, "feel like hell."

Akosua Adomako Ampofo's essay draws from her experiences of being raised in Ghana, Africa and raising her own children there, as well as from her research on Ghanaian trans-racial families. She argues that while motherhood and the socialization of children has been an important arena of theoretical inquiry in feminist analyses, very little attention has been given to trans-racial, trans-ethnic and trans-cultural motherhood and its effects on transforming majority cultures. Adomako Ampofo explains that although the dominant groups in Ghana are influential in determining socializing norms and practices (including through formal spaces such as schools), mothers of "multi-racial," "multi-ethnic," and "multi-cultural" children in Ghana may contest, subvert or reproduce existing ethnic politics, and that such may transform majority cultures.

Mothering Contradictions

Part III particularly emphasizes ambiguity, tension, contradiction, and personal struggle in feminist mothering. Confronting the inconsistency and ambivalence in their own lives and identities, the contributors illustrate the irresolvable messiness of feminist living and show how the frictions that emerge are tensions to be lived with, rather than problems to be resolved. D. Lynn O'Brien Hallstein locates the tension between empowered mothering and intensive mothering as a uniquely "postfeminist" third wave phenomenon. Hallstein discusses the ways that her struggle against intensive mothering, both in Switzerland and the US, was grounded, perhaps ironically, in her experiences of being raised in the second wave with feminist sensibilities. The second wave's emphasis on giving birth to oneself, she argues, created a problematic silence about giving birth to and/or raising one's children, leaving her ill-equipped to counter the ideology of intensive mothering.

In my own essay, I confront some of the messy complexities emergent from the placement of mothering on a sexuality continuum. Using the essay as a site of simultaneous celebration and contestation, I resist the erotic/maternal split, and examine the compelling and repelling dimensions of appropriate but intense intimacy that can emerge between mothers and children. I argue that the conceptual excision of the erotic from the maternal results in an impoverished understanding of mothering.

Wendy Nakanishi's essay illuminates the complexities of feminist living in Japan and her struggle against firmly entrenched cultural traditions and patterns. Characterized by the conspicuous absence of the father, the Japanese home is typically structured in ways that work to compensate for the relentless study regimentation meted out in Japanese schools. This demands much effort from the mothers, not only to prepare children for that regimentation, but also to compensate for it by offering safe haven in the home. Nakanishi discusses her efforts to navigate her way through public and "private" spheres in ways that might help her to avoid resenting the ways that issues of nationality, gender, and age preoccupy her life.

Emerging from her life-long confrontations with body image, Lorin Arnold's poem uncovers the complex layering of mothering, eating disorders, and feminism. Confronted routinely by the centrality of food in mothering practices—by the inability to escape even for a moment the conversations, the homework, the family activities about food, the daily dinner planning, buying, cooking, smelling, serving, coaxing—Arnold confronts the limits of feminist thinking and teaching. She questions the extent to which she is, and teaches her children to be, empowered.

Kelly Dorgan's essay works to de-stigmatize maternal "militancy" by explaining how traditional, nurture-only models of mothering are inadequate for effectively parenting special needs children. In her bold writing, Dorgan both argues for incorporating a militant mom image into our cultural representations of motherhood, and confesses her secret fear that she is reinforcing patriarchal models of discipline and control. She speaks for many mothers whose challenged and challenging children render the available models of mother-love less than effective.

Representing Motherhood

The essays in Part IV interrogate cultural texts and how they image motherhood and represent mothering practices. Interacting with Cherríe Moraga's poetic life writings, Susan Driver explores how Moraga's work articulates narratives and images of queer mothering that defy binary sexual, racial, and gender ideologies. Driver interrogates her own reading of Moraga as a feminist queer daughter craving resistant languages about mothering, and as someone becoming a queer mother with her butch partner. Moraga's work shows vividly how her own choices and investments in mothering as a Chicana lesbian propel her desires in multiple directions through networks of blood relations, friends, lovers, and political alliances. Interweaving her own experiences and voice with Moraga's, Driver details the significance of recreating meanings of kinship as sites of resistance and healing.

S. Alease Ferguson and Toni King discuss the mother distress and non-commitment emergent among the African-American teen mothers with whom they work. They illustrate the complex warp of tensions among traditional African American inter-generational/motherline values and hip hop culture, particularly in light of variables such as the global society's changing definition of adolescent development, dysmorphic societal imagery of young black women, and perceived permanent underclass status. Ferguson and King further ground this third wave dilemma for African-American teen mothers in the distractions produced by the "heady progress of second wave advances."

Rachel Epp Buller interacts with the work of feminist artists and women artists-of-color, and explores how women artists' representations of motherhood have found form, and offered nuanced insight, for mothers from the 1970s through the current era. Focusing her discussion on works by second wave artists Bettye Saar and Mary Kelly, and third wave era artists Renée Cox and Carrie Mae Weems, Buller layers her own experiences as an art historian mom within the artists' images of motherhood, the female body, power, identity construction, and generational dialogue.

Finally, Judith Stadtman Tucker draws from her experience as editor of *The Mothers Movement Online* to talk about how third wave mothers incorporate various dimensions of the internet into their lives as a way of making sense of both their families and their personal identities. She discusses ways that alternative mothers' media—both online and print publications—have emerged and proliferated; and examines the role of weblogs in creating mother knowledge. She also notes the potentially limited extent to which the digital realm may offer effective paths of resistance.

Conclusion

The contributors to this anthology—as feminists and as mothers; as activists, revolutionaries, and outlaws in our own ways; as women who mother in this third wave—want our children and our communities to feel rightfully entitled to gender, sexuality, race, ethnicity, and class equity and freedom. And we want them to recognize that a *sense* of entitlement is not enough. We want them to see through the postfeminist lie that the time for struggle is happily over; and to continue in their vigilance to guard against complacency. We also want them to feel happy, to dress up, to play the sports they want to play and wear the tiaras they want to wear—both literal and figurative—despite what dominant culture or monolithic feminist arguments might say. The women and men with whom we live or partner or parent measure up to our ideals no more than we ourselves do, no more than perhaps even our children do. Still, these are the families and selves that comprise our lives and we want to love and laugh with them; we want to have lived lives that we felt were worth living. We recognize the limits of feminism in ensuring all of that. And still we continue in our mother journeys, through feminism's liberations and constraints, through its confidences and doubts, through its clarity and haze, to build and nurture and emancipate our families and our selves.

¹There has been much discussion in electronic, print, and television news media and trade publications, not to mention blogs, about women "opting out" of paid work outside the home (see for example Lisa Belkin's "The Opt-Out Revolution"; also Linda R. Hirshman's *Get to Work ... and Get a Life, Before It's Too Late*). Similar discussion has proliferated about public and private battles fought between at-home and at-work mothers (see for example Leslie Morgan Steiner's *Mommy Wars: Stay-at-Home and Career Moms Face Off on Their Choices, Their Lives, Their*

Families; also Miriam Peskowitz's *The Truth Behind the Mommy Wars*).
[2]"Whoopsie" is a cheer that goes: "We're number one, can't be number two, we're gonna beat the WHOOP-sie out of you!" The "whoopsie" part is done in a singsongy high-pitch, with particular emphasis on the first syllable. This part of the cheer is further accentuated, to my unprecedented terror, with the girls, who are out on the court at halftime (a sports person would know whether "halftime" is one word or two without having to use spellcheck), turning around and lifting their skirts to stick their rear ends toward the audience upon "WHOOP-sie". The first time I saw this I gasped aloud, literally clutching my chest and looking around for a compatriot only to see parents and grandparents smiling proudly at how "cute" it all was. "Firecracker" is an age-old cheer that goes: "Firecracker, firecracker, boom boom boom [hips shaking side to side on this part]. Firecracker, firecracker, boom boom boom The boys got the muscles, the teachers got the brains, the girls got the sexy legs and *we* won the *game!*" I asked if we could omit these cheers on the grounds that they weren't age-appropriate. The leader said no, since no other parents had complained. This legacy of being the only one to "complain" has followed me all of my days. Jeanin and I did create alternative words to this cheer which she would mouth to me in the stands as she cheered from the court: Firecracker, firecracker blah blah blah.... "The girls got the muscles, the girls got the brains, the girls got the sexy legs, no WONDER we won the game!" This moment of resistance was but a small victory.

Works Cited

Anzaldúa, Gloria, ed. *Making Face, Making Soul/Haciendo Caras: Creative and Critical Perspectives by Feminists of Color.* San Francisco: Aunt Lute, 1990.

Asian Women United of California, eds. *Making Waves: An Anthology of Writings By and About Asian American Women.* Boston: Beacon, 1994.

Baumgardner, Jennifer, and Amy Richards. *Manifesta: Young Women, Feminism, and the Future.* New York: Farrar, 2000.

Baumgardner, Jennifer and Amy Richards. *Grassroots: A Field Guide for Feminist Activism.* New York: Farrar, 2005.

Belkin, Lisa. "The Opt-Out Revolution." *The New York Times Magazine* 26 October 2003: 42.

Bell-Scott, Patricia, Beverly Guy-Sheftall, Jaqueline Jones Royster, Janet Sims-Wood, Miriam Decosta-Willis and Lucie Fultz, eds. *Double Stitch: Black Women Writers Write About Mothers and Daughters.* Boston: Beacon, 1991.

Berger, Melody, ed. *We Don't Need Another Wave: Dispatches from the Next Generation of Feminists.* Emeryville, CA: Seal, 2006.

Chase, Susan E. and Mary F. Rogers. *Mothers and Children: Feminist Analyses and Personal Narratives.* New Brunswick: Rutgers University Press, 2001.

Chrystos. "I Don't Understand Those Who Have Turned Away From Me." *This Bridge Called My Back: Writings by Radical Women of Color.* Eds. Cherríe

Moraga and Gloria Anzaldúa. New York: Kitchen Table; Women of Color, 1981. 68-70.

Crittenden, Ann. *The Price of Motherhood*. New York: Henry Holt, 2001.

Dicker, Rory, and Alison Piepmeier, eds. *Catching a Wave: Reclaiming Feminism for the 21ˢᵗ Century*. Boston: Northeastern University Press, 2003.

Douglas, Susan J. and Meredith W. Michaels. *The Mommy Myth: The Idealization of Motherhood and How it Has Undermined Women*. New York: Free, 2004.

Findlen, Barbara, ed. *Listen Up: Voices From the Next Feminist Generation*. Seattle: Seal, 1995.

Harjo, Joy and Gloria Bird, eds. *Reinventing the Enemy's Language: Contemporary Native Women's Writings of North America*. New York: Norton, 1997.

Henry, Astrid. *Not My Mother's Sister: Generational Conflict and Third-Wave Feminism*. Bloomington: Indiana University Press, 2004.

Hernández, Daisy and Bushra Rehman, eds. *Colonize This! Young Women of Color on Today's Feminism*. Emeryville: Seal, 2002.

Heywood, Leslie and Jennifer Drake, eds. *Third Wave Agenda: Being Feminist, Doing Feminism*. Minneapolis: University of Minnesota Press, 1997.

Hirshman, Linda R. *Get to Work ... and Get a Life, Before It's Too Late*. New York: Penguin, 2007.

hooks, bell. *Teaching to Transgress: Education as the Practice of Freedom*. New York: Routledge, 1994.

Kadi, Joanna, ed. *Food for Our Grandmothers: Writings by Arab-American and Arab-Canadian Feminists*. Boston: South End, 1994.

Kinser, Amber E. "Negotiating Spaces For/Through Third Wave Feminism." *NWSA Journal* 16.3 (2004): 124-153.

Kristeva, Julia. "Women's Time." Trans. Alice Jardine and Harry Blake. *Signs: Journal of Women in Culture and Society* 7.1 (1981): 13-35.

Kristeva, Julia. "Stabat Mater." *Tales of Love: European Perspectives*. Trans. Leon S. Roudiez. New York: Columbia University Press.

Labaton, Vivien and Dawn Lundy Martin, eds. *The Fire This Time: Young Activists and the New Feminism*. New York: Anchor, 2004.

Lorde, Audre. "The Master's Tools Will Never Dismantle The Master's House." *This Bridge Called My Back: Writings by Radical Women of Color*. Eds. Cherríe Moraga and Gloria Anzaldúa. New York: Kitchen Table; Women of Color, 1981. 98-101.

Moraga, Cherríe. *Waiting in the Wings: Portrait of a Queer Motherhood*. New York: Firebrand, 1997.

Moraga, Cherríe and Gloria Anzaldúa, eds. *This Bridge Called My Back: Writings by Radical Women of Color*. New York: Kitchen Table; Women of Color, 1981.

Morales, Aurora Levins. "...And Even Fidel Can't Change That!" *This Bridge Called My Back: Writings by Radical Women of Color*. Eds. Cherríe Moraga and Gloria Anzaldúa. New York: Kitchen Table; Women of Color, 1981. 53-56.

Morales, Rosario. "We're All in the Same Boat." *This Bridge Called My Back: Writings by Radical Women of Color*. Eds. Cherríe Moraga and Gloria Anzaldúa.

New York: Kitchen Table; Women of Color, 1981. 91-93.

O'Reilly, Andrea. *Rocking the Cradle: Thoughts on Motherhood, Feminism and the Possibility of Empowered Mothering.* Toronto: Demeter, 2006.

O'Reilly, Andrea. "Introduction." *Mother Outlaws: Theories and Practices of Empowered Mothering.* Ed. Andrea O'Reilly. Toronto: Women's, 2004. 1-30.

Peskowitz, Miriam. *The Truth Behind the Mommy Wars.* Emeryville, CA: Seal, 2005.

Purvis, Jennifer. "Grrls and Women Together in the Third Wave: Embracing the Challenges of Intergenerational Feminisms." *National Women's Studies Association Journal* 16.3 (2004): 93-123.

Reddy, Maureen, Martha Roth and Amy Sheldon. *Mother Journeys: Feminists Write about Mothering.* Minneapolis: Spinsters Ink, 1994.

Steiner, Leslie Morgan. *Mommy Wars: Stay-at-Home and Career Moms Face Off on Their Choices, Their Lives, Their Families.* New York: Random House, 2006.

Thurer, Shari. *The Myths of Motherhood.* Wilmington: Houghton, 1994.

Turner, Victor and Edith Turner. "Performing Ethnography." *The Drama Review* 26.2 (1982): 33-49.

Valenti, Jessica, ed. *Full Frontal Feminism: A Young Woman's Guide to Why Feminism Matters.* Emeryville, CA: Seal, 2007.

Walker, Rebecca. *To Be Real: Telling the Truth and Changing the Face of Feminism.* New York: Anchor, 1995.

Warner, Judith. *Perfect Madness: Motherhood in the Age of Anxiety.* New York: Riverhead, 2005.

Part I
Motherhood Transforming

1
Of Motherhood Born

HEATHER HEWETT

I am more than a little embarrassed to report my disdain of mothers in my pre-motherhood life. Now, of course, I understand it as a symptom of my immense confusion and ambivalence toward motherhood, a contempt from which, thankfully, I have now (mostly) recovered; but then, I think, I mainly experienced my condescension as a product of my feminism (haphazardly assembled, and thus poorly understood), which set me apart (or so I thought) from the women of my youth.

Perhaps the words "disdain" and "condescension" are too harsh to describe the complexity of my experience; but they do get at the depth and intensity of those feelings, how the stories I told myself about my life were shored up against simplified notions of who I was and who I was not. I was the white, middle-class girl who left the conservative Christian suburbia of her youth for college on the East Coast and never went back. I was the one who was destined for greater things than motherhood and family life, the one who wanted to succeed because of her brains and her talents, the one who would travel the world and write. I was not the women I saw around me, mothers who seemed to lose their own lives in the service of caring for children. Most emphatically, I was not *my* mother, who was also not these women, but who never managed to refute the popular belief that women who "had it all" could only do so at some great cost. A performing artist and professor, my mother managed to survive the death of one child and the disability of another only to struggle daily with the burdens of the second shift and the pain of experiencing her talents and ambitions undercut by depression and alcohol. According to my unexamined childhood logic, by not becoming my mother—that is, by not becoming *a* mother—I would avoid these painful and self-destructive conflicts between self and motherhood, creativity and procreativity, and self-fulfillment and caregiving.

If I am to be completely honest, I must admit that I still know very little about the lives of those other women, the stay-at-home, upper-middle-class mothers who lived around us. I knew them only as the mothers of my childhood friends. I witnessed them driving carpools and attending church. I assumed from their clothes and their cars that they had more money than my family, and I supposed that many of them harbored very strict ideas about religion and gender roles. For example, I knew that I received much more positive attention for my behavior as a "lady" (though I never could figure out what I did to elicit such unasked-for praise) than for my bookish predispositions. Finally, while a few of these women exhibited concern for me, and great kindness toward my disabled sister, they were not my mother's friends; looking back, I suspect that they were avoiding the turmoil of my family, sinking slowly under the combined weight of alienation and alcohol.

As a result, many years later, when I had a child and, subsequently, read Adrienne Rich's *Of Woman Born*, I thought of these women. Rich, of course, differentiates between the practice of mothering and the institution of motherhood, the latter of which, Rich argues, perpetuates male power and privilege. With this phrase, "institution of motherhood," I began to understand the rigid notions of gender that constrained men as well as women in my hometown. I realized that many of these women likely found personal empowerment in their daily acts of mothering; but what struck me growing up was the rigidity of their designated roles. Then, however, I had no words, no perspective, no framework for understanding my experience. I simply felt anger at the injustice of my mother's situation (why was it her lot to struggle with so many burdens, and not my father's?), a righteousness muddied by my rage at both of my parents for seemingly having forgotten about *me*.

I would be different, I decided. I would not have children.

Yet in my rejection of a motherhood imperative—the cultural expectation that young girls, upon attaining womanhood, would (indeed, should) become mothers themselves—I unwittingly adopted a limited and impoverished understanding of mothering in the name of an equally limited feminism. True, the feminism that I cobbled together provided explanatory power for many of the experiences of my childhood, and it fueled my passion for gender equity as it propelled me to focus on my career. But it did not do many things. It did not fashion a lens through which I could examine how my own means of rebellion against strict gender roles—primarily, my embrace of achievement, which led to college and, eventually, graduate school and an academic career—depended upon certain privileges of class and race. It did not cause me to reflect upon the unseen, structural forces that led to my mother's solitary struggle with alcohol. Nor did it provide me with words to articulate my love for a man, or the vocabulary to understand the slow budding of my own desire to have children with him.

Thus, for years, I found myself at something of an impasse, knowing only that I was determined to write my own story differently, and suspecting that the tools for this rewriting lay in feminism. But feminism can hold vastly different meanings; and as I have suggested, mine was ill-informed on several fronts. Interestingly (though upon reflection, perhaps not surprisingly), the process by which I came to understand the limitations of this feminism, the feminism of my childhood, came through reading the work of women very different from me—women who did not necessarily define their feminism in the privileged spaces of university classrooms and libraries, but whose critiques of second-wave feminism left their mark on me, as well as on other members of my generation, thus expanding and changing how many of us think of feminism itself.

* * *

To my dear children,
Florence, Sylvester, Jake, Christy and Alice,
without whose sweet background noises
this book would not have been written.
—Buchi Emecheta, *Second-Class Citizen* (1975)

I am sitting upstairs in a drafty room, wrapped in blankets, reading. It is the mid-1990s, and I am in graduate school. Outside, dusk's stillness has settled upon the piles of autumn leaves, scattered on the sidewalk. My mind ranges, back and forth between the interior spaces of my solitude and the story of my book. I imagine myself a stranger in England, an immigrant from Nigeria, fed up with her husband and saddled with children who must be cared for, somehow, without the help of family or money—without anything, really, save the necessity to survive and a powerful ambition to write. Such is the story of my novel's main character, Adah, whose life reflects the experiences of its author, the Nigerian-British writer Buchi Emecheta. As Alice Walker explains in a 1976 book review, Emecheta is a writer "because of, not in spite of, her children" (66). For Adah-Emecheta, Walker argues, there is no conflict between her identities as mother and writer; rather, her cultural heritage as an Ibo woman enables her to sidestep the opposition created by Western culture's division of procreation (seen as physical, bodily, and female) and creation (seen as mental, spiritual, and male).

When I read Walker's review of this novel, I am readily willing to accept her attack on a split that has permeated so much of my own conflicted understanding of writing and motherhood. I sense hope in the possibility that these two identities do not exist in some kind of predetermined and ultimately tragic conflict with one another. And yet, I remain baffled by Emecheta's novel, by the assertion that the task of raising children does not present insurmountable obstacles for the artist, who needs time, money, and space of her own. Is it truly possible that someone can write a novel while her children play in the same room? I remember my own mother's thwarted attempts to practice piano in the living room while I, a small child, demanded her attention, lunging for her feet as she attempted to pedal through Mozart's concerti. Emecheta's experience seems unrealistic and foreign. I am angered and confused by it, even as my inner being thrills to its call. Aware of the presence of long-repressed desires yet still afraid of them, I am unable, finally, to embrace anything, either my desire for children or my desire for creative self-expression. I am not split so much as riddled by doubt, afraid at every turn that I am making bad choices. This fear prevents me from fully accepting any one part of myself, let alone mustering up the audacity to embrace them all.

* * *

Alice Walker challenged mainstream second-wave feminism with her embrace of "womanism," with its pointed inclusion of men and family and its attention to issues of race as well as gender. Her turn to Emecheta's novel in order to explore the interconnectedness of mothering and creative work (in *Ms. Magazine*, no less) defies the notion that women must choose between work and motherhood. Indeed, Walker's reading of Emecheta's novel enabled her to articulate an alternative vision of what it meant to be a feminist and a mother, and of how black women might imagine a world with different possibilities.

Historically, of course, the world that most black mothers have lived in has not been kind. Most black mothers have not had the privilege of choosing work or motherhood; they have had to work outside the home, particularly in countries such as the United States, often raising "other people's children as well as their own" (Berry 10). This necessity has arisen from such factors as the legacies of slavery and segregation, the persistence of discrimination and institutionalized racism, and the frequent interconnections between race and class. In spite of the realities of black motherhood, of the way that racist barriers have prohibited real choice, countless black women have mothered nonetheless.

For essayist Cecelie Berry, this history provides an important context for her own choice to stay at home with her children, an option unavailable to many of the black women who came before her. In her anthology *Rise Up Singing: Black Women Writers on Motherhood*, Berry claims motherhood as significant political work: to "build with love the home and the family of your dreams is the ultimate revolution," she writes (13). Alternatively, for journalist Lonnae O'Neal Parker, this history provides the inspiration for continuing to "balance" paid work and motherhood. As she notes in *I'm Every Woman: Remixed Stories of Marriage, Motherhood, and Work*, the long tradition of black mothers who have worked provides her with a "tradition [in which] I find inspiration and, often, a self-correcting mechanism that saves me from my whines" (33).

How different my own experience! Class and race privilege have left me vulnerable to cultural notions of the "good" mother, the rise of ideals surrounding middle-class intensive mothering, and the angst-ridden conflict—both real and staged—of the so-called "mommy wars." On more than one occasion, I have fallen victim to the comforting notion that choice, rather than unseen structural forces, governs individual women's lives. It is only through reading the narratives of those who have had to struggle with the barriers of race and class that I have begun to locate my own experience in the larger picture.

* * *

Speak, memory: the tiny, purplish hands, curled up in tiny balls; my own panic pressed down deep, as I watch for the quick up-and-down breath of her chest; the mewling cry, a siren that jerks me wide awake from thirsty sleep; the chapped lips, hungrily latched onto my swollen breasts.

I am a new mother of a baby girl. I am sleep-deprived and in love, maddened by my new bonds and enraptured by my tiny captor. The busy outer world appears as if in a haze. When I decide to venture outside our apartment, I spend what must be hours assembling the necessary accoutrements: bundling blanket, mittens, hat, pacifier, diaper bag, baby carrier. Once in a while I catch a view of myself on the way out the door: hair unbrushed, shirt spotted with milk, nursing bra unclasped.

I have not so much disappeared as forgotten myself; and while such forgetfulness provides moments of welcome laughter, a part of me finds my sudden self-transformation a bit alarming. After two years of trying to conceive a child (an experience that shocks me with the baffling realization that I am in control of neither my body nor my fertility), I have lived through an unexpectedly blissful nine months of pregnancy, an astonishingly painful sixteen hours of labor, and now this—this crazy, confusing, fog-filled existence which I cannot articulate, cannot describe, cannot even fathom.

Months later, I resolve to get a grip. I must understand what has happened to me. I am terrified by the power of this small creature, the way she pulls me into her aura. I am equally terrified by the moments when I long for my old life, when boredom and anger convince me that I am a bad, selfish, and terrible mother. I hear others—friends, mothers, grandmothers—tell me to enjoy it, not to worry, simply to be in the moment. I wish that I could; this advice resonates with what my yoga teacher used to say (back in my previous life, back when I used to take yoga).

But I cannot. I have too much fear, too many questions, too much at stake.

In pursuit of my newly formed goal, I do what I have been trained to do, as a scholar and writer: I search for books to read. I begin innocently enough, tiptoeing away from my sleeping daughter as I pick up the first title of this new project, *The Mommy Myth*. I read during what feels like stolen time, but resolve and conviction quiets the guilt. As I read, I am aware of the intermingled sensations of exhilaration and despair. Exhilaration as I puzzle through the intense experience of early motherhood, still in love with my daughter's small form, her fleshy cheeks, her intoxicating smell. Despair as I come to understand, deep down within me, the many hurdles facing mothers of all backgrounds. In my own case, I realize that what I have understood to be a privilege—my husband's salary—comes attached with strings, for his work keeps him away from home, and our new baby, for long days and nights. If this were to continue, I realize, we would find ourselves entrenched in the very same gender roles I have criticized and rejected my entire life.

In this way, reading begins to put my new existence in perspective. Titles such as *The Price of Motherhood, Maternal Desire, Unbending Gender, A Potent Spell,* and *The Truth behind the Mommy Wars* fill my shelves. Collectively, they represent a new wave of work by writers, journalists, and scholars asking why women across class and race still experience obstacles when they become mothers. These books seep into the gaps and corners of my days, and they sustain me as I grapple with what is happening to me. With the passing of time, I have become what is known as a "work from home" mom, which in my case means gigs as a freelance writer and part-time college instructor—work that barely manages to pay for our childcare. With the breathing room afforded by my husband's salary, I have found many reasons to work only part-time: the disheartening realities of the academic job market; my ambivalence about the demands of full-time work as a new mother; my sensitivity to the judgment of friends and family, many of whom express no misgivings about the new division of labor in my household. (Would they be so sanguine, I wonder, if my husband suddenly stopped working?) Most importantly, I want to spend time with my daughter.

And yet, I worry about where my present life is leading me. While I have willingly subscribed to a piece of wisdom so many of my peers have gleaned from watching our own mothers—our oft-repeated mantra that "you can have it all, just not at the same time"—I begin to worry that "taking time off" in the highly competitive field of academia actually means giving it up for the rest of my life. As time goes on, I realize that my driven and ambitious self longs for something more: a life that includes publishing books, teaching classes in my specialty, recognition from colleagues, a decent paycheck that will put an end to my financial dependency. I begin to think that perhaps I shouldn't feel so guilty about wanting these things in addition to motherhood.

The books I am reading help situate my life into an analytical frame that enables me to reexamine the institutions around me. I realize that what I want—well-paid, benefit-bearing, part-time work that will not penalize my eventual career aspirations as a tenured professor and write—does not seem to exist. That "taking time off" is both a class privilege and a "choice" stemming from the failure of many workplaces to accommodate parents who wish to ease up on their work lives in order to spend time with children. That, depending on one's location, quality daycare can be rare, and expensive. That in the urban area where we live, most nannies are women of color, usually immigrants, often illegal, who have frequently left their own children at home, a plane ride away. That these are not topics debated and worried over by politicians, but by individual families. That these problems remain, frustratingly, women's issues.

As a result, I can feel my own feminism shifting, expanding, and changing—perhaps not unlike what a reader of Adrienne Rich might have experienced, thirty years ago. I cling to the words of the writers I am reading amid the maelstrom around and within me, and I begin writing about motherhood for feminist and mainstream publications. Writing helps me puzzle through the morass I have found myself in, even as I adore my child and my new identity as a mother. I crave to know more about the experiences of other mothers, and I soon discover an explosion of autobiographical writing about motherhood—books, magazine essays, zines, and blogs by writers such as Ayun Halliday, Ariel Gore, Faulkner Fox, and Andrea Buchanan. I become indebted to these women, so freely sharing their own experiences of, and reflections about, motherhood in early 21st century America. In her own way, each writer explodes the myth that motherhood is somehow easy, natural, and always blissful. They honestly chronicle the stressful and unpleasant parts of motherhood, and some of them vent anger and confusion at the way that motherhood somehow seems to trigger traditional gender roles in previously progressive-minded partnerships. They become part of my conscious-ness-raising group, this tribe of writer-mothers who form my new community, these women who convince me that I'm not completely alone.

* * *

Third-wave mother writers speak in a voice familiar to me, fresh with new outrage and surprise at the way things are. Yet as indebted as I feel to these writers, I often wonder why we still seem to be having the same conversation about motherhood. After Rich published *Of Woman Born* during the heyday of the second wave—a controversial, ambitious, politically radical, and widely influential manifesto that keenly dissected both her own experience as well as the forces that have gone into the making of institutional motherhood—why are we still talking about feminism and motherhood in the same terms, and often in ways that are more personal and less political? I also wonder about who is having this conversation. Aside from a handful of women of color, why are white, middle-class women still dictating the terms of the discussion, and why does our culture continue to listen to these voices when it ignores so many others?

At times I worry that we are caught in a cycle of repetition, that many of the younger writers of the third wave aren't familiar with their feminist forebears, that a collective amnesia has wedged a gap between what the women's liberation movement was working toward in the 1970s, and what so many of us are working toward today. I worry that some of these young writers, even those whose work I admire, have lost Rich's political edge; that their writing, while well-crafted, has lost the bigger picture in their pursuit of the woof and weave of the everyday tasks of mothering. Most of all, I worry that an exclusive focus on the personal precludes the kind of systemic analysis so crucial for feminist activism.

At other times, I think that my generation is perhaps freer to explore the many different experiences of parenting. Not everyone is stuck on the idea, as I was growing up, that feminist liberation equals working outside the home. Indeed, some writers are quite willing to embrace caregiving as a means of empower-ment. Others express ambivalence and uncertainty, more in tune with my own experience. Collectively, however, they explore the lives of a widely diverse group of women (as well as some men)—mamas who are single, on welfare, teenage, lesbian, anarchist—in other words, anyone who challenges the dominant cultural images of motherhood (the white, middle-class, "good" mother). They reclaim formerly derogatory words such as "breeder," as Ariel Gore and Bee Lavender do in their anthology by the same name. Their sheer numbers, the expanding diversity of voices, the exploration of the political dimensions of the personal: I celebrate the multiplicity of this symphony, even when I wish that we could all tune into wavelengths aimed a bit more directly at social change.

Yet during hopeful moments, I think there might be links between third-wave writing and the surge of political activism among contemporary mothers, particu-

larly the new advocacy groups that have articulated a broad platform of policies
for mothers and families: a routinely familiar, but still frustratingly distant, agenda
that includes such items as changes in the tax structure, paid parental leave, universal childcare, and flexible work policies. And while I find myself angry at how
little progress we've made, these past thirty years (we're *still* talking about basic
issues such as childcare and paid leave?), I find hope in these new groups. Even
when they don't self-identify as feminist (which many of them don't). Even when
the majority of them squarely position themselves in the mainstream, focusing
on electoral politics rather than challenging the many ways in which notions of
biological motherhood are created and maintained by our culture. Even when I
fear that a general disengagement from a broader tradition of activism might cause
us to run the risk of repeating exclusions and mistakes from the past. Even when
they don't all show awareness of the long and diverse history of those who have
focused their energies on mothers' and caregivers' concerns across class, race, and
sexuality: the labor feminists who began advocating for workplace changes in the
1940s, the poor women who started the welfare rights movement, the women of
color who have worked for a wide range of interconnected social justice issues,
the gay and lesbian parents who have fought for the right to have a family, the
immigrant rights advocates who are attempting to address the effects of transnational migration on parents and children.

Even so, I place hope in these new mothers' advocacy groups, in their focus on
the need for structural and institutional change and their attempt to change the
terms of the debate in our country, which has focused for so long on women's
"choices" and family "values." In many instances, these new groups represent col-
laborations between second- and third-wavers, suggesting how often the "waves"
of feminism overlap in our misnamed era of "postfeminism." For these reasons,
I find myself hopeful that the renewed interest in mother- and family-centered
activism will help us to achieve—finally—some of feminism's most far-reaching
visions for social and structural change.

* * *

As a child of the era following the decades of the second wave, I am a member of
the third wave. Yet my feminism, while defined by historical events and the present
realities of our globalized age, is also marked by other factors: by the voices of the
women whose work I have read, by my own experience, and by the experience of
my mother. For the impetus underlying my journey really begins with her and
with my own attempt to understand her experience as well as my own.

What I have come to see is how much my mother needed but didn't have
when she was trying to work and mother. As a woman who preceded the second
wave, she had very little available to her as she made her way: no maternity
leave, even unpaid; no social net for helping her raise a disabled child; no
sympathetic peers willing to pitch in; no partner truly prepared to help her
with the ominous task of raising children and running a household while she
continued to teach and perform. No wonder she broke under the burden of

performing her superwoman act; no wonder she fell apart, and then blamed herself for failing at it all.

Years later, when we speak about my life, I sense my mother's fear for me. Although she would never call herself a feminist, she understands the deep isolation that stems from the burdens she carried. She appreciates the tremendous strain that flows from the belief that mothers—and only mothers—are the ones who can sufficiently care for children. She knows this because she has lived it, and she wants to spare me the pain of an existence torn between caring for others and caring for myself.

* * *

The tyranny of biological motherhood is one reason that I, like so many other feminists, have found myself attracted to alternative ways of thinking about, and creating, families. Perhaps this is why so many third wavers have claimed alternative models of mothering and parenting, creating subcultural communities featuring "alternative" family roles and formations. (Zines such as *The Future Generation*, *Punk Parent*, *East Village Inky*, *Placenta*, and *Rad Dad* provide a glimpse of how some individuals are doing just this.) Another model is the tradition of nonbiological and community "othermothering" within many African American communities. Aunties, grandmothers, friends, fictive kin—anyone who shares parenting responsibilities with mothers can be considered an othermother. A practice with roots in West Africa, othermothering often results in what Stanlie James calls a communal "ethic of care" as well as political activism (47). James, for example, views motherhood as an experience that can fuel "social transformation" (45), and Patricia Hill Collins argues that motherhood often "*politicizes* Black women*" (194).

Still other communities have created alternative models for mothering and caregiving. Gay and lesbian parents are remaking the nuclear family, embracing two, three, even four parents who provide care for children in different ways. Some scholars argue that these forms of caregiving, like othermothering, challenge institutional motherhood. For example, Andrea O'Reilly argues that lesbian mothering, like African American and feminist mothering, often functions as a mode of "empowered mothering" that enables women to resist oppressive stereotypes of the "good" or "sacrificial" mother (5). Likewise, Laura Kessler finds that many groups historically denied the privilege of familial privacy have created practices of "transgressive caregiving" that transform family care work into political resistance (2-4).

These expansive ways of creating and caring for family contrast with the way so many middle- and upper middle-class families (including mine) define family as a private unit, something that must be sustained with one (or two) incomes that enable the purchase of clothes, food, educational opportunities, and the services of paid caregivers. Objectively, I understand many of the reasons why so many families organize themselves in this way; realities such as the geographical separation of extended families, the development trend toward sprawl and McMansions, the increase of economic pressures, the escalation of work hours, the pressures of intensive mothering, and the increasing abandonment of ideals such as the public domain and the public commons make it difficult, if not downright impossible, to embrace community-based notions of family and caregiving.

And yet, I wish I could figure out how I could somehow use these alternative models to inform my own family life. How can those of us who find ourselves in more traditional family arrangements shake things up and transform mothering into something different—something a little more community-minded, a little more political?

From time to time, I've run across writers who hint at ways to do this. In *Crossing the Color Line*, for example, Maureen Reddy argues that the notion of othermothering provides a model for white women to reimagine motherhood. By "committing herself to a particular child (or children) for reasons other than bourgeois individualism," Reddy writes, "a woman commits herself to the future and strikes a blow against a social system that tries to push us all into rigidly bounded nuclear families that compete against each other for even scarcer rewards" (155). For Reddy, othermothering provides an important model for feminist alliances across difference.

I am attracted by Reddy's argument, by the allure of community-based othermothering, by the promise of alliances across difference. Yet I am still not sure, much of the time, of precisely how I might put this into practice.

* * *

When I finally land a full-time teaching job, I am thrown back into rigid distinctions between work and family. My husband, daughter, and I move out of the city and become a two-commuter family, halfway in between his workplace and mine. We live in an idyllic, green town that I grow to love; and yet, I am well aware of how supreme the private ideal of the family reigns here.

Every morning, I kiss my daughter goodbye when her babysitter arrives. She throws her small frame around me, demanding kisses and hugs, at times clinging to my legs and crying, at other times requesting that we shake hands, bidding me goodbye. I stroke her soft cheek and her blondish brown hair, which I manage to pull back into a ponytail only once in a while, when she permits me. I feel such pride in my daughter, so sure of her desires at age three. I drive off to a wonderful job, at a university more than an hour away that could not offer me on-campus daycare when I needed it. Sometimes, I drive to a café in town, where I sneak in an hour of writing. The uninterrupted time a cup of coffee buys me is well worth it; and unless I have no other option, I do not choose to work at home.

We have adapted and adjusted to our new life, and I am grateful for my job and our childcare situation; but still, it is not the life I had imagined. For while I derive great satisfaction from my work, I am well aware of its price—long hours spent driving, constant fatigue, and (worst of all) a deep division between my life at work and at home.

It is not the life I had imagined, the life I still think is possible, the life I tell myself we are still working toward.

As a result, I find myself living with contradiction and ambivalence, the place explored with courage and compassion by so many of the young feminists in my generation. I hope that my allegiance to my career and an institution does not dilute my commitment to social change or my passion for my family. I also hope I am not deluding myself in placing hope in such things as teaching classes in literature and feminism, or in seeking ways of integrating my lives as a mother, teacher, scholar, and writer—whether this means undertaking research that explores motherhood/mothering and feminism, or bringing feminist research and inquiry into the public arena, or searching for spaces (if not physical, then metaphorical) where I can write and mother at the same time.

* * *

As I put these words down on the page, deadline fast approaching, I face yet another due date: the arrival of my second child. And so I have stolen away again, laptop plugged in at a café, thinking about this essay, my teaching, my daughter; but most of all, feeling the movement in my pregnant belly, taught and bruised and spilling over into my chair.

Within days, I will give birth, a mother about to be born again.

I am poised to begin anew the cycle of these past three years, a cycle which has led me through periods of upheaval, bafflement, and understanding. And yet nothing is resolved; much remains uncertain. I have not achieved integration or balance; if anything, I have simply come to understand the elusive hope of these words, the painful struggle involved in caring about them, and the ongoing search for spaces in which I can be myself at the same time that I mother.

Writing propels me on this journey. In this essay, it has forced me to think about the process of traveling back and forth between reflecting on personal experience and developing systemic analyses of the world around me. The act of crossing back and forth has proven challenging, and I have often felt these two modes of thought dueling in my struggle to write. And yet I cannot survive with only one of them; each is too integral to me, as a writer making her way as a feminist and a mother. For this reason, I come back, again and again, to the figure of Adrienne Rich, with her powerful and poetic insistence on looking hard at both her own life and the institutions of society, one always in relationship with the other.

It is not too much to believe, I hope, that the many different stories of the current wave will come together, not unlike those of an earlier era; that perhaps the cumulative effect of this outpouring will be to change our assumptions, our narratives of what has happened, and our imagination of what is possible—both individually as well as collectively. If we can see our stories in tandem with those around us, allowing both differences as well as connections to crystallize in our view, then perhaps we can continue to work toward change.

I believe this. If I didn't, I would give up hope. Even so, the road ahead appears lonely and uncertain, the descending winter dusk reminding me of how very alone this can feel, this birthing of children, this birthing of who and what we want to be.

Works Cited

Berry, Cecelie S. "Introduction." *Rise Up Singing: Black Women Writers on Mother-hood*. Ed. Cecelie S. Berry. New York: Harlem Moon, 2004. 5-13.

Collins, Patricia Hill. "Black Women and Motherhood." *Black Feminist Thought: Knowledge, Consciousness, and the Politics of Empowerment*. 2nd Ed. New York: Routledge, 2000. 173-199.

Crittenden, Ann. *The Price of Motherhood: Why the Most Important Job in the World Is Still the Least Valued*. New York: Henry Holt, 2001.

de Marneffe, Daphne. *Maternal Desire: On Children, Love, and the Inner Life*. Boston: Little, 2004.

Douglas, Susan and Meredith Michaels. *The Mommy Myth: The Idealization of Motherhood and How It Has Undermined Women*. New York: Free Press, 2004.

Emecheta, Buchi. *Second-Class Citizen*. New York: Braziller, 1975.

Gore, Ariel and Bee Lavender, Eds. *Breeder: Real-Life Stories from the New Genera-tion of Mothers*. Emeryville, CA: Seal, 2001.

James, Stanlie M. "Mothering: A Possible Black Feminist Link to Social Trans-formation?" *Theorizing Black Feminisms: The Visionary Pragmatism of Black Women*. Eds. Stanlie M. James and Abena P. A. Busia. New York: Routledge, 1993. 44-54.

Kessler, Laura T. "Transgressive Caregiving." *Florida State University Law Review* 33.1 (2005): 1-87.

O'Reilly, Andrea. "Introduction." *Mother Outlaws: Theories and Practices of Empow-ered Mothering*. Ed. Andrea O'Reilly. Toronto: Women's Press, 2004. 1-28.

Parker, Lonnae O'Neal. *I'm Every Woman: Remixed Stories of Marriage, Mother-hood, and Work*. New York: Harper, 2005.

Peskowitz, Miriam. *The Truth behind the Mommy Wars: Who Decides What Makes a Good Mother?* Emeryville, CA: Seal, 2005.

Reddy, Maureen. *Crossing the Color Line: Race, Parenting, and Culture*. New Brunswick: Rutgers University Press, 1994.

Rich, Adrienne. *Of Woman Born: Motherhood as Experience and Institution*. 1976. New York: Norton, 1986.

Smith, Janna Malamud. *A Potent Spell: Mother Love and the Power of Fear*. Boston: Houghton, 2003.

Walker, Alice. "A Writer Because of, Not in Spite of, Her Children." 1976. *In Search of Our Mothers' Gardens: Womanist Prose*. San Diego: Harcourt, 1983. 66-70.

Williams, Joan. *Unbending Gender: Why Work and Family Conflict and What to Do About It*. Oxford: Oxford University Press, 2000.

2

An Open Letter to the Lesbians Who Have Mothered Before Me

MAURA RYAN

Mothers & Sisters,

There are so many of you. You are birth mothers who have chosen to get pregnant when you were always taught that lesbians aren't capable of being mothers; you are birth mothers who came out as lesbians when you were told that your children would hate you for it, or that your lesbianism would ruin their lives, maybe make them unable to cope with the real world as adults. You are women who had your children taken from you by ex-husbands, ex-boyfriends, donors, family members, or the state; they assumed they knew better than you what was best for your children because you are a lesbian. You are mothers who have other-mothered without recognition, without the smiling nods from strangers who see you as a mother; you are women who have had your mothering ignored because you were not biologically related to your children, and because you loved their biological mothers. You are women who may have socially mothered for a time, had a falling out with the biological mother, and (with no legal claim to them) never saw your children again; or maybe you have loved the children of women you once loved, and continue to raise them as community mothers. You have been kicked out of your families of origin to start new and creative ones of your own; or you have created new families to the joy of your families of origin, bridging the divide between where you've come from and where you can go. You have served as activist mothers in organizing against sexism, white supremacy, and homophobia. You have been mother to motherless queer kids who have needed guidance and support. You are women who have mothered me by changing the world I came into, and have made it possible for me to be a mother.

I can't imagine how you must have felt. I came out in 1996 when I was 14 years old in Fort Lauderdale. I had a teen support group at our local GLBT community center; I had the resources to start a gay-straight alliance at my high school whose presence was unchallenged by homophobic peers and their parents; seeing Pride flags downtown was normal; seeing gay people on MTV was normal. Still, I never felt more alone or more scared for my life, or more like the life I expected could no longer be counted on. People harassed me at school; administrators did nothing, even when I told them the names and class periods of the boys who threw rocks at my car, my locker, my head, or when my head was bashed into my locker, or when they threatened to rape me. I didn't tell my parents what happened at school because I thought they might kick me out, or lock me up for being a lesbian. All of this was still better than the culture in which you grew up, came out, and raised your children. I can't imagine how you must have felt.

Even now, dykes who want to mother are inundated with cultural messages that tell us that lesbians are not as capable of mothering, that we need male parents as role models for our children, and that our children will suffer by abuse, peer ridicule, or becoming gay themselves. These things still get to me, even when I think I'm over them. Like last year—every time I got my period it felt like somebody was taking an axe to my lower back. Because of the sexist nature of medical understandings, general practitioners and emergency room physicians insisted that it was either a problem with my gallbladder or kidney stones; the pain being initiated every month during my period didn't make them wonder if it was gynecological. I got ultrasound after ultrasound until my mother suggested I see a gynecologist.

So, I went to the gynecologist my insurance company sent me to see. I express the expected feminine gender for my biological female sex; I can say that much for my privilege. For this reason, when the male gynecologist walked into the exam room, meeting me for the first time, he kindly held out his hand to shake mine. I was wearing a paper towel-like gown that barely fastened in the front; the nurse had asked that I take off all of my clothes and wear only the gown. He asked that I lay down. To perform the breast exam, he opened the whole gown so that my body was entirely naked. The nurse looked down and away, seemingly embarrassed. He looked down to my right hip bone, on it my tattoo in swirled black lettering read "DYKE," he smirked and said, "You're a clever one. What would make you get that? Do you have any other tattoos?" I answered, "One on my lower back." "I shudder to think," he said while entering me for the pelvic exam, "what that one says."

After the exam we had a short consultation in his office. "I can't be sure at this point. We'll need more tests to be sure, but I think you have fibroid tumors in your uterus." "What does that mean—I mean what do we do in that case?" "What we would do in that case is perform a complete hysterectomy." He looked at me blankly, but squarely in the eye and said, "Would that be a problem?" I was 22 years old.

I talked to feminist activist friends who organize around women's health issues and found out that radical hysterectomies are not the prime solution for fibroid tumors—especially for women in "childbearing years." It is perhaps the easiest solution for physicians, especially when they assume that you do not need your uterus for any practical use. I did not know this, though, in the weeks I spent trying to find another gynecologist. My mother researched alternatives endlessly, my dyke professor shook her head and said, "And you wonder why dykes are afraid to go to the doctor," and I cried every time I could be alone.

I didn't even have fibroid tumors (the second opinion gynecologist told me). I had a large growth on my right ovary that needed to be removed. It had gotten too big (from neglect) to be removed by laser so I would have to have surgery.

The day before the surgery my gynecologist told me that the growth was probably not cancerous. If it was, (and they needed to see it before they could determine its status) he told me, "We'll just go ahead and perform a hysterectomy while you're still open."

I told myself that I could still mother. I had other options: my partner could give birth or we could adopt children. Still, some small part of me, planted by our culture's homophobia and reinforced by both of my physicians assuming that I am not as entitled to keeping my uterus as other women my age, believed that this was my body's way of telling me that I should not be a mother. After all the personal and emotional work I've done to prove that I can be a mother like other women, they still got me. There are still those nasty nagging feelings hiding in the recesses of my memory that believe what I learned before I was a lesbian: lesbians are not meant to be mothers. The tumor was not cancerous. They closed me without taking anything that was mine. The light pink scar rests in the layers of skin above my vagina and under my dyke tattoo.

Even though nothing really changed in my ability to get pregnant, it made me realize my deep internalization of anti-lesbian motherhood rhetoric. After all this time, it still happens. Not only have I had to negotiate my feelings about mother-hood with society's feelings about lesbianism, I have had to deal with the fear a lot of dykes have that by becoming mothers we leave the queer community.

When I first started thinking about being a mother, I was watching a documentary where this gay activist said that *all* gays and lesbians are parents because we all have the responsibility to parent the next generation of queer kids. I fell into a panic, thinking that I was going to be slacking on my responsibilities to help queer kids in the interest of raising (probably) straight kids. I thought that it was impossible to mother children *and* to mother younger queer people. My biggest fear became that I would gain children and lose a community. I feared that I would be ignor-ing young queer kids who would need me. I believed that (instead of adding to a diversity of mothers) I would only make myself more acceptable to society while further pathologizing queer women who do not choose to mother.

Thinking this way is disrespectful. The first older dyke who held my hand while I cried to her about being a lesbian in high school had children; women who organized with me in the Lesbian Avengers had toddlers and teenagers. By thinking this way, I had given in to both the cultural idea that someone has to love their biological children more than they can love family members of choice; and the either/or misconception that one is either a mother *or* an activist—a homebody who fulfills her role, *or* somebody who cares about social change. I ignored that having our families *is* social change; I ignored the social change you created in feminist, anti-racist, and queer activist organizations; I ignored what it has taken you to build your families, and create the change that allows me to have a family.

It's true—every one of you who has had the courage to create a queer family has contributed to social change just by doing that. In addition, so many of you have also been activists. Young dykes are thankful for this legacy but there are some undeniable problems in the mainstream feminist and gay organizations we have inherited. I bring up our social movements for a couple of reasons. I bring them up because of their disturbing similarities—feminist and gay organizing have historically shared more than just lesbian activity in them—they have also shared serious critiques from people of color for their racism. I bring them up to convey the importance of thinking about our public presentation of our social movement beliefs, goals, and methods of achieving these goals. After all, this presentation tells people who is in our community and what we want for these community members. I also bring them up because I think we have to be honest about the mistakes we've made so we can do a better job in the future. I bring up their problems because I think we can change them.

We all know that feminist organizations, gay and lesbian communities, and gay and lesbian social movements have been criticized widely for their white, European focus. We probably also know that, unfortunately, a standard response to this criticism has been one of the following: "That is not true of my group because there are several women of color in our organization;" and "My community/organization reaches out to people of color specifically, and if they do not wish to be active, we cannot make them be a part of things." Women of color have always been a part of feminist and queer organizations; and they also had to choose their battles within these organizations in order to stay in them. Some people of color have chosen to ignore the pleas for inclusion that have recently come from feminist and queer organizations because of the obvious tokenism in such sentiments. The point is this: having people of color in your organization/community does not mean that your movement holistically includes them or the political goals that will fulfill their needs.

Terry Boggis points out that the "self-elected representatives" of the gay parenting community are white, upper-middle class people who take pride in planning their families, and that these people have painted a picture of a whole community by talking about themselves (176-177).

This doesn't just happen around issues of gay parenting. A recent public relations slogan that nicely summarizes the white-oriented goals of the mainstream gay/lesbian movement is the argument, *we are just like you*. The statement *we are just like you* is practically copyrighted by gays and lesbians. While feminists don't exactly say this, its logic can be seen in feminist undertakings. It can be seen in the (white) liberal feminist demand for equal access to education for women (ignoring racism in education) or now in the (largely white) demand for gay marriage (ignoring the ways in which marriage is used as leverage against poor people). When we say "you," we mean a specific "you." As Joanna Kadi points out, the "you" we mean is white, middle-class, and male (37-38); when we say this we do not mean we are just like single Chicana mothers. If this is true—and it has been for some time, the "we" that we are attempting to encompass barely covers any of us. The queer community needs to create a "we" statement that recognizes the queer, single, Chicana mothers in our community; and we need to develop a theoretical starting point that recognizes heterosexual single Chicana mothers as part of the "we" when we talk about struggle, revolution, and change. When we think about "our" movements, we should always include movements that focus on smashing white supremacy, poverty, unfair labor practices, advantages for the able-bodied, and war (to name a few). We should think of them as ours because all of these things affect queers, and because even when they're affecting people who aren't queer, it's the right thing to do.

We need to heal the wounds of exclusion that we have inflicted, and begin to conceptualize a future of progressive politics and inclusion. To do that, we have to move beyond prioritizing sexuality as *the* oppression.

I went to a conference recently where a femme dyke told the group in the workshop that she had worked hard to be a dyke. We do. We work to maintain ourselves in a society that says we are inhuman because we are queer. We work to maintain relationships with family members of origin. We work to not be scared that someone might kill us or rape us every time we walk down the street. When we want to become mothers we have to work on all of the anti-lesbian mother sentiments we've heard all of our lives. I know you know what she's talking about. Maybe it's because of all this work, or maybe it's because it's difficult for most people to empathize—whatever the reason, too often white middle-class lesbians assume that their gender and sexuality oppression make them the most oppressed people on the planet. We especially believe this when we talk about how difficult it is for us to mother. We forget that the dominant discourse on "the perfect family" exists along many categories—sexuality is just one of them. The idea of the perfect mother is also race and class specific. Not only is the perfect mother heterosexual, she is also white, middle-class, monogamous, and legally married to one man for her whole life.

Most white lesbians would tell you that because of racism lesbians of color might have a more difficult time with motherhood than they do; but it may be difficult for these same women to imagine the ways that heterosexual women of color are discouraged from motherhood.

If lesbians have been ignored as potential mothers, Black women, Patricia Hill Collins tells us, have been historically vilified for being the wrong kind of mother. Black mothers are culturally represented as mammies (who warmly care for white children), matriarchs (who badly care for their own children), or welfare queens (who do not care for their children). Since the institution of American slavery to modern times, Black motherhood has been feared, ridiculed, and repressed as much as possible (69-97). These ideologies have tangible effects. For example, in 1965, Senator Daniel Patrick Moynihan published his infamous government document *The Moynihan Report*, blaming the so-called overbearing matriarchal structure of Black families for the believed low achievement of Black men. In a modern example, we learn from Gwendolyn Mink's work, that the (second) Bush administration's Healthy Marriage Initiative[1] has specifically targeted women of color, who are perceived to be promiscuous and irresponsible mothers (495-500).

Lesbian women (who are probably white and middle-class in popular imagination) are constructed as being dangerous to their children because of their sexual orientation. Heterosexual women who are poor, and/or women of color, are constructed to be dangerous to their children because of classist/racist images that say they are promiscuous and irresponsible. Dominant ideology's best women—who are white, middle-class, documented citizens, and heterosexual—must have children (in a socially desirable way) to be thought of as good women. These things have something to do with one another. These ideologies keep all women from living up to their full potential as people and as mothers. The persistence of all of these things means that we have a lot of work left to do.

It's time that all queer women—irrespective of our political generation—work together. We have to create a world where no one fears for their lives or their safety when they come out as queer; we have to create a world where no queer girl who wants to mother thinks mothering is impossible for her. We have to work together to create a place where our families are taken seriously, and where that is reflected in our languages, family ideology, and law. We have to move beyond thinking that people are either queer or people of color, and incorporate practical political ways to be both. We have to be vigilant in our project to unearth the ways that sexism, racism, and homophobia intersect for all of us in all moments of our lives. We have to reinvent the ways in which we work across lines of race, nation, and class. I know I can take this on because you have done so much already.

For young dykes in the third wave, your work in your families and in activist organizations has created a world where, more than ever, motherhood is a choice, and not an expectation of all women; there's more of an understanding that there should be no good or bad women; we recognize privilege and teach revolution; we do not conflate love, sex, reproduction, and family; the sexual plurality of mothers creates a motherhood plurality that will change the world by changing the children who are raised in it; we keep ourselves and teach our children who we are.

The reason I write this letter has to do with my wanting to be a mother. In wanting that I have had to take on several other projects. Besides fighting the infrastructures and symbolic boundaries that keep queer women from having children, I also choose to take on the project of remembering the women who have made it possible for me to mother. Your choices, your political legacies, and your motherhood battles have made it possible. You are some of the women who have shifted the definition of the word mother, and continue to change the definition of the word woman. You are my sisters and my mothers. I can offer you a small return and that is that the conversation between us about the future of motherhood, feminism, and queer rights will continue as long as we both have voices.

In Love & Solidarity,

Maura

[1]The Healthy Marriage Initiative is a reform to welfare that encourages women to marry the biological fathers of their children in order to continue receiving state aid.

Works Cited

Boggis, Terry. "Affording Our Families: Class Issues in Family Formation." *Queer Families Queer Politics: Challenging Culture and the State*. Eds. Mary Bernstein and Renate Reimann. New York: Columbia University Press, 2001. 176-177.

Hill Collins, Patricia. *Black Feminist Thought*. New York: Routledge, 2000.

Kadi, Joanna. "Homophobic Workers or Elitist Queers?" *Queerly Classed: Gay Men and Lesbians Write about Class*. Ed. Susan Raffo. Massachusetts: South End, 1997. 37-38.

Mink, Gwendolyn. "The Lady and the Tramp (II): Feminist Welfare Politics, Poor Single Mothers, and the Challenge of Welfare Justice." *Feminist Frontiers*. Eds. Verta Taylor, Nancy Whittier, and Leila Rupp. New York: McGraw-Hill, 2006. 495-500.

Moynihan, Daniel Patrick. *The Negro Family: The Case for National Action*. Washington, DC: US Labor Department, 1975.

3

Dispatches from a Displaced Mama

Mothering Through Disaster or Re-membering Home

LAURA CAMILLE TULEY

Recently I was asked by Amber Kinser, another writer on feminism and mothering, whether feminism held any significance for me during my period of exile from New Orleans after Hurricane Katrina; or if, given the personal, social and environmental scope of the tragedy, feminist concerns had been relegated to a distant back burner, to be re-addressed at a more emotionally and intellectually settled future point. Specifically, she asked, "Was it even on your radar?" "Yes," I told Amber without hesitation. Not only were feminist issues "on my radar," they were, in many respects, even more apparent and vital to me than they had been in my former and consistently ordered life.

I grew up with a sense of feminist priorities (and by that I mean, in part, with a sense of the value of equal opportunity to work, and at work, and a sense of the need for equal partnership in all things private). In college, I became a consciously feminist woman by way of Women's Studies courses and went on to refine and actualize those values in my graduate school training and research. Since the beginning of my career as a teacher, I have always incorporated, to some degree, either feminist writings or

September 13, 2005

My sister-in-law, Brenda, is one of those women who make the comfort of the others a priority.

In the first week of my family's exile from New Orleans, Brenda set about the task of easing our transition from life in the Victorian double gallery we own in an historic neighborhood across the river from the French Quarter to squatting in a room of her well-manicured suburban ranch house in a subdivision south of Houston, Texas. And to her credit, she made significant headway in paving a trail through what was, to us, thorny and uncharted territory. Namely, she enabled me to create what I hoped would be a reassuring environment for my son, Dylan, in his make-shift new "home."

First, Brenda secured a position for him in the Methodist daycare center down the road, which offers a "Mother's Day Out," three days a week. Dylan is accustomed to daycare and to interacting with other children, so, naturally, I was concerned about him in his week "off" after our evacuation, during most of which he was subject to the stressed company of stunned parents. The center, obviously organized to accommodate stay-at-home mothers, whose presence is legion here, was generous enough to allow Dylan temporary free residency in its small and appropriately nurturing domicile. In addition, Brenda's own sister-in-law brought over a box of books and toys to donate to my refugee toddler. Soon, my brother's office was overflowing with toy cars and other plastic objects, while stacks of children's books lined Dylan's bed. And there was more. Upon hearing of our plight, a haircutter at the local salon refused payment after cutting Dylan's hair. As residents of Louisiana, we were given a 25 percent discount at the nearby "Buckle" store and 20 percent off of our

38

writings by women (whether it be the authors I include to supplement the largely male western canon in survey literature courses, or in the form of actual women's studies and feminist theory courses). More concretely, and recently, in my choice of a mate, and in the rearing of my young son, I have also endeavored to embody feminist values (e.g., my husband assumes more than half of the domestic responsibilities in our home, and half of the responsibility for parenting).

After the storm, in the absence of immediate professional responsibilities (other than one online composition course), for the first time since the first few months of my son's infancy, I might have taken a break simply to focus on mothering and spousal support. However, this was not, by instinct or inclination, what I elected to do. I chose to sustain myself first, which, ultimately, meant sustaining my work and cultivating my creativity. As something of a "third-wave feminist" in orientation (though I'm a few years older than most third-wave "girls"), the either/or dichotomy between mothering and work, is not an option. Rather, the freedom to pursue my interests and to use my mind is a given and is, without question, necessary to my survival. And yet, as with most Katrina "refugees," coping with our collective trauma was everything; most of us wandered around for months with mild depression or low-grade anxiety disorders. So how was I to recover what I needed? The answer, I found, was to use my experience, which included that self-doubt or ambivalence triggered by the choices I was making. I learned to use the very trauma of loss and its

breakfast at the neighborhood diner. Such acts of goodwill peppered our days. For her part, Brenda would turn up in the evening with a new outfit or pajama set, purchased from baby Gap on her way home from work, to supplement the few items of clothing I managed to stuff in Dylan's suitcase on our way out the door. Occasionally, she'd throw in a bottle of wine to pacify his parents.

Meanwhile, we watched on television as desperate evacuees from New Orleans' Superdome and Convention Center were finally bussed out of the city to Houston's Astrodome. We were all, it seems, benefiting from the prosperity of Texans. The odd thing about all of this generosity for me, on a personal level, was, simply, that it felt quite odd; at once necessary and excessive. Here we were, my family of three, essentially in need of support and compassion and yet, not truly "refugees," with all of the third world (racial and economic) connotations that that term suggests. We did have a place to stay and nutritious food and childcare services. Moreover, we are white and middle class. And so, when, on the second day of "Mother's Day Out," I showed up with Dylan's lunch in a Kroger bag, and his teacher looked at me with a mixture of pity and embarrassment and told me, "I bought him a lunchbox over the weekend," I felt both weirdly insulted and vaguely inadequate. I had not provided well for my son, did not even think to pack his lunch in a lunchbox to match the care and attention to detail of other, less nomadic mothers, the stationary mothers of suburbia, whose children would grow up to be sturdy, productive citizens of America, or, at the very least, of Texas. Perhaps, as an individual, partnered or not, I could more easily stomach this period of impotence and limbo, venture across the country to embrace new and surprising opportunities. As a mother, I am troubled by my association with "them," the multitude of homeless and poor, flooding the state and desperate for handouts. Leaving Dylan's "Dolphin Room" at the daycare center, I observed that, without exception, every cubby housed a solid little lunch box bedecked in bright colors.

September 18, 2005

Giving, like taking, is rarely straightforward.

At the end of our first week in exile, my family was invited to a pool party at the home of my sister-in-law's brother, Brandon. Brandon and his wife Kelly live deep into the southern suburbs of

aftermath in order to resolve it.

Soon after evacuating our home in Algiers Point, on the west bank of New Orleans, I was invited by Sheri Reed, the editor of *mamazine.com*, to document my experience of mothering through displacement. I accepted her invitation and became a weekly contributor to her online 'zine. Moreover, I became a participant in a cyber-community of feminist mothers, grappling with the multi-layered challenges of contemporary parenting. As Jennifer Baumgardner and Amy Richards note in their *Manifesta,* "In exchanges with one another, women learn that we are the real experts—often more so than the paid experts, who have studied but not experienced the subject" (17). The forum and my participation within it became both a space for me to translate my experience of displacement by one of the worst (un)natural disasters in the history of the United States and, paradoxically, a means to preserve a sense of self beyond that of merely or primarily mother. Thus, my columns functioned in a couple of ways. First, as an exploration of the physical, economic and spiritual loss to my family, friends, and community, of how I was faced, suddenly, with the critical gaze of stay-at-home mothers in our conservative suburban retreat outside of Houston, Texas, and of how I was confronted with the often uninformed and condescending political views of our host community. I also exploited, through writing, my experience and the tools available to me (in this case, my computer and cyberspace) to re-invent or re-member (in the sense of Plato's idea of *anamnesis* or dis-forgetting as the recognition of something essential

Houston, in a planned community of newly snapped together mansions, abutting a lush and expansive golf course. Kelly, herself a mother of two boys, five and three, was particularly anxious in that first week to provide us with a luxurious distraction from our worries and grief. And, in fact, by the end of the week we had suffered both relief and horror to learn, almost simultaneously, that our house had been spared and that bands of looters were roaming the neighborhood, which was being defended by a "militia" of armed neighbors who had refused to evacuate during the storm and were engaged in gun battle with the intruders. What this meant to us was that, although our home was intact, our community, as we knew it, had, effectively, dissolved. Not only did we face the prospect of looting and damage to our home, we were confronted with the reality of living in the future with a population of homeowners who were, at the very least, permanently altered, if not deeply scarred, by the violent aftermath of Hurricane Katrina.

Not that the storm actually caused any of the unnerving social dynamics that ensued in the city or elsewhere. Rather, I believe, it shed a glaringly bright light on those normally neglected—or repressed—regions of our country's collective psyche. But none of this was at the forefront of my or my husband's thinking on that Sunday afternoon as we parked our Subaru Outback at the edge of Brandon's virtual castle of a house amid a sea of nearly identical houses nestled a long and comforting way from the battleground of New Orleans. Instead, we gathered our towels and waited eagerly for the security gates that protected Brandon's drive and property with iron posts to magically part, a sign that our hosts' relief effort had, indeed, begun.

Inside, we found a curvy and capacious saltwater pool and hot tub, complete with rocks and waterfall, ensconced in the fantasy of a tropical garden. Before either of us had a chance to exclaim our thankfulness for this vision of paradise in the suburbs, Brandon handed each of us a beer and directed Dylan, who was already tugging at his T-shirt and kicking off his shoes, to join his 3-year-old, Hunter, frolicking in the pool. Soon the three of us were enjoying the deeply inviting oasis; Dylan on my lap as I lay in a floating recliner, my husband, Chris, on a raft gazing up through the trees at an almost painted blue sky. Gradually, our troubles began to recede. "This is really surreal," my husband observed, almost guiltily. "New

to oneself) what my house or home really is; namely, the cultivation of that creative center which enables me to live in healthy and thoughtful relation to others.

That I was writing for a primarily female audience made my venture "pro-woman" in the third-wave sense that Baumgardner and Richards articulate. That I was "claiming ownership" of traditionally male domains (i.e., the media and technology) also placed my work in the realm of third-wave strivings for power and recognition. As Kinser notes concisely in her own writing on third-wave feminism, "What is most influential in defining a 'third wave' is its position relative to, and therefore how it is poised to respond to, the current so-cio-cultural, technological, and political climate" (133). Or, as Amy Anderson, co-editor of *mamazine.com* put it to me: "We are third-wave feminists—women who grew up in the 1970's being told we could be whatever we wanted to be and basically still believe that. However, there were not many representations of feminist mothers in the mainstream media. We wanted to hear the voices of other feminist mothers like us, and ta da! *mamazine*…." That my feminist impulses coincided then, and coincide now with my life as a mother and a writer for *mamazine,* informs and reflects my practice of empowered mothering, and puts me in vital contact with those voices to which Anderson refers.

When I think back over a year of writing—samples of which I share with my reader here—I recall that many of my columns contain questions related to feminism (i.e, what it means to live as both a feminist and a mother). I also recognize that they raise, implicitly, and

Orleans is in total disorder, thousands are homeless, and we're practically on vacation."

After an enchanted spell, however, a deeper reflection of our relation to our hosts and their relation to New Orleans began to emerge. "Dylan seems to be doing great!" Kelly exclaimed, wide eyed from her seated post on the patio. "Yes," I nodded, gratefully, watching Chris and Dylan as they danced through the water. "I'm so happy you could come…this whole thing is so disturbing!" she added emphatically, refilling her glass from a bottle of Pinot Noir. "Well, thank you for having us and yes, it is," I confirmed. "My biggest concern is that they're going to try to pin it all on Bush!" she asserted, cocking an eyebrow knowingly and spearing an olive. I had to admit that this was not my biggest concern. "Would you like a glass?" she asked, motioning towards the bottle. "This was all the rage in Wine Spectator last month." "Thanks, but no," I answered, holding up my beer. "Cheers!" she smiled, leaning back in her chair. "You know, you should feel free to drop by some afternoon with Dylan next week." "Thanks," I answered, trying to conjure an image of Kelly and I alone with our sons."

This image became even less tenable for me as the afternoon wore on. Ignoring Dylan for most of the afternoon in the pool, Hunter became openly hostile when the children retired to the plush second floor of Brandon and Kelly's home. Here in two spacious connecting rooms Dylan discovered a smorgasbord of toys, a child's fantasy of the good life. In front of a big-screened TV, their older son, Hartzen, sat frozen before a game of Nintendo, with two of his friends, who were shouting competitively, while Hartzen maintained control of the joystick. Dylan stood in fascinated delight before a vast and intricate train set, occupying another corner of the room. However, almost as soon as he began to maneuver a line of cars around the track, Hunter, who was hovering protectively in the background, dashed over and smashed up his train. Dylan stared at Hunter for a moment and then glanced at me, questioningly, before resuming his play. Once again, Hunter sent his cars flying across the table. At this point Dylan verbally protested—"STOP!"—in response to which Hunter shoved him. "It's alright, baby," I assured Dylan, swooping over to pick him up as he began to sob. "These aren't our toys." "He should go home and play with his train," Hunter declared ruefully, glaring up at me. "He will," I answered back, more defiantly

at times explicitly, the closely connected issues of class and race, the politics of which are inextricably interwoven in the fabric and history of New Orleans culture and which were starkly, sometimes brutally, apparent after the storm. I did not, personally, suffer the extremes of desperation and the loss that many people did. I was not rescued from a rooftop nor did I go for days without water or food in the Superdome or Convention Center. My family was displaced from New Orleans for three months, but when we returned, it was to a neighborhood and house that had sustained relatively minor wind damage and no flooding. Nevertheless, my view represents a piece of that grander narrative in which everyone connected with the event has suffered and continues to suffer to some degree. Even within the relatively plush and protected environment of my initial evacuation site, I struggled with the jarring realization that I too was a "refugee," in need of some assistance psychologically and socially, if not physically. Further, by virtue of my sudden dislocation and inability to control my environment, I was confronted with the ubiquitous stay-at-home suburban culture from which I had managed to shield myself through my own professional and feminist choices; a culture that continues to situate and define the lives of many middle- and upper middle-class American women.

Baumgardner and Richards contend that "there is never one feminist issue that dwarfs all others" (47). True to form, their list of what counts as a concern for third-wave feminism encompasses a range of issues and problems—from the educational to

than I had intended, and moved, with Dylan, away from the room.

November 20, 2005

As with shoe styles, I firmly believe that no one parenting style—color, size, or shape—fits all despite what the experts may tell you. This isn't to say that we should not, upon occasion, heed the advice or recommendations of others. It is also not to say that we can't experiment, from time to time, with new brands or colors; life is dynamic, after all, as are we. What I am saying, quite simply, is that the choices we make as parents may not always suit or appeal to everyone. For mothers, however, as those who have historically assumed the ethical burden of responsibility in childrearing, the reality of our differences is often difficult to bear.

Early in the week my son Dylan developed a virus known as "Hand, Foot and Mouth Disease." The illness is the universal dread of childcare centers and schools as it is highly contagious and can take up to seven days to run its course. Its primary symptom is painful little sores that develop, initially, in the mouth and later, although not always, on the hands and feet. Such an illness can, naturally, wreak havoc in the lives of working parents and their children. In our current situation, it posed a mere inconvenience. Dylan was exposed to the virus through a new buddy at the Montessori school in which we had enrolled him after moving from my brother's home to our own apartment in Houston and within four days developed sores in his mouth and scattered little bumps in the palms of his hands. His mood was otherwise good, his energy high. But because of the risk of contagion, we elected to keep him home from school for the rest of the week.

Because I am teaching online and had a few more pressing responsibilities that week than my husband, Chris, he agreed to watch Dylan for the four days during which Dylan was out. Although he was tired at the end of each day, Chris assumed this responsibility calmly and with few complaints, for which I was enormously grateful. Better yet, by the end of the week, Chris remarked that, to his surprise, he had enjoyed the exclusive and extensive time he had spent alone with Dylan, especially knowing that, soon after we return to New Orleans in December, he will resume full-time work and a schedule that will afford him with few such opportunities. I found myself simultaneously pleased and slightly envi-

the sexual or the environmental to the ethnic. A common agenda, except in the broadest terms, seems not to be on their agenda. Broadly speaking, however, what is consistently vital to third-wave feminists, as to their second-wave foremothers, is political awareness. That the personal experience is always indicative of a collective political is still assumed. "Historically, women's personal stories have been evidence of where the movement needs to go politically and, furthermore, that there is a need to move forward" (Baumgardner and Richards 20). My experience of others' interpretation of the aftermath of Katrina, particularly those in my overwhelmingly conservative retreat during and after the storm, reaffirmed for me the relevance of political engagement for women. Namely, the way in which class differences and political affiliation in American society are feminist issues. That is, they are the issues that divide women, determine one's style of mothering, either enable or delimit one's sensitivity to the plight of others and, by extension, either enable or delimit one's capacity for growth.

In her volume, *To Be Real: Telling the Truth and Changing the Face of Feminism*, Rebecca Walker writes of a generational gap between second and third wave women, "For us, the lines between Us and Them are often blurred, and as a result we find ourselves seeking to create identities that accommodate ambiguity and our multiple personalities: including more than excluding, exploring more than defining, searching more than arriving" (xxxiii). It seems to me that the searching, exploration and inclusion to which Walker refers are as essential to the growth of feminism, and

ous at his disclosure; suddenly I was aware of how absorbed I had been in my own work that week, and how little time I had, in fact, spent with my son. Suddenly, I could hear the somber ticking of an ominous metaphysical clock, visualize the days slipping by, feel, with an acute sense of loss, the passage of time during which I was estranged from my baby, the very wellspring of my existence, and I was plagued by remorse.

In this vulnerable state, I went to see my therapist. Like many of my friends, during the past two months since evacuating for Katrina, I've consulted, periodically, with a psychologist who is doing pro-bono work for Katrina evacuees. As one who is training to become a counselor, I am a big proponent, given the right circumstances and the right "fit," of therapy for both the mind and body. So, I did not hesitate to check in from time to time this semester to monitor my emotional health. This particular session, however, evolved into something that was more about the often-contentious battleground of mothering styles than the health of my psyche.

After describing my week and the ambivalence I had experienced in wanting to work while missing my child, my therapist, who had just come off of a five-year stint of stay-at-home motherdom with two young sons, boldly asserted, "Your first responsibility is to your son." "Well, yes," I consented, willingly, "Dylan is my first priority, but I do, also, have to do my work." "You choose to do your work," she interrupted, "As parents, we make all kinds of choices. But your son needs you now. And there's no one who can better raise him, better understand him, better handle his illness, or his moods, than you." "Well," I hesitated, aware that I was becoming defensive, "my husband did a great job this week." "And I commend him for that!" she interrupted again. "But your son needs both of you." I could not exactly disagree with her; Dylan needed me, of course he did, as I needed him. Yet, I explained to her, I also needed my work outside of him, was not cut out to be a stay-at-home mom. Even as a child, my role model was the pretty and endearing, yet seriously working, Mary Richards. Only, I always imagined, in my perfect universe I'd be Mary Richards with a kid. With the help of my husband, I'd have it all. I tried to explain this to her; the centrality of both work and family, my sense that my personal fulfillment could only enhance my effectiveness as a mother. "You can always work later. Get another

to the ongoing cultivation of relationships between women, as they are to any discussion of the complex dynamics that gave rise to the issues New Orleans faces today.

My own meandering exploration of life as a working mother and equal partner is rarely neat. Rather, I tend instinctively to resist those social pressures that would lead me to define my priorities too purely or narrowly, and thereby to sacrifice vital aspects of my "multiple personality" and complicated self. In this sense, to borrow Walker's now famous declaration, I too "am the third wave." I am of a community and, to an extent, generation of feminist women who strive to live up to our potential, intellectually and creatively and to identify and cultivate mates who appreciate that desire and ambition in us. At the same time, we feel entitled to participate in those aspects of traditional women's culture—motherhood and domesticity—from which we also derive pleasure. During my family's evacuation, I worked to re-invent and sustain my variegated nature in our temporary new "home" environment. Yet, the ambiguity of whether or not I was doing the "right" thing for my family, whose needs were, in many ways, compounded, engendered in me both a tremendous ambivalence—a simultaneous certainty of my needs and nagging self-doubt—and a realization that I had returned to the same tension that underwrites the identity of every contemporary feminist daughter. That is, that we can neither rebel against nor embrace the legacy of our mothers without misgiving. Rather, our journey through adulthood is fraught with inevitable potholes, much like

degree later," she responded tersely. "But you will never get back this time with your son. You don't get a second chance." I was beginning to sweat. "He's been in daycare—a good daycare—full time, since he was eight months old," I told her. "And it works for us. Both Chris and I need some time for ourselves" "Then why have children?" my therapist shot back.

So, here it was again; that same old furious question, cast, like so many stones, from woman to woman. Why have children if you aren't willing to be there twenty-four seven? Why have children if you aren't able to happily sacrifice your identity? Why can't you give up yourself, I have suffered and so should you! As the veil of professionalism fell away, we sat, my therapist and I, locked in the familiar stand off between stay-at-home and working mothers. At this point, I realized, we were both far too invested in our chosen paths and too self-conscious about how things might have been different, how like or unlike our own mothers we were, how sad we sometimes felt, how anxious we were that other women were doing it otherwise and that we, somehow, were missing the boat. My therapist suddenly flushed, aware I suspect, of her own less than therapeutic engagement, and hastily added, "I'm sorry. This is an issue I am passionate about." "I am, too," I answered, managing to smile, in response to which she smiled tentatively back. We talked for a while longer, moving to other, less provocative subjects. As I left, she gave me a list of children's books she thought I might enjoy reading to Dylan. Books, she claimed, that were imaginatively written and challenging intellectually. Books to stimulate me, as well as him. I took this list and thanked her. It seemed to me to be a gesture of reconciliation. A compromise from across intensely contested borders. Folding it carefully and placing it in my bag, I made a mental note to revisit the list, and, possibly, a local bookstore, at some future date.

June 25, 2006

On many levels, life in New Orleans post-Katrina is about death. For many people, that death is the literal physical death of family or friends, whether during the storm or in the health crisis that has ensued. Many are struggling with the death, so to speak, of their flooded homes, and all of the attendant possessions and memories therein. Many have suffered or are witnessing the death of careers. But everyone in New

a drive through the streets of New Orleans….

One of the biggest potholes, or challenges, I confronted upon returning to New Orleans in December, and in attempting to remake our lives there in the months that ensued, was how to cope appropriately with the specter of death. That existential dilemma, which always already awaits us as human beings, awaits us, as parents, with sudden and startling immediacy. In some ways, I feel it is our biggest hurdle: namely, the question of how to prepare our children gracefully for the fact that life is, ultimately, groundless (no parent or parent figure can protect us forever), chaotic (there is little that is truly in our control) and tragic (we are, after all, mortal), but that it is possible to thrive nonetheless. Overwhelmed by mold, debris, and wreckage, and awash in a communal sorrow that almost everyone I knew was attempting to medicate, for the most part, with alcohol, New Orleans reminded me of all three of these basic principles. My struggle to shield not just my increasingly perceptive son, but also my own psyche from the sheer magnitude of physical destruction, violence, and loss was ongoing. But my struggle to filter and digest the fragile and transitory core of the human condition was, by far, the greater. In the first year of life post-Katrina, New Orleans presented a neat microcosm of the insight at which we all, eventually, arrive: namely, that nothing you make in this life is guaranteed, everything that you build can, without a moment's notice, be taken away; and in every hopeful beginning, lies an inevitable end. And yet, somehow, we persevere, often passionately

Orleans now lives with the death of an environment and of life as they knew it before.

So, it's not surprising that children are also struggling, perhaps prematurely, with death anxiety or a budding knowledge of their mortality. This said, eight months after Katrina, my son Dylan seemed to remain blissfully and somewhat miraculously oblivious of death and, by extension, blissfully anxiety free. That is until one fateful day at the zoo.

Dylan and I set out one Saturday in May to see the many animals that consume so much of his time and attention as toys and in books. And, after making our usual loop around the enclosures of the "African Safari," pausing in ritual pit stops to observe the tigers, lions, elephants, and a lone toucan, Dylan announced with conviction that he wanted to ride on the carousel. So, we made our way over to the ticket booth, purchased a ticket, and waited in line. The way it works is that if a child is under a certain height a parent or other guardian is required to stand by the child while he or she rides at the cost of only one ticket. So, Dylan and I climbed together aboard the colorful merry-go-round, replete with zoo animals of every shape and size. Dylan carefully scoped out the leopard he wanted to ride and, after strapping him on, I climbed onto a neighboring ostrich, confident that Dylan was positioned securely atop his jungle cat, from which I was only an arm's length away.

As luck would have it, mommy was busted by the employee scanning the carousel to ensure that everyone was properly situated. "Ma'am, you need to stand by your son," the man in uniform advised me brusquely. I blushed as I slid shamefacedly from the ostrich's back and assumed my position by Dylan's side. I feel certain that Dylan observed my discomfort, especially as I explained to him somewhat tensely, and before I had had a chance to think, that the man thought it would be dangerous for him to ride alone.

Nevertheless, the moment passed and the two of us moved on to other sights and sounds. That is, until I sat with him on his bed at the end of the day, folding a sheet around his tired body and kissing him lightly on his forehead. "You had to get off the ostrich," Dylan remarked. "Yes. Yes, I did," I answered, bemused. "The man at the zoo thought it might be dangerous for you to ride alone, but really I think you were fine." "What other things are dangerous?" Dylan pressed on, ignoring my attempt to reassure

and with a sense of infinite possibility, despite ample evidence of our practical impotence. It seems that, given the means—a hammer and nails, saw and some wood or, to use a more traditionally feminine metaphor, a needle and thread, scissors and cloth—women, men, and children are bound to create. As Albert Camus writes in "The Myth of Sisyphus," "The struggle itself toward the heights is enough to fill a man's heart" (120). And so it was with many of the hearty and dogged survivors who returned home to pick up the trash and assemble anew.

Granted, my family's capacity to contemplate death from a position of relative safety, during the event and after, is a reflection of our relative privilege; we did not, as I've noted, lose either our home or our neighborhood. Moreover, we had the means to evacuate; we are white, middle-class, and insured. I was forced to drive, with Dylan, through virtual mine fields on our daily pilgrimage to and from work, school, and home, and to field from him persistently anxious questions. It was also in this fragile period of recovery that my son first became aware of death as a concept. But it remains to be said that we were then and are now able to absorb, contemplate, and learn from the death of our former existence and environment without, as it were, dying. This was not, obviously, the case for many. Katrina not only took the lives of hundreds of poor, elderly, and unlucky when it hit (recent estimates put the death toll at 1,577 in the New Orleans metropolitan area alone), but the toll has continued to rise in the years that have followed via a proliferation of mental and physical

him. "Well, gosh, I don't know...I mean, lots of things are dangerous; that's the nature of life," I stammered. "Crossing the street without looking both ways is dangerous. That's why you should always always wait to cross the street with me or your dad, um, driving cars can be dangerous. That's why mommy can't retrieve your toys while she's driving...yes, lots of things are dangerous, but as long as you're careful, you'll be okay." I was becoming palpably nervous. "Tell me about the hurricane. Tell me about going to Texas," Dylan proceeded, not missing a beat.

I paused to catch my breath. "Well, every year there's a hurricane season, and we happen to live in a city near the water, sooooo, we sometimes—but only sometimes—get a hurricane, you know, a really big storm, and have to leave for a few days while the hurricane passes through, but last year, the city got a really, really big hurricane and some of the city was broken. Remember? And so we had to stay in Texas, with Uncle Aaron and Aunt Brenda, for a while." Dylan contemplated my expression, the rush of my words. "But you should know that you will always be safe with us. I mean, we will always evacuate—you know, leave—before the hurricane gets here," I hurried on, hoping to contain the damage, reverse the tide. "And our house is really safe. Very strong. Like the brick house in The Three Little Pigs. You remember that house, don't you? Strong." Dylan seemed to consider this. "Read me a book," he answered, finally, presenting me with a welcome segue out of the conversation.

But the exchange left me unsettled. I felt certain that the incident on the carousel had triggered in him a budding awareness of death and related anxiety. When, however, I consulted with a play therapist I know, recounting the conversation and what had occurred previously, she observed, simply, that Dylan was asking whether or not he was safe. Well, sure, I thought to myself. But what lies beneath our desire for safety but an incipient knowledge that, ultimately, none of us is safe or protected because—ding ding ding—every one of us dies? And was it not appropriate for Dylan to connect this nascent awareness to the hurricane, that big, unwieldy symbol of finitude? Moreover, it was I who had, unwittingly, provided the catalyst for this grim recognition, a fact about which I felt extensive remorse.

What I learned a week later was that a "real" apprehension of death, one that is conscious anyway, looks quite different from Dylan's introspective line

illness, suicide, addiction, divorce, and domestic violence.

And so, in the searching spirit of third-wave feminism, which recognizes at once the limited nature of "women's issues," particularly those of the white bourgeois variety, *and* our intricate connection, as feminist women, to the palimpsest of political problems that compose American life, I want to qualify my narrative with the recognition that this is, after all, just one story, and hardly the worst. At the same time, I proffer my narrative, as it is, as a rubric of the vastly complex and painful arena wrought by this disaster within which I sought and seek to remember my home.

Works Cited

Baumgardner, Jennifer and Amy Richards. *Manifesta: Young Women, Feminism, and the Future.* New York: Ferrar, 2000.

Camus, Albert. *The Myth of Sisyphus: and Other Essays.* New York: Vintage, 1991.

Kinser, Amber E. "Negotiating Spaces For/Through Third Wave Feminism." *NWSA Journal* 16.3 (2004): 124-153.

Walker, Rebecca. *To Be Real: Telling the Truth and Changing the Face of Feminism.* New York: Anchor, 1995.

of questioning. That one doesn't, in fact, apprehend death either easily or openly.

One evening, while Dylan and I were discussing the characters in the Disney movie Finding Nemo, on which he had found a fairly insubstantial little book at the local library, Dylan asked if Nemo was a girl. "Well, no, honey," I answered. "Nemo is a boy." "No he's not." Dylan insisted stubbornly. "Nemo is a girl." "No, really, honey, trust me on this one—Nemo's a boy." "He's a girl!" Dylan repeated, his voice growing louder. "Well, why don't we just go watch the movie?" I offered smugly, gesturing towards our DVD collection. "Okay," he agreed readily. So, while Dylan settled on the couch, I put Finding Nemo into the DVD player. In the first few moments of the film—those memorably disturbing ones just before Nemo's mother and all of his siblings are obliterated in several swift bites—Dylan proclaimed cheerfully, "SEE! Nemo is a girl!" "No, Dylan," I explained gently, "that's Nemo's mommy." "Nemo's mommy???" Dylan asked, mystified.

Oh lord, I thought. Disney's penchant for killing its mothers was finally coming home to roost...We had been watching the movie for nearly two years and I had always felt relieved that Dylan did not appear to notice. Now, he seemed alarmed and confused as he watched Nemo's father whimper as he cradled that last little egg. "But what what—WHERE is Nemo's mommy?" "Well," I replied thinking that I had to tell him the truth and nothing but, "Dylan's mother was eaten by that creature." "WHY?" Dylan gasped. "Why was she eaten by that creature?" "Well, I guess it was hungry," I responded, wincing internally. "WHY? WHY IS THAT CREATURE HUNGRY?" Dylan cried insistently. "Well, I don't know," I answered. "WHERE ARE THE EGGS?" he pressed, scanning my face. "They were eaten, too," I confessed, feeling genuinely sad at the cruelty of the world. "WHY?" Dylan wondered again. "I want Nemo's mommy back!" This continued off and on for another half an hour at which point I suggested that we turn off the movie and get ready for bed, a proposal to which he quickly agreed.

And on this night, as I tucked him in and kissed his forehead, Dylan was strangely quiet. I cursed Disney as I cursed post-Katrina New Orleans and, moreover, myself for our seemingly conjoined roles in his flustered awakening. Could I turn back the clock, in all of us, I thought, I certainly would.

4
Mothering in a Time of Terror

LARA LENGEL, ANCA BIRZESCU AND JENNIFER MINDA

In her look toward what she calls a new politics of motherhood, a politics that favors egalitarianism over divisiveness, support over disregard, Melissa Benn and other feminist scholars (see Kinser and others in this volume) remind us of the complex relationship between feminism and mothering. Concerned about this alliance, Benn asks, "If the story of feminism is the story of ideas about women, then mothers and motherhood should, surely, be one of its natural subjects? After all, no woman is born without one; most women still become one" (190). Clearly, feminisms celebrate mothers and mothering, as evidenced by the work in this collection, and by the other feminist scholarship upon which we build (see Anzaldúa). Less clear are the feminist voices; they are often so subtle they create a nearly imperceptible undercurrent that seems to have little to no interest in the enterprise of motherhood. It is the silences that are most perplexing (see O'Brien Hallstein in this volume), as if feminisms are reluctant to give voice to their interest. Maureen Freely explains, in her *Open Letter to the Mothers Feminism Forgot*, "It is through well meaning silence that Mothers became the Others of feminism—in much the same way that women become the Others of patriarchy" (13).

We use the term "enterprise" of motherhood specifically here to underscore the risky and life-altering endeavor of mothering, a venture so testing to women, and to some feminisms, that there have been numerous moments, particularly palpable in the first and second waves, when thoughts about mothering shifted along a spectrum of attitudes from love to contempt, inciting ambivalence, self-doubt, even self-hate in both women with and *sans enfants*.

Feminism's relationship to motherhood is a "kind of hypocritical poseur, the engaging friend who talks about you behind your back" (Benn 191). That hypocritical poseur is less threatening than the duplicitous work of big media, government, and other instruments of dominant ideology. They have instigated another type of hypocrisy, the "mommy wars" which situate mothers against "non-mothers," women who work outside the home against at-home mothers (who, apparently, do no work), and mothers against the childcare professionals they employ. The "mommy wars" demand that women (and men) take sides and, as a result, reduce a multifaceted phenomenon of lived experience, multiple identities, and overwhelming responsibilities down to a simplistic bipolar opposition. Placed unwillingly on either side of this clash when asked to defend their choices and claims, women in the third wave wonder how they got involved in this conflict; they don't recall enlisting to serve in this war. Others take the divide to heart, asking of their perceived enemy, "why do they hate us?" as they silence certain identities and activities over others, depending on which squad the interlocutor appears to be fighting.

More worrisome are the unasked questions, the assumptions that all's well. Could it be the soothing effect of dominant discourses surrounding new millennium prestige mothering, with its corporate work-life balance policies, its shiny egalitarian landscape of middle class professionalism? Ambitious fantasies abound in advertising, entertainment media, even shareholder reports: the young professional reaches into her late model family van to pick up her toddler out of his high-end car seat/booster/stroller transportation "solution," while supportive husband/father stands holding their infant, all a-smiles in the doorway of the four-bedroom suburban colonial. All is beautiful in this land of family values; the "new" (illustrated by the active, professional mother and her helpful partner), yet traditional, heteronormative family is wrapped in a cocoon of invulnerability, safety, promise. The future looks bright even to those young women and men whom we have taught and with whom we have learned in gender and women's studies classrooms, spaces where questions about dominant ideology *should* be asked. Many of the tough questions about how they will negotiate their future parenting choices are left unasked; instead the invulnerable make optimistic claims about equal opportunities and commitment to conflict-free shared parenting; they're confident that they will easily secure all the *ecoutrements* of heteronormative "success" required to place themselves in the privileged panorama described above. All will be well when they embark upon their parenting project.

This imagined landscape adds to the divisiveness propelling the "mommy wars" in Western Europe, the United States, and other rich nations, since so many mothers are excluded from the opulence these rich nations embody. While the prosperity and material comfort is promised to all in these lands, it is provided to a select few who have access to various forms of power including, but not limited to, class standing, economic stability, health insurance, and safe and reliable childcare. The transnational telecasts of this landscape, too, contribute to broader global divisions characterized by tangible evidence of marginalization and enactments of exclusion. In turn they incite other wars—chasms between have's (the global power elite) and have-not's (the billions living impoverished under the rule of the elite). But these chasms suffer from the inattention of all kinds of hypocritical poseurs who claim that a powerful "us" cares about the disenfranchised "them."

The war that has suffered no inattention whatsoever is, of course, the mammoth "us" and "them" scheme known as the "War on Terror." It locates "us"/"patriots" against the terrorist "them," leaving no space for options in between. This war has painted a clear *visage* of the Other (see Boyd-Barrett; Cassara and Lengel), but terrorism used to be seen as politically-fueled violence or threats of violence instigated by a nameless, faceless Other. Could it be only several years ago when terrorism was the domain of the Other, doing its dirty work in its distant Other place? Perhaps it is not so startling, then, to reflect upon the confusion emanating from the cocooned invulnerable citizens of the land of "us" who asked on a certain sunny day in 2001, and continue to ask, "Why do they hate us?"

It is the multiple layers of the discourse surrounding "us" and "them" that need to be more closely examined, to understand how they intersect and correlate, despite their seemingly disparate nature and characteristics. As we interrogate the "us"/"them" dichotomy, we first examine ourselves, and our own markers of privilege: our whiteness, our education, our claim to at least a few of the elements incorporated into the portrait of privileged parenting (a tenured position, house in a college town, high-tech kid stuff, even if acquired second-hand), our professional identities (offering access to learning, guidance of encouraging mentors, a few yet vital institutional benefits such as health insurance, and opportunities for travel to research the challenges and immense accomplishments of mothers in Asia, the Middle East and North Africa, and Eastern Europe).

We question the hierarchy of citizenship in the "nanny state"—a term used for a type of excessively protective political rule, but also for a state embodied and ruled by socio-economically and professionally privileged mothers (and fathers) who employ, often, underpaid and overworked caregivers, and our own identities as mothers who have needed daycare and caregivers who have provided it. We attempt to raze power rifts, between mother and carer, mother and Other. We acknowledge that mothering is best when it is a collaborative experience incorporating the love, expertise, and capacity of many mothers. We honor the ways women care for the children we have come to love, whether they emerged from our own wombs or from those women whom we have also come to love.

We choose to ignore the various rungs on which the academic hierarchy places us, and the ageism inherent in some third wave feminist thought; we write not as an associate professor in her forties, a graduate student in her late twenties and a recent undergraduate in her earlier twenties, but as three women who have nurtured a bond of collaboration emerging from all sorts, parenting, writing, thinking, and caring. Through our collaboration, we create a powerful alliance, a power *with* rather than a "top-down" or power *over* (see Albrecht and Brewer; Hartsock; Macy). Sharing their ideas on feminist leadership and alliances, Lisa Albrecht and Rose Brewer remind us that "power, derived from energy and strength in people, requires an openness and vulnerability" (5). We attempt, writing as British, American, and Romanian citizens, to maintain this openness and vulnerability, to seek ways to diminish the partitions between nations and different global feminisms, and to question the politicized alliances which advance the borderless nature of a world organized in an increasingly transnational power hierarchy of "us's" and the "them's."

Most crucially, in our commitment as mothers, as daughters, and as sisters, we aim to interrogate and, in even some small way, break down the blockades—the cultural, economic, political, ethnic, religious lines of defense—that have contributed to the experiences detailed here. We write of the horrific, the senseless slayings of those who, in their mundane negotiation of urban space commuting from home to work or school, stepped into the wrong place at the wrong time. We also write of the everyday, the "mundane" lived experience that is nearly invisible when all's well, the same everyday moments (an ice cream cone, a quick farewell hug) to which we cling in a time of terror. We also think of the mothers of those who implement suicide bombings. They lost a son, they bear the grief of many other mothers whose sons and daughters he killed, they bear the divisive Other-ing bestowed upon them not only by the powerful "us," but also by their own disenfranchised communities. We consider, as well, those who have been wrongly identified as terrorists, like Jean Charles de Menezes, an unarmed 27-year-old Brazilian electrician who was shot to death by the London Metropolitan Police Service when suspected of involvement with the July 21, 2005 bombing attempts on the London Underground.[1] We wonder if those of us who are peace activists (and, thus, "anti-patriots"?) are under the watchful eye of the state.

We wonder how the overwhelmingly male domain of terrorism is situated within a discourse of motherhood in mainstream media. Headlines like "The Mother of all Terrorism Battles" (Boehlert) and "Israel is The Mother of Terrorism in The Middle East" (Akleh) suggest it's all about mothers. In "Mother Nature, terror-ist" in *U.S. News and World Report*, Bernadine Healy writes, "With our minds focused on war and political terrorism, Mother Nature proves to be the worst of all terrorists in the horror of her sudden assault on vulnerable innocents." In "'Mother of Satan': The New Terror Weapon of Choice," ABC News writers Burke, Setrakian and Cuomo define "Mother of Satan" as acetone peroxide, a liquid bomb ingredient that could pass for hair gel, could be inserted into a tube of toothpaste, and detonated with a flash of a simple disposable camera. The same substance used by the fathers, brothers, and sons in the London Underground on July 7, 2005. Not mothers. Our children were in London, scheduled to return just weeks after 24 male suspects planned to set off the "Mother of Satan" explosives on ten flights from London to the US, ripping them apart over the Atlantic or, worse, sending the shards of metal and bodies down upon the citizens of major US cities (Barr). Why is this explosive a "mother"? Would a mother create this? Would a mother detonate this?

What mothers do is try to understand, to help heal, to protect. Our stories here illustrate just a few instances of violence; there are many mothers who endure state-governed terrorism, occupation and oppression on a daily basis (see Anzaldúa; Giacaman and Johnson; Lentin). Our stories illustrate that we have been merely observers to trauma, and that one can only begin to try to understand the horrific pain of losing a loved one to such violence, let alone losing your own child. We remain untouched, at least bodily, by the petrol and nail cocktails that killed 52 and injured upwards of 700 in London on July 7, 2005, by the attempts to kill many more with similar home-made explosive devices hidden in backpacks on July 21, 2005, or by the arsenal of explosives found in a Mercedes in Piccadilly Circus just a few days before we sent this essay to be published. Have we (the two of us who happened to be in the US, Italy, and Romania at the time of these incidents) been spared either by vast geophysical distances or (for the one of us who was traveling to Central London by public transport on both of those July days with two young children) by a few meters, by the choice of this bus over that one?

As we reflect on these choices, and how fortunate we are, we share these letters and, in our alliance, we refer to the young persons who learned of bombs on those days as our children. One of us gave birth to them. All three of us have mothered them. We are connected by a common thread of our love for them and for each other, and for the many mothers who have been affected by all kinds of violence. The letters begin with those written by Jennifer, who was with the children during the two days of bombings in London. They are followed by those by Anca, writing from Romania and reflecting on the violence in her own nation. Finally, Lara writes with hope for a more peaceful future for our children.

Remembering London
London, 8 July 2005

Dear big cat and little cat,

You woke me up after sneaking into my room, trying hard to stifle your giggles, then jumping on my bed yelling "Up, Up Kitty! Hello Kitty!" I had been with you in London for one month the first week of July.[2] At this point we were all feeling comfortable in our summer routines of morning BBC Kids, then park, then shop, then back home to prepare tea, or our special days of an outing to a museum or far-away park. London being new to me, I was just as excited as you, my little jumping kitties, as we planned another day on the town.

At book-reading and happy thoughts time the previous evening, we had talked about getting up extra early and heading all the way across London, to the Bethnal Green Museum of Childhood to check out the collection of toys and games throughout history. We had hoped to be on the Northern Line (you remember that one—the black lines on the subway map. The Tube line that's so deep and old that the train pushes out extra dusty air onto the train platform as the train arrives) heading northeast from home by 9:00 a.m., but ended up running behind and watching some morning shows on BBC Kids while filling up the "nanny pack" with the day's supplies: wet wipes, a book or two, a few colored pencils, and "wawoo-baboo"—do you remember that was your name for water bottles?

As we were heading out the door, I got a text message alert about a power surge on the Tube; it said that it would be better to take the bus, due to the train delays. I looked on the computer and, despite your insistence on checking out your favorite "computers" (what you call kid-friendly websites like BBC Kids Online and BobtheBuilder.com), I managed to get a quick glance at BBC News Online which at that time also mentioned the power surge and subsequent outage on the Tube.

With no easy way to cross from West London all the way eastward to Bethnal Green, we chose to take the bus towards Piccadilly Circus instead. There were no signs of distress or upset among any of the passengers on the bus, only slight mumbles of annoyance about the disruption in the morning commute. After about 15 minutes riding on the upper level of the big red number 94 bus, we entered Shepherd's Bush. Pulling to a stop outside one of the Tube stations, I noticed several busses stopped up ahead, unmoving. Our driver pulled up behind one of the busses, put our bus in park, walked quickly off the bus, down the street, and out of view. No one around us made any motion to get up, or appeared concerned. I remember smiling as you looked out the windows, looking for shepherds and their sheep. A man behind me complained about how inconvenient these driver switches were, so I assumed that was what was going on. After several minutes, a driver still hadn't appeared, and several passengers became restless and left the bus in a huff. I was proud of how patient you were and how quiet and attentive you were when a police officer stepped aboard and shouted a warning.

"The busses are stopped, get off now!" The mass of bewildered passengers headed toward the bus doors and spilled out onto the streets. I asked the nearest officer what was going on, and got a gruff, "Transportation's not safe today in London. We are under attack." Confused, I asked why the power outage on the Tube was shutting down the bus routes. The answer I received was, *"Power surges don't kill people or blow the roofs off busses, missy."*

Then, it was as though word of terrorist attacks began to spread through London in a matter of seconds—the time it takes to detonate a bomb. Time simultaneously sped up and slowed down. People quickly tried to reach their loved ones on their phones to share the news of the attacks. But no one was moving much, nor seemed to be in a hurry to get to work. It was as though there was a clear break in the crowd, measured in terms of those who had gotten the news about the bombs and those who hadn't. Standing alone with both of you, holding your hands firmly along a busy street in the unfamiliar area of Shepherd's Bush, I protected you even though we were jostled along with a crowd uncertain where it was headed. We needed those shepherds now, to guide us peacefully to a safe haven.

Since our cell phone couldn't make or receive calls, I sent a text message to Daddy to tell him we were safe and were going to look for a place to wait for information from police or other helpers. I was concerned about what to tell you but there wasn't really time for questions, and there wasn't really panic, just a sort of aimless wandering and "What now?" attitude among the crowd in general. I looked for the nearest place we could sit down and gather more information as we tried to figure out what was going to happen next. Amid the confusion and mild chaos, I spotted a McDonald's up ahead. I knew it would be somewhere you'd find familiar. Looking back now, I can't believe that I was concerned that Dad would be angry that I had exposed you to processed chicken nuggets, french fries, and a toy to calm you in a time of crisis. However, those were my thoughts as I headed toward the familiar golden arches. We sat down with our Happy Meals, while I cautiously observed the crowd around us. It seemed that news of the attack was still trickling slowly into everyone's awareness. Cell phone lines were jammed, and the people surrounding us were cursing and furiously punching numbers into their phones. After a long series of failed attempts at communicating with Dad, we agreed to go to our park in the square, wait for him to meet us, then all to go home together.

As we were leaving McDonald's, we struck up a conversation with a friendly woman working there as she wiped the tables. She commented on what an inconvenience the power outages were, since her daughter was on a field trip in Windsor, and she was concerned that it may take her daughter longer to get home with all of the evening commuters jamming the busses. Here I was alone in an unfamiliar place, and together we bonded over concerns for the safety of the children around us. She was a single mom who sent her daughter off on her field trip and headed off to work at McDonald's that morning.

As we talked, I realized that I was the first person from whom she had heard about the attacks. What she previously thought was a not uncommon situation of public transportation disruptions was, in fact, a series of bombings. In a matter of seconds, her demeanor went from annoyance to pure panic. With the buses no longer running in Central London, she wondered if her daughter was safe and if she would be able to get home at all. This mummy was stuck at a McDonald's, with no way to reach her daughter by phone or transportation, and complete uncertainty about whether or not either would be able to return home that night. The three of us gave her a big "family hug," then sent happy thoughts to her and her daughter. We talked about how scary it must be for that mummy and sent thankful thoughts that we were safe and together. I reassured you that I would always keep you safe.

I was also trying to reassure myself that we could be safe in a world that unkind people have made unsafe. I felt powerless in the face of man-made explosives. I thought about the notion of man-made; were there any woman-made bombs exploded on this day? Somehow I thought not.

I continued asking myself these questions, trying to maintain a comforting smile for the moments you looked up at me, with questioning expressions on your lovely faces. We walked to the center of the park, a small triangular patch of grass, waiting for Dad. The swings swayed in the wind, as though abandoned suddenly. Our park seemed sad; you didn't even ask to play. I think it was clear that something was wrong in London that day. The three of us stood there all alone on our little green triangle, a big sky turning increasingly gray above us.

Just as the sky threatened to release its tears, mine began to well up in my eyes. I tried to suppress them so that you wouldn't worry. But, little cat, you're like a barometer, you always sense when tears are about to flow. You asked, as you do when your inner barometer gives you a tear warning, "Are you crying, Aunt Jen?" I responded, "A little bit, but not too much," just like you tend to say, trying hard to blink away the waterfall before it could flow in earnest. I tried to explain that I felt how you feel when you say, "I feel only a little bit good" (And, I must say, your positive focus makes me smile when you say things like this).

I said that I was crying with relief that we were okay, but sad that others were not okay. I also tried to explain to myself the complex, conflicting set of feelings washing over me. Was I really crying out of relief, that we were lucky that time, far away from the bombs? Was I crying because I feel an overwhelming sense of wanting to show you the world, but, especially now, keep you out of it? Was I crying because I want to keep you safe, but am entirely uncertain if that's even possible? Was I was crying not out of fear, but in anticipation of the fears that were to come, the changes in the way we look at the world? I thought about how alone I feel here sometimes, with mainly you two to talk to. I thought about the sudden rupture to lots of people's worldviews, not so long ago at all, on the day when the airplanes crashed into the tall towers in New York. You don't remember that day, little cat, because you weren't even a half-year old. The bad things happened at about the same time of day as today, on the same kind of sunny, warm morning, the same promise of a lovely day, a lovely future. You may have some very distant memory, big cat, of that day in the first half of your third year. I remember your mommy calling me from London. She got a phone call from another mommy at the university whose students came in to her class and said something really bad was happening. Some kind of horrible accident in New York. The news traveled quickly across the Atlantic, but details were still hazy on that London afternoon—that New York morning.

Canceling class and picking up her 1-year-old son, your friend "E," from his carer, she rushed over to your house. She and mommy took turns holding baby cat and/or the phone, while they tried to simultaneously keep the toddlers doing crafts at the dining room table, out of view of the BBC's transmission of the falling towers, and keep their fingers on the redial button, frantically and continually trying, in vain, to reach their mothers, your grandmas, across the big ocean. The international phone lines were blocked for hours. Mom said she was worried most about grandma; she was alone, thousands of miles away from you all in London. Suddenly the world seemed disconnected and entirely uncertain. With all flights cancelled, would you ever be able to leave the island and see your extended family again?

And the next question the mommies thought was: Is London the next target?

The sound of a car horn jolted me back to the present, the park, the graying sky. All around the square, the streets were becoming crowded with an unusual amount of traffic. Londoners who rarely used their cars were out in full force, left with no other way to travel once the trains and busses stopped running. Once we were safely in the family car after being picked up by Dad, I began to hear snippets of what had happened on the radio. The information I had heard so far began to have even deeper meaning as the bomb locations and details began to surface. As I was piecing all of the information together, it was almost as if I was studying for an exam, absorbing the places, the names, all the details so I could remember, and so I could situate us in the day. If we hadn't been watching a second episode of Teletubbies that morning, we would have left the house on time and could have been much more geographically close to the bombs. The

Underground lines now closed were trains I had taken as recently as the night before the attacks.

That night, when the busses began running again, I headed to Central London. I felt compelled to see what was left behind. Walking through the West End, at a time when the nightlife should have been booming, the space was empty, in total silence. For the first time, I felt scared to be walking alone. All of the West End shows had been cancelled. Just a day earlier, Trafalgar Square had been bustling with celebration and confetti as London won the bid to host the 2012 Olympics. You'll remember watching the pigeons thinking the confetti was food. Now, the square was silent, celebrations cancelled, pigeons plucking at the aftermath. People everywhere seemed unsure of what to do. Walking home, I came upon a gathering in a parking lot. It was a gathering of police officers, standing near the open boot of a car. As I got nearer, and observed the scene up close, I saw the entire rear of the car was filled with big guns.

In a city where the police had previously not carried firearms, firearms were being distributed to the police force, as though an afterthought. It struck me then, that this was just one of the many changes London would see. I have a month left with you here in London, and I am determined not to let fear keep us from exploring everything London has to offer. While I am deeply shaken by the events that took place here, I'm confident that the city will stay strong. We got through the confusion, you are safe, and we will be as careful as possible while we continue to explore the city, and seek peace.

Love, Aunt Jen

Remembering Childhood in a Land Under Siege
Bucharest, Romania, 14 July 2005

Dear, dear, children,

I am writing to let you know how relieved I am to hear that you and Aunt Jen are safe and well in London. I want to write because what happened this week brought back bad memories, hidden inside me but not lost, of incidents that took place sixteen years ago in my country, Romania. I believe in the healing gift of writing, in its power to release the burden of our fears that begin in our childhood and sometimes continue. I don't want your memories of this time of your young life to be sad or scary, but to be joyful and full of peace and sunshine. Sharing these experiences of my childhood through writing helps not to bury and forget the past, but to accept our painful memories, and to regain hope and commitment to create a better world for you, our children, and our future.

The similarity between what happened in my country sixteen years ago and what happened in yours this week is that the people who hurt and killed others were like an invisible enemy. The difference is that there was already a clear enemy in Romania and other countries under communist rule. This enemy was the government, political leaders who stopped us from saying what we felt, doing things we believed in. We had hoped that communism would end at some point, so that we were free to say and do as we wanted to. But after fifty years of communist rule, our hopes were thrown in a swirling pool mixed with hopes for a happy future, and then fears of a more dangerous and sad life than we were already living, then back again to hope. It was like life was playing games with us. In December 1989, our emotions and experiences started to be flung together chaotically, in a quick chain of events lasting just a couple of weeks, even though at the time it felt like forever. Once you get even older, we can talk more about all these things—Heroism and Revolution, heroic deaths, horrible lies and orchestrated diversion, a stolen revolution, a coup d'etat, mass manipulation of citizens, and impressively persuasive incidents of what was called terrorism, all resulting in irrational but not less tragic death.[3]

I travel back in my mind, taking you on a journey to a place and a life I lived sixteen years ago, when I was nine years old, just a few years older than you at this point. Once you can read this letter on your own, without mommy's help, maybe you will be this very same age. I want you to close your eyes and picture a place, maybe your favorite park, your bedroom filled with the glow of your sparkly night light, a place you could never imagine being anything other than peaceful and quiet. That's where I'm taking you now. We're traveling to an old, old town. Older than anything you've seen in the US, old as some of the old castles you have seen in London. At some point you'll learn in history classes about colonization. This town was colonized by the Saxons in the Middle Ages, many hundreds of years ago. On our journey in this old town, we go to an old street that bears the name of a nineteenth-century French novelist. That had been a place where nothing bad or out of the ordinary happened. Children like you played in the streets, and grandmas and grandpas visited on park benches stroked by the gentle late afternoon sunlight. When memories like these are joyful and peaceful, you are fond of them, you are proud of them, you cherish them, ordinary or extraordinary. I used to be fond of my memories about this place, so every time I was sad or distressed I would recall one by one, those precious images and moments. And it would work miracles—bringing healing and peace.

The days before Christmas 1989, looking forward to a restful time with my family in this wonderful town, I did not have the slightest idea that the events that were just about to happen would forever change my memories about that place. It was such a joy to celebrate Christmas together with my grandparents, in my wonderful childhood town. Celebrating Christmas and Easter under communism was a bit different from the charm of Christmas trees, lights, presents, and Easter egg hunts you enjoy. But even though we celebrated these important events silently, these family celebrations brought us strength to go on and hope that the political situation would change sooner or later.

I remember my aunt telling me about the four-hour train ride she took on December 18 and the brief exchange of words she had with a colleague at the railway station in Bucharest, just before getting on the train. She was told about rumors that civilian anti-government riots started in the streets of Timisoara, a city in the western part of the country, and that armed forces were firing at the demonstrators. My family already knew about this rumor that was to be confirmed just days later, when the protests would spread throughout the country, eventually reaching the heart of the capital. Suddenly, preparations to celebrate approaching Christmas became unspoken hopes for a long awaited miracle of liberation from the totalitarian regime. We were frightened, but we also dared to hope.

Our hope escalated on December 21, during the officially held mass assembly in Bucharest. Broadcasted live on national television, the official agenda was punctured by the voices of small resistance groups who shouted "Down with the dictatorship!" and, though the televised coverage was taken off the air a few moments after the shouting began, citizens across the country caught an important glimpse into the resistance efforts sweeping through Romania. They also saw the anxiousness on the face of the dictator trying to quiet the crowds from his balcony. This was the sparkle that prompted citizens to get out in the streets and protest during that very night. On the next day, the president and his spouse took off in their personal helicopter and were later arrested, and on Christmas day they were executed.

It appeared, thus, that our enemy was gone. But then, in a chaos of confrontations involving army, intelligence services, militia, "terrorists," and civilians so confusing, an invisible enemy emerged. The rumors and "official" news suggested, however, that these enemies were terrorists. We were frightened because we didn't know who this new, faceless, nameless enemy was. Was the enemy against the former ruler fighting for the people, or aligned with the ruler and, thus, attacking the citizenship in order to shut down our new nation?

We didn't know until years later, what started as a spontaneous anti-communist protest in Timisoara, suppressed in blood by the ruling government and its army, transformed into a conspired attack of the regrouped communist forces against civilians for the sole purpose of seizing the power. Communists spread word of "terrorism" to justify their intervention.

Years later, newly liberated Romanian newspapers reported the number of citizens hurt and killed before December 22 was approximately ten times smaller than the casualties registered after that date (Vasile). We were still trying to answer questions like: Who killed who? Who are the terrorists? and Who is accountable for these horrible crimes? Reports after the fall of communist rule stated, "There haven't been any terrorists identified, but only the armed cadres and civilians who fired as a result of manipulations, and of orders given by some of their superiors…. It was an attack against country's citizens" (Vasile).

But, children, I don't want to write to you what I now know about these events. I want to write what I lived and felt during those days, when everyone experienced fear, confusion, despair, terror, and a glimmer of hope. I want to write what I remember about being a child in the middle of this situation that, for someone so young, was very hard to understand. I remember so intensely the beginning of the nightmare—deafening sounds of sirens and machine gunfire at night, shouting of people in the streets, piercing lights coming from the helicopters patrolling above us. I also remember how my mother tried to keep my sister and me calm by having us draw pictures and do crafts.

How did I understand all that was so suddenly happening? I first thought of the family members who were not with us, afraid that we would never see them again. I felt so helpless. Terror and panic were approaching from everywhere, from the streets and from television and radio. The "news" and rumors about terrorist snipers and intelligence services forces fighting back became fanatical—the oil refinery close to town was going to be bombed; the drinking water reserve had been poisoned, and for a time the color of tap water did become dirty-brown. I remember how frightening the idea of poisoned water was to us children. We take for granted safe water, just like when you enter your classroom, wash your hands, and then take a sip of cool, clean, clear water from the water fountains. Think about what life would be like if there was no safe water. Though untrue, the rumors debilitated our thinking, and made us fearful of everything and everyone. These "terrorist" attacks were meant not only to mutilate people physically but also to cripple our soul and courage.

Other images remain with me, trucks passing in front of our house, carrying new coffins made of white polished wood. Mothers and fathers dressed in mourning clothes grasping the coffins as they slowly moved along the street, as if in a last desperate attempt to hang on to their children. It is that kind of image that mutilates mothers' spirits and makes them question the purpose of bringing new lives into the world.

I didn't see the far scarier images that happened that time; I only heard of them years later, when I was a teenager. I don't want to scare you needlessly now, but help you understand how much we love you, how much mothers love their children. How life would never be the same if we lost you. And how I hope that as you grow older you will work hard to create a world where people live peacefully, instead of a world where people kill children. I thus learnt the youngest victim in what was once such a peaceful town was only 3 years old—Paul Alin Chirca, killed at a checkpoint by Military Unit 1205, the military base where his father had fulfilled his military stage. After he, his father, and his mother, seven months pregnant with Paul's sibling-to-be, were initially given permission to drive on, the Military Unit started to fire at the car. Little Paul was killed instantly. Afterward, investigators found 37 bullet holes in the Chirca family car. Both parents were wounded. The mother was taken to the emergency under military escort. The father was arrested under suspicion of terrorism (Popescu-Oprea). I feel now more than ever the anger your mother felt when she shared with me news reports on terrorism that used "mother" terms. How could anyone liken the source of life with the very force that negates it? What was left for Paul's mom, this pregnant and mourning mother, to hope for and believe in?

Everyone was scared. I was trying to persuade myself that we would be safe because we stayed inside the house. With its large basement the house became in my mind a neutral, untouchable place that protected us; I imagined that we were staying in one of the enchanted palaces I used to dream about and read about in my bedtime stories. Years later though I learnt how death had peeked through windows and walls in the town of my dreams, how people had died in their own houses, shot by bullets that came through roofs, windows, and walls.[4]

Many families mourned their departed, without even having the closure of knowing who killed them. A Romanian journalist wrote, "To each of those who died then we owe our life. They left this world instead of us, just because they were there to meet death. And today, our steps are leaning on their shoulders. We owe today's Romania to "Romania in Heavens" (Popescu-Oprea).

This is my story I wanted to share with you, a story of another child in another place in another time, who experienced the same fears, and asked the same questions. Our stories are placed in different global contexts, and yet the similarities are striking. Your mother sent me the stories of those in London who did not live. Mihaela Otto, I see her as a lovely young woman who could have been a neighbor of mine in Bucharest.[5] I was thinking about her 78-year-old mother, Elena Draganescu, who lived with Mihaela, her husband Matthew and their two teenage sons. I think about what other needless devastation Elena might have seen in Romania, sixteen years ago. I believe that sharing these memories with other mothers and their children is the right step to make known our justified anger, and to our mission to stigmatize terror of any kind that can be inflicted upon human beings, upon Daughters and Sons of Mothers.

All my love, Aunt Anca

Remembering Our Strength
London, July 22, 2005

Dear kittens,

We are safe once again. But there were more bombs today in London. I'm writing to you to let you know what has happened today so that you can remember how close we were this time. We were spending this beautiful and sunny day at Kensington Garden in Hyde Park. I was talking with a mother and her teenage daughters who had just arrived from the US for a visit. They were curious about what it was like to be in London during the attack on July 7. You and her daughters were playing in the sand near the giant pirate ship when we heard helicopters roaring overhead. Two large black military helicopters came into view and circled the area a few times, drawing a crowd. You were in awe of the big, black machines, and the adults around us seemed to wonder what was going on. As the helicopters circled overhead, the teenage girls discussed whether or not Princes William and Harry were likely to step off the helicopters. Two weeks earlier, prior to 7/7, I might have shared in their wishful and whimsical thoughts. However, this London was a city changed, on edge about any disruption in routine. Seconds later, a text message arrived from Daddy. The message was simple but definitive. "It's happened again. Stay where you are."

The big black metal birds landing on the lawn at Kensington Palace weren't here for a friendly visit or for a show of ceremony. Blinded by the sun, I snapped a picture as they began to descend, and the image captured showed a large black mass shielding the rays of the sun. When the helicopters touched down, military men dressed in black clamored out with drawn rifles and ran towards Shepherd's Bush. We later found out this was one of the sites where one of the "rucksack bombs," as they were being called, was found. This time, during the frightening minutes of uncertainty, mothers, nannies, and families surrounded me. I think we all shared a kind of unity and solidarity. I definitely felt more of a sense of belonging, and less pushed out of the way or jostled down a busy street. Whatever it was, whatever had happened, the term "again" weighed on my mind. We had already dealt with the fear, uncertainty, and shock of a terrorist attack once. I didn't feel as though we were completely unprepared. Many Tube stations and the entire Piccadilly line were already shut down. London was becoming a city readjusted. Today, there was a sense of calm. Whatever had occurred, I had confidence that the situation was being well-handled.

There was no sense of urgency to head home, and again there were Tube line closures and throngs of passengers re-routed and displaced. When we did head for home, our only option was to cross the entirety of Hyde Park, a journey that would have previously seemed way too long for both of you to walk. Along the way, we shared weary smiles with other pedestrians, as we waited in the queue for ice cream, and we looked for the nearest functioning transportation. These smiles were smiles of resignation, as though they were saying, "This is it, this is our lives now, these detours, these bomb scares."

To you, this was an adventure. Going from one end of the park to the other and the added treat of ice cream along the way in the hot sun were a change of scenery. We even picked a few flowers along the way to put on the dinner table. That night I sat down with you, to try to find out what you had gathered about what was going on. You were clearly excited by the sight of the huge helicopters and soldiers climbing off, but I wanted to see what was beyond your wonder. You didn't seem scared or concerned, but it was now clear to you that some bad people had put bombs on the trains. That was why we had to take different trains now, or the bus. To me, the most important thing was that you weren't scared. Your naiveté was a blessing, something I wish I still had. Together, we looked at a website titled werenotafraid.com. On the website, people from around the world had submitted pictures in response to al Qaeda's claim that "Britain is now burning with fear." Instead, London is declaring, "We are not afraid." At first sight, during those critical first few hours as the uncertainty and carnage set in, our London may have been afraid. I know I was momentarily scared, but this city's unity made me stronger inside. Sharing these pictures and this message of support and strength with you made me feel as though we were all healing together. We were declaring our strength and our refusal to be scared. In a small way, I felt like you were able to understand. This website was a positive media outlet that I could share with you to demonstrate strength and solidarity. You would not have benefited from the scenes of bloodied victims escaping Tube stations, or the debris and carnage that flooded the television news and newspapers. Although these images were necessary and factual elements needed to report on the attacks, it was seeing the strength, unity, and support of people around the world that helped to alleviate our fears. Let's continue to be strong and help others to do so, too.

All my love, Auntie Jen

Hoping for a Peaceful Future
7 July 2006

My dearest children,

You cannot yet read this; I write for myself now, perhaps as a record of how much I'm thinking of you, how much I love you. Perhaps, as well, I write to relive the relief I felt when I knew you were OK, to calm my fury. I know you're doing well, sweet smart son, with your ABCs and, my super bright girl, in your reading at school, but you can just figure out a few "sight words" now, so I'm writing for you to read this in the future. I write to celebrate that future. I write to celebrate your lives.

At 5:10 a.m. one year ago today, Daddy called. He said there were bombs in London. You were there, with Aunt Jen on your way to a museum. Communication systems were down; he was unable to get through to Jen and Jen couldn't call me internationally. I didn't know if you were safe for nearly an hour. Nearly an hour of not knowing. He called back as soon as he heard from Aunt Jen, who told him the three of you were safe. I can't describe the sense of relief that second call gave me.

All this past year, I've been thinking about being a mommy, raising children in a world where scary things happen, where each day promises both joys and risks. I've also been reading other mommies' stories of joys and risks. Victoria Hardie, for instance, is a British mommy who writes about how "The World Became a More Dangerous Place" after she brought children into it. And she was just writing about having an infant in the leafy English countryside in the 1980s, not about making sure children are safe in a land under siege. But what she wrote resonated with how I felt about the bombings, the danger in that mother's bones, just like the chilling damp that runs through your back and chest while you wait for a bus on a London autumn evening. After giving birth to the first of her two sons, that mother "was to discover as time went on that it wasn't just emotional vulnerability that hit me, but physical and economic vulnerability as well. *The world suddenly became a much more dangerous place once I had a baby dependent on me for his very life*" (53, emphasis added).

There are fifty-two other mothers who, one year ago today, came to a sudden and sorrowful realization of what a dangerous place the world can be. I share with you their names, and their stories, both to honor them and to help you understand what those mothers felt when they lost their children. Children who, like you, were on public transportation in London that day. Mothers like Pam Daplyn, who lost her 26-year-old daughter Elizabeth. The mother of Gamze Gunoral, 24, who traveled with her daughter's earthly body back to her native Turkey for her funeral there.[6] And the parents of Anat Rosenberg, who traveled from Jerusalem to bring her body back for the funeral. Even though Anat was planning to visit her parents later that year, she was hesitant to do so—fear of suicide bombers on busses. Ruth Parathasangary, whose last memory of her daughter Shyanjua was the sweet smile she gave to her mother as she left for work. Ruth and her husband said in a statement, "We adored our daughter. With so much to live for she paid the price of man's wickedness to man."

The mother of Shahara Islam, who said that her daughter was an "Eastender, a Londoner and British, but above all a true Muslim and proud to be so." For the mother of Benedetta Ciaccia, who is pictured weeping at the casket that held her daughter who, two months from her wedding day, was buried in her bridal gown. For the parents of 26-year-old Shelley Mather, who traveled from Auckland, New Zealand to search in vain for their daughter. And upwards of 700 other mothers, whose children were injured by the bombings.

I write about the children, to help you understand what they must be feeling when they lost their mothers who were travelling just like you were that day. The two daughters of Anna Brandt, a Polish woman who had lived in London for three years. On her way to work as a cleaner, she took the Piccadilly Line at 8:00 a.m. toward a neighborhood very close to your London house. She never made it. One of her daughters had just arrived that day from Poland to visit her. Another woman from Poland, Monika Suchocka, who worked minutes away from where we used to live. Her parents and brother brought her ashes back to her homeland. For the three children of Ojara Ikeagwu, a 56-year-old social worker who had helped hundreds of adults with learning disabilities and who engaged in a great deal of voluntary work among her community, those of Nigerian descent living in Britain. For Azuma and Zakari, the two children of Gladys Wundowa, who attended her funeral in her home village in Ghana with 2,000 others who grieved her death.

For Daniel, aged 25, and Jamie, 23, sons of Susan Levy. Like mother June and daughter Carrie Taylor, Jamie and his mother enjoyed sharing their commutes into the city each weekday. On the morning of the seventh, she had said goodbye to her son, who exited at Finsbury Park station, while she remained on the Piccadilly Line, a train blown up underneath Russell Square. Susan's cousin Jason said, "Sue was very much a loving mother. They were the most tight-knit family imaginable. They did everything together. I feel for the two boys—they are absolutely devastated."

For two other sons, aged seven and one, and how they are going to make sense of why their mummy, Marie Hartley, was on the bus that was bombed at Tavistock Square.

For the children, husband, and friends of Iranian-born Behnaz Mozakka, who was described as a "mum" to everyone, particularly those at the Great Ormond Street Children's Hospital where she was a biomedical officer.

I write about the children who may never be touched by someone who would have helped birth them, and who would have loved them from their first moments out of their mothers' wombs. Emily Jenkins was training to become a midwife, just like the wonderful midwives that helped bring you both into the world.

Others who have left a legacy of providing peace and understanding in the face of suffering. Like Helen Jones, who helped her close friend, the Reverend David Thom, when he was preparing to preside over a funeral of a child he witnessed dying in an accident. Helen told him, "In tragedy, it is never God's will. God's is the first heart to break and God is the first to shed a tear." In Helen's honor, nearly £1 million (nearly $2 million US) has been raised to build the Eden Valley children's hospice in Carlisle in the peace of England's Lake District. Like Hyman, who volunteered to raise funds for a cancer charity and to build bridges of understanding and compassion between Palestinian and Jewish communities.[7]

I also share with you stories of survivors of the bombs. One, in particular, the story of Gill Hicks, a 37-year-old Australian native who was the last person to be carried out of one of the Tube stations alive. She missed traveling on the safe train, the one right before the bombed one, because of a pushy male commuter. Waiting for a Piccadilly Line train at King's Cross station, Gill was pushed aside by a man getting on the first train that approached, leaving her to get on a train that was bombed. Two police officers, Aaron Debnam and Steve Bryan, helped her out of the train station as she struggled to stay alive (Barrett). After they turned Ms. Hicks over to the medical team, they headed back to assist other injured travelers. They were later told she had died.

Officers Debnam and Bryan later learned she had survived, although crippled by the loss of both of her lower legs. They also learned she was the last person to be carried out alive from the wreckage. Three months after the bombings, the two officers and Gill were reunited, and all three cried because it was very sad, all their experiences, but also because it was happy that the officers and doctors saved her life and they were able to meet again.

What I thought was most touching about this survival story was that when asked if she was angry, Gill thought of a mother: "I don't feel any anger at all toward, toward the, the poor guy that was susceptible enough to, I guess almost be a victim himself, you know and I feel, I do feel deeply sad for their families and particularly for the guy that, that killed himself on my tube who has now, I believe his wife has had a little baby, and I just, I just think that there's something so sad about that, that she's unable to show grief publicly, that this child now will grow up, with an understanding of what his father has done and just the lives that have been destroyed for no apparent reason."[8]

While I do honor her for not harboring anger, I must admit I'm still angry and scared, because like that British mother said, our world can be a dangerous place. I will do my best to keep you safe in this world. I will guide you to do the same as you give birth sometime in the future. Then we will be linked in the process of giving birth to our babies. Each day of our newborns' lives presents so much wonder and change that we treasure each and every one of them. We note their every movement, every moment when their deep eyes slowly open, every time their tiny mouths clamp down with surprising ferocity on our breasts.

But then we send them out into the world. We watch as they walk or run away from us, into the future, new journeys, new places. When I kiss you goodbye, as you walk towards your school, or as you travel across the world, I fear that you will leave me forever. So I make certain to give that hug and kiss, and make sure you know I love you, each time we part.

Another mommy did this, too. June Taylor and her 24-year-old daughter, Carrie, kissed as they parted at Liverpool Street station during their commute together. "We travel together every day," June said. "I know it sounds silly but we have a little farewell ritual. Carrie gives me a kiss goodbye before we go our separate ways. Then I watch her as she heads off for the tube. Every few steps she turns and waves before she disappears into the crowd. I always watch until she's out of sight. It's a funny little mum's habit—but I'm so very glad that the last picture I have of her is smiling and waving at me."

You have to put trust in your higher power(s) when you kiss your children farewell. There is so much that can go wrong; so many ways that you can be taken from us. Car accidents, child abductions, fatal illnesses, terrorist attacks. You are so strong, and so very, very fragile.

I am strong today, but tomorrow I could be just as fragile. Today I am privileged to be able to write to you; I am humbled by my good fortune to have two hands with which to type out these words and to hold you, and two eyes to reflect on my letter to you as it appears on the screen and to see your smiles when you return from London next month. I am humbled as I honor those who live with the attentiveness, pain both emotional and physical (that empty gap that forms in one's abdomen, that hunching of the shoulders, the wave of pain that washes away, only to hit you again with full force), that accompanies the loss of a friend, family member, mother, sister, child.

What most compelled us, Aunties Jen and Anca and me, to write these letters to you is to record your stories and to help you understand our experiences and emotions during and immediately after these events. We write to invite you to continue to reflect, as you grow older and increasingly more aware of the abuses of power, of the possible divisiveness of difference, of the lasting benefits of peaceful resolution to conflict. Finally we write to help you understand the gendered nature of terrorism and women's resistance to it, and women's courage to stand up and face the deadly artillery in efforts to save their children. We want our children to know about women's efforts toward conflict resolution, to inspire them to embark upon their own future efforts in building peace.

They are written, too, for the many mothers who fear they will lose their children in this time of terror, and the children who hug their mothers a little more tightly once they begin to learn what's happening in the world; they, too, fear death—the loss of others who are in the center of their worlds, perhaps more than their own. They are written for remembering how strong, and how fragile we *all* are.

Sometimes these stories are too much to bear. But not enough to stop mothers from bearing our children, bringing them into a world that we hope will be safe. For now we will continue to work together to create that world. You are doing this now, by learning about peace in school, and seeking peace at home. I wish that others in the world would do the same, so that you will grow up, and have children and grandchildren of your own in a safe, happy, and peaceful world.

All my love, Mommy

[1]At various moments in these letters, we refer to the London Underground and London transport system. The "Tube" is Londoners' term for the London Underground, named for the cylindrical shape of the train tunnels. With operation beginning on January 10, 1863, it is the oldest and one of the busiest underground railway networks in the world. It is part of Transport for London, which also runs the bus system.

Commuters on Tube trains and a bus at Tavistock Square were victim to suicide bombers on July 7, 2005. On July 21, 2005, small explosions occurred at tube stations Shepherd's Bush, Warrens Street, and Oval. One of the authors of the letters in this essay, Jennifer Minda, and the children to whom the letters are written were on a bus traveling by Shepherd's Bush station at the time of the explosion. For more information on Jean Charles de Menezes, who was killed on the London Underground on July 22, 2005, please see < http://www.justice4jean.com >.

[2]To protect our children, we have omitted names and most identifying details.

[3]The Romanian revolution in December 1989 started as a popular revolt against the country's communist regime, but many commentators argue that the revolution was hijacked by former communist apparatchiks that seized power in the days following the overthrow of the communist dictator, Nicolae Ceausescu. For more on the events leading up to and including December 1989, see McFaul who explains the Romanian transition from communism and its "powerful leaders from the ancien régime." After "'people power' destroyed the last communist regime, communist apparatchiks motivated by their own interests and not committed to democratic norms dominated the first postcommunist regime" (McFaul 241).

[4]Reports of how unsafe citizens were in their own homes emerged after the fall of the Romanian communist regime: "Ceausescu's capture had just been announced on TV. Tiberiu Nedelca opened up a bottle of wine to celebrate the moment with his wife. "Freedom, a new life, everything we've dreamt about...this is what we're going to have from now on," he told his wife. And then a neighbor came and told them there were two soldiers firing from the roof of their flat, and he went up on the roof to announce to the two about the dictator's arrest. But the soldiers shot him, in the right kidney; he lived only through the evening." The report continues with others who were killed on December 22, 1989: "Hans went to his brother's house, and together with his father and sister-in-law got closer to the window to see what was happening outside. Suddenly they heard a sharp snap in the window. The other two turned their eyes and saw how a second bullet hit Hans's wedding ring and then ricochet in the wall. A third bullet hit him in the

neck, exploding at the base of the brain. Hans died in the arms of his father" (Popescu-Oprea).

[5]To maintain a narrative flow, certain references have been placed in the endnotes. All the obituaries in this section can be found in the several references listed under the authorship of BBC News Online (2005). This particular reference is to one of the obituaries of those killed on July 7, 2005. BBC News Online (2005). "Obituary: Mihaela Otto." Retrieved December 12, 2006, from <http://news.bbc.co.uk/1/hi/england/london/4738199.stm>.

[6]The children believe that when a person dies, their "earth body" is buried, but their spirit goes to their higher power.

[7]The report on the Eden Valley children's hospice in Carlisle, England, founded in honor of Helen Jones, can be found at "Work Begins on Children's Hospice," 3 Aug. 2005. BBC News Online. 27 Oct. 2006 <http://news.bbc.co.uk/1/hi/england/cumbria/6146550.stm>.

[8]Gill Hicks, the last person to be carried out alive from the London Underground on July 7, 2005, is quoted in an article by Stephen Barrett.

Works Cited

Akleh, Elias. "Israel is The Mother of Terrorism in The Middle East." 26 June 2006. Jewwatch.com. 12 Sept. 2006 <http://www.jewwatch.com/jew-occu-piedgovernments-israel-mother-of-terrorism.html>.

Albrecht, Lisa, and Rose M. Brewer. "Bridges of Power: Women's Multicultural Alliances for Social Change." *Bridges of Power: Women's Multicultural Alliances for Social Change*. Eds. L. Albrecht and R. M. Brewer. Philadelphia: New Society, 1990. 2-22.

Anzaldúa, Gloria. "En el Nombre de Todas las Madres Que Han Perdido Sus Hijos en la Guerra" ["In the Name of All the Mothers Who Have Lost Children in the War"]. *Gloria Evangelina Anzaldúa Papers*, 1942-2004. Box 34, Folder 1, 1984.

Baron, Nancy. "Helping Children Feel Safe in this Time of Global Terrorism." Unicef.org. September 2004. UNICEF: Child Protection from Violence, Exploitation and Abuse. 25 Apr. 2006 <http://www.unicef.org/protection/files/Nancy_Baron_on_children_in_crisis.pdf >.

Barr, Robert. "19 Suspects in British Terror Plot ID'd." ABCnews.com. 11 Aug. 2006. ABC News International. 28 Jan. 2007 <http://abcnews.go.com/International/wireStory?id=230041>.

Barrett, Stephen. "Priority one." BBC News Online. 15 Nov. 2005. BBC News. 15 Mar. 2007 <http://news.bbc.co.uk/1/hi/magazine/4435172.stm>.

Benn, Melissa. *Madonna and Child: Towards a New Politics of Motherhood*. London: Jonathan Cape, 1998.

Boehlert, Eric. "The Mother of All Terrorism battles." Salon.com. 29 Nov. 2001. Salon. 15 Dec. 2006 <http://archive.salon.com/news/feature/2001/11/29/war_on_saddam/index_np.htm>.

Boyd-Barrett, Oliver. "Cyberspace, Globalization and U.S. empire." *Communications Media, Globalization, and Empire*. Ed. Oliver Boyd-Barrett. London: John Libbey, 2007. 53-76.

Boyd-Barrett, Oliver. "Doubt foreclosed (2): U.S. Mainstream Media and the Attacks of 9-11." *Terrorism, Globalization & Mass Communication*. Ed. David Demers. Spokane, Washington: Marquette, 2002. 3-33.

Burke, Mary Kate, Setrakian, Lara, and Cuomo, Chris. "'Mother of Satan': The New Terror Weapon of Choice." ABC News Good Morning America. 11 Aug. 2006. ABC News. 2 Oct. 2006 <http://abcnews.go.com/GMA/Terrorism/story?id=2300460&page=1>.

Cassara, Catherine and Lengel, Laura. "Move Over CNN: Al-Jazeera's View of the World Takes on the West." *Global Media Go to War: Role of News and Entertainment Media During the 2003 Iraq War*. Ed. Ralph Berenger. Spokane: Marquette, 2004. 229-234.

Freely, Maureen. *What About Us? An Open Letter to the Mothers Feminism Forgot*. London: Bloomsbury, 1995.

Giacaman, Rita, and Johnson, Penny. "Palestinian Women: Building Barricades and Breaking Barriers." *Intifada: The Israeli Uprising Against Israeli Occupation*. Eds. Zachary Lockman and Joel Beinin. Boston: South End, 1989. 155-170.

Hardie, Victoria. "The World Became a More Dangerous Place." *Balancing Acts: On Being a Mother*. Ed. Katherine Gieve. London: Virago, 1989. 52-72.

Hartsock, Nancy. "Political Change: Two Perspectives on Power." *Building Feminist Theory: Essays from Quest, a Feminist Quarterly*. Eds. Charlotte Bunch et al. New York: Longman, 1981. 3-19.

Healy, Bernadine. "Mother Nature, terrorist." USNews.com. 1 Oct. 2005. US News and World Report. 14 Dec. 2006 <http://www.usnews.com/usnews/health/articles/050110/10healy.htm>.

Lentin, Ronit. "'No Woman's Law Will Rot This State': The Israeli Racial State and Feminist Resistance." *Sociological Research Online* 9.3 <http://www.socresonline.org.uk/9/3/9/3/lentin.html>.

Macy, Joanna R. *Despair and Personal Power in the Nuclear Age*. Philadelphia: New Society, 1983.

McFaul, Michael. "The Fourth Wave of Democracy and Dictatorship. Noncooperative Transitions in the Postcommunist World." *World Politics* 54:2 (2002): 212-244.

"Mother shook chocolate tin bomb." The Search for Peace, Latest News. BBC News Online. 1 Mar. 1999. BBC News. 10 Apr. 2006 <http://news.bbc.co.uk/2/hi/events/northern_ireland/latest_news/288636.stm>.

"Obituary: Anat Rosenberg." BBC News Online. 3 Aug. 2005. BBC News. 1 Oct. 2006 <http://news.bbc.co.uk/1/hi/england/london/4738127.stm>.

"Obituary: Anna Brandt." BBC News Online. 3 Aug. 2005. BBC News. 25 Oct. 2006 <http://news.bbc.co.uk/2/hi/uk_news/england/london/4741547.stm>.

"Obituary: Behnaz Mozakka." BBC News Online. 3 Aug. 2005. BBC News. 28 Oct. 2006 <http://news.bbc.co.uk/1/hi/england/london/4741117.stm>.

"Obituary: Benedetta Ciaccia." BBC News Online. 3 Aug. 2005. BBC News. 1 Oct. 2006 <http://news.bbc.co.uk/1/hi/uk_news/england/london/4741399. stm>.

"Obituary: Carrie Taylor." BBC News Online. 3 Aug. 2005. BBC News. 3 Oct. 2006 <http://news.bbc.co.uk/1/hi/england/london/4741441.stm>.

"Obituary: Elizabeth Daplyn." BBC News Online. 3 Aug. 2005. BBC News. 25 Oct. 2006 <http://news.bbc.co.uk/1/hi/uk/4741261.stm>.

"Obituary: Emily Jenkins." BBC News Online. 3 Aug. 2005. BBC News. 27 Oct. 2006 <http://news.bbc.co.uk/1/hi/england/london/4741375.stm>.

"Obituary: Gamze Gunoral." BBC News Online. 3 Aug. 2005. BBC News. 25 Oct. 2006 <http://news.bbc.co.uk/1/hi/uk/4741213.stm>.

"Obituary: Marie Hartley." BBC News Online. 3 Aug. 2005. BBC News. 28 Oct. 2006 <http://news.bbc.co.uk/1/hi/england/london/4741063.stm>.

"Obituary: Miriam Hyman." BBC News Online. 3 Aug. 2005. BBC News. 3 Oct. 2006 <http://news.bbc.co.uk/1/hi/england/london/4738123.stm>.

"Obituary: Monika Suchocka." BBC News Online. 3 Aug. 2005. BBC News. 28 Oct. 2006 <http://news.bbc.co.uk/1/hi/england/london/4741215.stm>.

"Obituary: Neetu Jain." BBC News Online. 3 Aug. 2005. BBC News. 23 Sept. 2006 <http://news.bbc.co.uk/1/hi/england/london/4739655.stm>.

"Obituary: Shelley Mather." BBC News Online. 3 Aug. 2005. BBC News. 28 Oct. 2006 <http://news.bbc.co.uk/1/hi/england/london/4741409.stm>.

"Obituary: Shyanuja Parathasangary." BBC News Online. 3 Aug. 2005. BBC News. 3 Oct. 2006 <http://news.bbc.co.uk/1/hi/england/london/4738107. stm>.

"Obituary: Susan Levy." BBC News Online. 3 Aug. 2005. BBC News. 25 Oct. 2006 <http://news.bbc.co.uk/1/hi/england/london/4737787.stm>.

Popescu-Oprea, Adriana. "Romania din ceruri [Romania in Heavens]." Jurnalul. ro. 19 Dec. 2004. *Jurnalul National.* 1 Feb. 2007 <http://www.jurnalul.ro/articol_24499/romania_din_ceruri.html>.

Vasile, R. "Romanian revolution: An aggravated diversion." *Romania Libera.* 20 Dec. 2005 <http://www.romanialibera.ro/a53449/revolutia-romana-o-diversiune-calificata.html>.

"Work begins on children's hospice." BBC News Online. 3 Aug. 2005. BBC News. 27 Oct. 2006 <http://news.bbc.co.uk/1/hi/england/cumbria/6146550.stm>.

Zaatari, Zeina. "The Culture of Motherhood: An Avenue for Women's Civil Participation in South Lebanon." *Journal of Middle East Women's Studies* 2.1 (2006): 33-64.

**Part II
Mothering Resistance**

5
Con el Palote en Una Mano y el Libro en la Otra

LARISSA M. MERCADO-LÓPEZ

On a recent evening in April of 2006, my daughters and I stood, holding hands, in front of the university's "Border Crossing" statue, created by the late Luis Jiménez. The university's conservative student organization was petitioning to have the statue removed because, according to them, it allegedly depicted "illegal activity," and the Chicana/o graduate student group I belonged to was having a peace vigil in honor of the immigrants the statue represented. As we stood, I could not help but feel that my history was being effaced and that my family and I were being personally attacked, and I knew that my failure to act would render me complicitous in that attack. I gazed at the woman huddled on top of her husband's shoulders, her child's hands wildly reaching out of the hand-made rebozo she clutched around her shoulders, and I empathized with that woman—a crosser of borders, a protector of children, a vehicle of tradition, a survivor who goes against the current and stays above the water. As the conservative student group whispered their opposition to our vigil, I looked over and noticed some of my own raza in that crowd. I wondered how many of them were carried by their mothers across those very same literal and figurative waters. Clutching my daughters' hands, I resolved that my decision to include my children in la lucha was not one of simple choice, but of necessity: if we don't involve our children in our own movimientos, they will surely become a part of someone else's.

Atravesando y Llorando

I like to think that I am una traviesa, one who traverses the boundaries of destiny and tradition, what Gloria Holguín Cuádraz would refer to as an "adulteress to our class and culture" (217). I have followed the Chicana's traditional path in an untraditional way, becoming the expected wife and mother while maintaining a space in the academy. I've made tortillas while reading Anzaldúa; nursed babies with my left hand while typing with the right; carried a diaper bag on one shoulder and a backpack on the other; tickled baby feet while typing out footnotes. A pejorative term, "traviesa" has become who I am, an identity that allows me to find strength in the contradictions that I embody as a Chicana mother-scholar.

However, from combating demoralizing feelings of guilt and inadequacy as a mother to feeling out of place and illegitimate as a scholar, my journey as a Chicana mother/activist in graduate school has not been one without struggle. Criticized for her decision to pursue fulfillment *outside* of the home, the Chicana mother in academia at times suffers from the "Llorona complex," a stigma that shrouds Chicanas who choose not to have children in order to pursue their career or who 'sacrifice' their children to pursue other personal passions (Castillo 186). But the wail of the academic Chicana mother/Llorona is not for the children she leaves at home, but for those others who complicate her existence, who refuse to allow her to occupy that space where she can negotiate her identity as a mother, a scholar, an artist, and an activist. Before I began to embrace my maternity as an intersectional, politicized identity, I struggled to negotiate my spheres of scholarly, artistic, and maternal identities, problematically attempting to perform these identities one at a time. However, I have come to realize that the only way to avoid becoming una Llorona is to perform my motherhood as a function of my politics and my politics as a function of my motherhood.

In her essay "The Mother-Bond Principle," Ana Castillo questions and challenges constructions of motherhood, examining the structural, cultural, and religious underpinnings that have reduced women to mere wombs in the nationalist project. Castillo advocates for Chicanas to appropriate a Xicanista consciousness to examine their perceptions of motherhood as performed by their mothers as they begin to form their *own* identities as mothers. She states, "We are daughters of women who have been subject to a social system—compounded doubly by Mexican traditions and U.S. WASP dominance that prohibited them from opportunities that may have challenged their creative and intellectual potential in more ways than being wife, mother, and assembly line worker" (188). This systematic refusal to recognize a "creative and intellectual potential" is one that has confined the Chicana mother to her home, to her children, to her position in the labor market. Whether by the demands of capitalism or the guilt from Catholicism, the Chicana mother has learned to quell her yearning to create in ways other than producing the goods of capitalism or birthing children.

Chicana mothers are not expressionless, however. Case studies, ethnographies, and our own family histories and memories provide ample evidence that Chicana mothers are usually the primary agents of cultural production. However, such productions, or traditions, are typically those which are able to be performed within the parameters of the mother's domestic sphere and that support or emphasize the qualities, practices, and expectations of "the" traditional mother. As a result, our Chicana mothers have been more likely to channel their creative energies not through the paintbrush or the plume or the instrument—at least not in *public* spaces—but through the intensive care of their gardens, the beautiful hand-knitted estrellitas in their tapestries, and the perfect symmetry of their tortillas. I have witnessed this act of creation in my own abuela, whose incessant rose gardening, knitting, and stitching baffled me as a teenager. Small stacks of tablecloths and pillow cases always lay strewn about; the table cloths that actually made it to the table were covered in plastic. She knitted in the day and late at night, in the dining room, guided only by a distant kitchen light and the glow from the television I watched in her living room. And as I fell asleep, I was almost always sure to hear the creaking of the floorboards as her soft steps approached me to cover me with one of her many holey, knitted colchas, blankets that offered no protection from the cold but always warmed me inside.

Nationalism has co-opted the rhetoric of motherhood to keep Chicana mothers from searching for fulfillment outside the home, demanding that the woman remain all-sacrificing for the good of the nation and cultura. Virgin/whore or Guadalupe/Llorona, the Chicana mother constantly finds herself navigating between these binaries, searching for that space where motherhood can be performed in ways that are meaningful and fulfilling.

Chicanas Working in M/otherly Ways

The first "official" attempt to reconstruct Chicana motherhood occurred in 1971, when 600 Chicanas gathered in solidarity in Houston, Texas for the first national Chicana conference (Vidal 21). It was the first time that Chicana leaders of the Chicana/o Movement had gathered in a safe, non-sanctioned space to discuss the issues not being discussed by their male counterparts, particularly those concerning their needs as women and mothers. The Chicana leaders resolved, "Chicana motherhood should not preclude educational, political, social, and economic advancement," challenging the socially and culturally constructed definitions and limitations of "motherhood" (21). This articulation marked the beginning of the Chicana's efforts to liberate Chicana mothers from their nonnegotiable confinement to their homes, husbands, and children. Ideally, the Chicana mother was now "free" to pursue personal, intellectual, and artistic development, and to seek the fulfillment and happiness that motherhood alone could not always satisfy.

The Chicanas of the Chicana/o Movement expanded the definitions of 'woman,' 'wife,' and 'mother' through their work in the public sphere as political organizers and scholars. Taking to the streets and the classrooms, these Chicanas involved themselves in shaping the policies that affected their households and their ways of living. As the personal became more political, the parameters that defined their domestic sphere grew past their tiny yards and past their streets, surpassing school districts, cities, even counties. Their political work was inextricable from their personal work, and almost always one and the same.

It is now more than thirty-five years later. Binaries of Chicana motherhood still exist, so I am forced to articulate my own conceptualization of Chicana motherhood, which I have come to call third-space Chicana maternal praxis. Theory informs my mothering, but my mothering/maternity has the potential to challenge theory. As a Chicana mother-scholar I am an embodiment of discursive and cultural contradiction; nothing is stable. I continue to carve out ways to be the feminist that I am by confronting these contradictions, by acknowledging my maternal, brown body—not as an organ for patriarchal movements, but as a body of knowledge(s). I am constantly reminded of my body's materiality when I return home between semesters to my tiny town of 2,400 in South Texas. When asked how my degree is coming along, I cannot help but imagine that when I state, "I'm a full-time student," my tia or tio really hears, "I'm a part-time mom." I find it frustrating that the work I do as an academic is not considered intrinsic to my work as a mother. My desire to expend my energy in Chicana feminism, theory and literature is kindled by my love for my daughters and my concern for (and fear of) the world in which they live. Whether I am articulating Chicana third-space maternal pedagogies in the writing classroom or questioning the absence of Chicana representation in university committees, the work I do in the university is to ensure the inclusion and *validation* of my children and all other Chicanitas from the first day they set foot on a college campus. As an instructor of English Literature and Women's Studies, I am already shaping and training the social actors who will, or have already begun to interact with future Chicana university students. My influence, my work, my *mothering* begins now and here.

My decision to continue with graduate school and enter a P.hD. program after having children was fueled by a very different reason from my decision to go to graduate school prior to my children's births: then it was about what I wanted to do; now it is about what I *must* do. As women, under the law we have the choice to become mothers; as mothers, however, *we have no choice* when it comes to doing the *work that matters*. And this is where my frustration lies. I cannot comprehend why my work as an academic and an activist is not considered work that matters to the well-being of my family, when my family—biological, cultural, and global—is the reason I do this work. I do not understand why a mother's work must always be restricted to that which is necessary to maintain the environment of the home, when the climate of the home is so contingent on the work that is done in the external social, political, and ecological environment. When I vote as a mother, I am influencing policies that determine whether or not I will receive assistance with food and medical care, or maintain protection of my reproductive rights. I may not resolve the immigration debates or end domestic violence by voting or marching in the streets, but I am part of the solution, and my children will gain the sense of understanding that they, too, can work to improve their world.

Perhaps what is needed is not only an extension of "work" but also an extension of "home;" maybe then the work (artistic, political, and domestic), the skills, the strategies of living that mothers have so finely honed and developed to ensure the survival of the home and family will be applied to maintain the survival of the cultural community, the city, the world.

Dolores Huerta, one of the great Chicana civil rights activists and mother of eleven children, has advocated throughout her life for the involvement of the mother and children in politics and the movimiento. "Lower your homemaking standards," her official website states; "I always like to say that for every unmade bed, some farm workers got a $1 an hour or more" (par. 6). As a graduate student and activist I have come to the realization that I will never "get ahead" in my housework, much less keep up with it. But the work I am doing is not like the laundry that can be done late at night before I go to bed: the urgency of the society we live in is much too great to be ignored or postponed. Chicana mothers must be involved because they are most in tune with the needs of the family. If they are not involved, the Chicana/o family runs the risk of being under- or misrepresented, which often leads to being underserved.

Towards a Libratory Paradigm of Chicana Motherhood

I call for a reconfiguration of Chicana motherhood, a motherhood in which the academic/political work that I am doing now—and that I will continue to do in the future—is considered just as important to the health and development of my children as the food I am putting on the table. It will be a motherhood that is as much about nurturing the body, spirit, and mind of the mother as nurturing those of the children; a motherhood that extends beyond the socially constructed parameters of the home, and flows across city, county, state, and national borderlines. Whereas the resolution on Chicana motherhood once read, "Chicana motherhood should not preclude educational, political, social, and economic advancement" (Vidal 21), it is vital that it now read "Chicana motherhood *must include* educational, political, social, and economic advancement."

Chicana mothers today are situated on the cusp of tradition, a location of potential empowerment where they can negotiate the traditions handed down to them as well as the possibilities of creating new ones. Chicana motherhood is a site of conflict, where values of the past come into contact with those of the present; it is a site of contradiction, where brown, maternal bodies must negotiate their identities within public spaces. But rather than dwell over her fragmentation, the Chicana mother can approach her position as an opportunity to create new models of motherhood, and to help others achieve transcendence into a motherhood that allows for personal and political development.

Chicana mothers today are slowly becoming aware of this space of empowerment, and are turning to public service and the arts to affect social and cultural change. Organizations such as Latina Mami in Austin, Texas, and Chicana Mama in Phoenix, Arizona, were created to fill the void for support and resources for Latina and Chicana mothers. From maternity clothes to ESL classes to culturally enriching playdates, these organizations are committed to the care and physical, intellectual, and cultural growth of both mother and child. In addition, testimonios, such as Nina Marie Durán's *Elijah on My Mind*, are opening up possibilities for dialogue and consciousness-formation. Duran's short testimonio on young motherhood is one of few accounts of Chicana motherhood to forge its way into the exploding scene of "Mommy Lit." While Duran's book does not specifically address the complexities of *Chicana* motherhood, it is the absence of the recognition of these complexities that demands the writings of Chicana mothers. Cherríe Moraga's *Waiting in the Wings: Portrait of a Queer Motherhood,* a memoir about Chicana lesbian motherhood, and Ana Castillo's essay "The Mother-Bond Principle" are two of the only works to specifically address Chicana motherhood, and while they are seminal contributions to mother of color scholarship, more work is needed to attend to the multiplicitous identities within the maternal Chicana community. My sister and I recently had a conversation about the lack of literature on motherhood that features *Chicana* mothers on and between the covers, besides the occasional, government-issued "how-to" manual on infant nutrition and development. While the physical experience of pregnancy and childbirth is, for the most part, transcultural, the ways (myths, religious beliefs, etc.) in which we *interpret* and make meaning of the childbearing and child-rearing experience vary greatly across cultures. Third-wave efforts to free women from essentialist identities have yet to fully attend to the *semiotics* of the pregnant body, especially that of the brown Chicana. The absence of Chicana mothers from this scene obscures the cultural and social differences between Chicana motherhood and the dominant perception of (Anglo) motherhood, necessitating that Chicana mothers take up the pen to write their way back into literature, into the social fabric, into motherhood.

Chicana motherhood is not simply a vocation but a call to action; it is an opportunity to pass on important traditions, as well as an opportunity to discard those that do not benefit the family and to create new traditions that do. As I continue in my graduate studies I will approach everything I do as a responsibility of motherhood, and along the way I will share my story with the hope that others will share theirs. I will write, I will create, I will protest: I will mother. The work I will do for my global and cultural families will be inextricable from that which I do for my biological family, for the work I do as a mother-scholar is a labor of love, and anything one does for love is truly the work that matters.

Works Cited

Anzaldúa, Gloria. *Borderlands/La Frontera: The New Mestiza*. San Francisco: Aunt Lute, 1999.

Castillo, Ana. *Massacre of the Dreamers: Essays on Xicanisma*. New York: Plume, 1994.

Cuádraz, Gloria Holguín. "Diary of a Llorona Ph.D." *Telling to Live: Latina Feminist Testimonios*. Ed. The Latina Feminist Group. Durham: Duke University Press, 2001.

Durán, Nina Marie. *Elijah on My Mind: A Little Boy Who Loves Me More Than Any Man Ever Could*. Deadwood: Wyatt-MacKenzie, 2006.

Huerta, Dolores. "Parenting Guidelines." 14 Mar 2006. <http://www.doloreshuerta.org/Parent%20Guidelines.htm>.

Moraga, Cherríe. *Waiting in the Wings: Portrait of a Queer Motherhood*. Ithaca: Firebrand, 1997.

Vidal, Mirta. *Chicanas Speak Out*. New York: Pathfinder, 1971.

6

My Life as a Transgressor

Memoir of a Lesbian Soccer Mom

MARLENE G. FINE

I recently served as a co-facilitator for a dialogue on race and ethnicity among lesbian, gay, bisexual, and transgendered people (LGBT). On the first evening, I introduced myself as a lesbian who married her partner of 28 years in May 2004, when same-sex marriage became legal in Massachusetts, and who has two adopted African American teenage sons. I revealed my identity with more than my usual pride because I assumed that I was among people who shared my pride. My assumption was wrong.

Over the next several weeks, I discovered that the LGBT community is fractured by identity wars among those who are gay, homosexual, queer, gay by birth, lesbian by political choice, once male now female (or the reverse), bi-sexual, older, younger, single, partnered—the list goes on. And my co-facilitator's notes from a subsequent week when I was away made clear that my identity as a "lesbian soccer mom" (the group's term, not mine) was offensive to everyone in the group. I represented all that was wrong with the LGBT community in Massachusetts. I was married, living in the suburbs, raising children, and driving a Volvo station wagon. People like me distorted the work of the movement; rather than undermining existing social mores, we reproduced them. We were different, but not really different.

In this memoir I explore the implications of living a conventional life in an unconventional way. What does it mean when two "out" white lesbians raise two African-American sons in a primarily white suburban community? My spouse and I are double transgressors. We transgress the norms of the community in which we live and raise our children by being lesbians. We also transgress the norms of the LGBT community by living a conventional lifestyle, including getting married. Although we inhabit the margins of both communities, however, I believe that how we live our lives positively affects individual and community attitudes. Our daily practices serve as a powerful form of social activism.

Before I say more about my present life as a transgressor, I need to go back to an earlier time in my life. Feminist theorists share a belief in the subjective nature of knowledge (Belenky, Clinchy, Goldberger, and Tarule; Gilligan; Keller). My subjectivity serves as the lens through which I see, experience, and understand the world. To understand my perspective, you need to have some sense of what feminist theorists call my "standpoint" (Collins; Harding; Hartsock; O'Brien Hallstein, "A Postmodern Caring"; Wood). Standpoint, however, represents more than subjectivity that is based on experience. Standpoint is achieved through self-reflexivity, dialogue with others, and active involvement, and gives one the tools to think critically about one's own experiences and the experiences of others (Litwin and O'Brien Hallstein; O'Brien Hallstein, "Where Standpoint Stands Now"). What follows is my journey to achieve my standpoint.

Born in 1949, I came of age in the late 1960s. Although I knew as a teenager that I did not want to become a suburban New Jersey Jewish housewife, my initial forays into activism were with the anti-war movement, not feminism. I experienced sexism in my anti-war work (the New Left was notable for its patriarchal structure and poor treatment of women), but didn't become a feminist until I went to graduate school. My feminism was forged not in consciousness-raising groups but in classrooms where my classmates and I read the second-wave feminist works of Susan Brownmiller, Simone de Beauvoir, Betty Friedan, Germaine Greer, and Kate Millett, and talked about the ways that women were excluded from the academy. I endorsed being a lesbian as a political choice: women needed to be separate from men in order to become equal to them, as Ti-Grace Atkinson and Jill Johnston had argued. It wasn't until 1977, however, when I fell in love with a woman, that I "came out" and saw my choice as more than a political act.

Forging my identity as an adult woman through the feminism of the 1970s, which is generally seen as part of the second wave of feminism, gave me a particular understanding of feminism and its commitments. Feminism was about improving women's lives: equal pay for equal work, opportunities for employment in fields traditionally dominated by men, access to contraception and abortion, political and economic power. Although I didn't believe that men were necessarily my enemy, I wasn't interested in men. I didn't want to spend my time educating them. My focus was on women.

Although I considered myself a strong feminist, I often felt constrained by that identity. I was also often criticized by other women, especially lesbians, for not looking the part. We lived in western Massachusetts, a stronghold of the feminist movement in the 1970s (rumors abounded that Patty Hearst was hiding among us). Our lives centered on a small group of feminist intellectuals, mostly white and mostly academics, many of whom identified themselves as radical feminists. Most of the women were childless, but a few lesbians who had been married previously had children. (Artificial insemination had not yet become a commonplace option for single women and adoption by lesbians wasn't legal). Those who had boys were often the subject of heated arguments about whether you could raise a male child and still be a radical feminist. In this culture, make-up, skirts, and high heels were verboten.

I was an anomaly. Known in college for my bright blue eye shadow and later in graduate school for my heavily frosted hair and polished nails, I was a long-time subscriber to *Vogue*. Not a femme, but most definitely not a woman most people would assume was a lesbian. My non-conformity to feminist expectations of how I should look and behave came to a head when I was cast in a local feminist theater production as a straight woman. The lesbian feminist community was aghast, and many protested my taking the role. Although I chafed under these constraints, I didn't know how to resist them. I both understood and endorsed the feminist analysis of the beauty industry (de Beauvoir; Greer) and I even wrote academic articles about the ways that male definitions of "woman" denied women their genuine identities. When we left the "Happy Valley" in 1988, part of me breathed a sigh of relief that I would no longer be questioned about my daily presentation of self.

My exclusive focus on women changed in 1989 when my partner and I adopted our first child, a boy. Suddenly, at age 40, I was a mother, and not just any mother. I was the white lesbian mother of an African-American son. And I wasn't just any lesbian mother. My partner was the vice president for academic affairs of a major private university. We were a visible couple—not only as the white parents of a black child, but as the lesbian couple who often represented the university at public functions, including trustee dinners.

Having been an "out" lesbian on both my campus and my partner's for over 10 years, I thought I understood what it means to be visible. In fact, I had no idea. When our son was three months old, we traveled to Maine on vacation. Although we stayed in a small fishing village, we made frequent day trips up and down the Maine coast. Wherever we went, people greeted us and commented about the restaurant where we had eaten the previous evening or the town we had visited a few days before. I had no recollection of meeting them before. How did they know us? It took me several days to realize that we hadn't encountered any other black people in our travels—and the people we encountered hadn't seen any other white women with a black baby. The people we saw all looked alike—and their families didn't look like ours.

I also thought I understood the concept of privilege. Parenting a black child, however, taught me otherwise. When we were out with our son, strangers, white and black, would come up to us and almost tearfully tell us what wonderful people we were and how blessed our son was because we had adopted him. Would they have said the same if we were two black women with a white baby? I was doubtful. I also learned about not having privilege. As a tenured college professor with a Ph.D. and two master's degrees, I experienced the world at the top of an intellectual and social class hierarchy. I tumbled quickly to the bottom of that hierarchy the day that I took our son to the local Social Security office to apply for his Social Security card. When my name was called, I approached the desk, a white woman in jeans carrying a black baby. The clerk assumed I was there to pick up my monthly welfare check. I was so shocked I couldn't speak.

Being a lesbian had made me aware of heterosexual privilege. I understood the danger inherent in casual Monday morning conversation about what I did over the weekend and with whom. I had felt the personal slights when I received invitations for me and my spouse, but no acknowledgement that I, or others, had partners or lovers or significant others—whatever term covers those who could not be spouses.

Awareness of the privilege of being white was new to me, although it was not new in the sense of knowing that it existed. Along with feminists and academics all over the United States, I had read and shared with my students Peggy McIntosh's seminal essay, "White Privilege and Male Privilege." As a woman, I had experienced the consequences of male privilege, but white privilege was a theoretical concept, an abstraction. I understood theoretically that as a white person I had privileges that black people didn't have—I could buy a house in any neighborhood (assuming I had sufficient money); I could walk the streets of my town without having someone call the police; I could drive my car without getting pulled over simply because I looked suspicious; I could shop in upscale stores without being followed by security guards. That is, I could do these things before I became the mother of black children and experienced white privilege, or the lack thereof, as the "outsider within" (Luke; see also Frankenburg 135).

It is not that having black children erased all of my white privileges. I still had many—and these spilled over and protected my children, especially when they were young. But white privilege became viscerally real rather than theoretical the day that my partner and I, now with two black babies in tow, stopped to look at a beach house on Cape Cod. The owner assured us that the house was available for rent that summer. We told her that we had a few other houses to look at and that we would call her the next morning if we still wanted the house. I called early in the morning; she told me the house was no longer available. I got off the phone convinced that she would not rent to us because of the children. She proved me wrong a few hours later when she called back to say that she had convinced the people who had rented the house to change their rental dates because she thought our boys were adorable and would love staying in her house. The damage was done, however, because the moment she told me that the house was no longer available to rent, I understood the horror of believing that everything that happens to you might be because of your skin color. I understood how that belief would constantly haunt me and would distort my understanding of events in my life and my children's lives. Why didn't he get a solo in the band concert? Why was he left out of the team photograph? I even questioned the good things that happened, thinking that the boys received good grades or accolades simply because they were black and other people either had low expectations for them or were afraid to judge them fairly for fear of being called racist.

Over the years my partner and I settled into our lives as lesbian mothers. We lived in a suburban development of new homes. Although we were the only lesbians in the neighborhood, we "fit in" because we were parents. Our boys played with the other neighborhood children. We talked with the other mothers as we gathered in our driveways and along the sidewalk watching the children play. The neighborhood fathers joined us as we built a backyard swing set one Mother's Day. We were invited to birthday celebrations and family barbecues. I even coached one of the local soccer teams. Heading off to soccer practice with two small boys in my Volvo station wagon every Saturday morning, I was, indeed, the quintessential suburban soccer mom.

Our awareness of our differences, however, remained a constant part of our lives, especially regarding issues about race. We sent our children to private school because we worried that, as African-American boys, they would be overlooked or not sufficiently challenged in our local public school. We worried about ensuring that the boys would learn about and appreciate African-American history and culture, and we worried about whether they would have the personal resources and knowledge to confront racism when it inevitably reared its head. And we worried about more mundane issues—finding a black barber who could cut their hair properly, keeping their skin moisturized, making sure that our pediatrician was familiar with the medical problems of African-American children. I was far too busy, however, to worry about my identity as a lesbian. Apart from laughing about the incongruity of my present life, especially in light of my earlier incarnation as a radical feminist, I didn't spend much time reflecting on being a lesbian. Most of the time I was just a mom.

In that frame of reference, being called a soccer mom, or even a lesbian soccer mom, was just fine with me. But hearing a group of LGBT activists call me a lesbian soccer mom as a way of excluding me from the group made me stop and think about who I am (the thinking came after my initial surprise, anger, and then sadness). Self-reflection is an essential component of feminist theorizing, which recognizes the truthfulness of personal knowledge (Fine 129-130). So I reflected, and began to ask myself questions about my identity, my values, and my personal commitments. Had I really abandoned my connections to the LGBT community? Was it possible to maintain an identity as a lesbian and also as a suburban soccer mom? Was it politically incorrect for my partner and me to marry after 28 years in a committed relationship? Did that marriage certificate and our matching gold wedding bands mean that we had been co-opted by the larger culture and its traditional values and gender roles?

In my effort to answer these questions and respond to their challenges, I turned to the works of other feminist writers for insight. I looked at essays and books by younger feminists (who often identify as third wave feminists) to see what they had to say about identity (Anzaldúa and Keating; Henry; Hernández and Rehman; Jones; Labaton and Martin; Morgan). Although I was initially put off by the fierce, and, I think, overstated, rejection of second wave feminists in their writings, many of these women spoke directly to the kinds of questions that I was asking. Four third wave feminist ideas in particular helped me grapple with questions about my identity and my commitments: the interlocking nature of identity, the acceptance of paradox, the process and place of activism, and the position of mothering.

Lisa Jones, in a powerful series of essays titled *Bulletproof Diva: Tales of Race, Sex, and Hair*, questions the portrayal of black women in pop music as either "all powerful or all vulnerable" (106). Jones says that she should be able to negotiate both identities. As I read her account of her discomfort with the bipolar representation of black female identity, I realized I could substitute my own discomfort with the bipolar identities allowed me as a lesbian. As a young woman, I couldn't wear make-up and be a lesbian; as a grown woman, I couldn't be a mother and a lesbian—at least not a married lesbian soccer mom.

Many women attempt to negotiate multiple identities, and often we find that we don't fit neatly into any one of those identities. Adriana Lopez, a young Latina, says that she straddles "the contradictions of U.S. and Latin American identities." She says, "I'm not curvaceous and polished enough for Latin American standards and I'm too sexy and well-dressed for white-American standards" (131). This sense of not fitting into a particular identity runs through third wave feminism, and it opens the door to an understanding of the interlocking nature of identity. Astrid Henry elaborates the concept: "gender, race, ethnicity, sexuality, and class never function in isolation but work as interconnected categories of oppression and privilege" (32). Because we have multiple identities, each of us walks in the shoes of both the oppressor and the oppressed. As a white lesbian soccer mom, I am privileged because I am white and that privilege oppresses those who are not. I am also privileged because I am a mother. I am accepted at work—by colleagues and students—and in my community in ways that I was not before I became a mother. Being a mother gives me a legitimate identity in a heterosexual, coupled world. But I also walk with the oppressed. I am a lesbian and my children are black. Cristina Tzintzun, daughter of a white father and Mexican mother, asks, "Who am I?" and answers: "I am mixed. I am the colonizer and the colonized, the exploiter and the exploited. I am confused yet sure. I am a contradiction" (28).

The acceptance of this contradiction and the paradoxical nature of women's identity in particular and the world in general is a hallmark of third wave feminism. Feminists have long identified the paradoxes that women encounter (Wood and Conrad). In the 1970s, women who wanted to be successful in business were exhorted to dress and act like men. But women who did were called "bitches." Damned if they did and damned if they didn't. When I was younger, I railed against the unfairness of the double binds these paradoxes put me in, and I struggled to find ways out of the contradictions. Now I find it comforting to accept the contradictions. I am who I am. I am a lesbian mother who drives a Volvo station wagon, has two teenage African-American sons, is married to her partner of thirty years, subscribes to *Vogue*, and writes about feminist theory. I live both a conventional and a radical life. I conform and I transgress. I celebrate the contradictions. And through that celebration, I teach my children that they, too, can be contradictions.

During the first session of the LGBT dialogue series that I mentioned earlier, I told the group that I valued talk and its transforming power. I quoted Martin Luther King—"the ends are the means in process." I was immediately challenged by a young gay man who said that he was tired of talk without action and that even King had changed his position near the end of his life. This young man challenged my credentials as an activist. His comments and the subsequent references to me as a lesbian soccer mom made clear that the group saw me and others who lived lives similar to mine not as activists but as "sell-outs" to the system, people whose conventional lifestyles simply reproduced the status quo.

Again, a young third wave feminist gave me a different lens through which to see my life. Leah Lakshmi Piepzna-Samarasinha says that revolutionary change happens not only through laws and guns, but also "through the families and communities we build to replace the dead life we want to flee" (5). My partner and I have built a family, one that is both conventional and non-traditional. When our sons were younger, we acquired our first dog, a chocolate Labrador. Our youngest son, who had longed for a dog for many years, happily informed us that we were now the typical American family—two parents, two children, and a dog. He seemed completely nonplussed when my partner replied, "not quite." We are not the typical American family, yet, in many ways, we are. And it is precisely because we transgress the norms while simultaneously embodying them that we are able to participate in revolutionary change. The paradoxical nature of our lives creates the power to change the social structure—not through sweeping political reforms or social movements, but through daily acts of resistance to established cultural norms.

Although we are married, neither my partner nor I perform the traditional gender roles within our relationship. Our sons see us cook and clean, do the yard work, paint the house, handle the finances, and go to work everyday. They know that we each have our strengths—I handle the finances, my partner keeps track of household repairs, but our division of labor doesn't reproduce gender roles. Our sons and others in the community see us at parent-teacher conferences, school sporting events, local fundraisers, and social gatherings. We chaperone school dances, have birthday parties at our home, and do volunteer work in town. We try to arrive together and always introduce ourselves as the mothers of our sons. We wear matching wedding bands. We protest forms that ask for the name of our sons' father and mother, and we insist that the forms be changed. When asked if I'm married, I say yes—to a woman. We perform similar acts of resistance with respect to race. When our oldest son was an infant, I attended a trustee dinner at the university where my partner was the vice president for academic affairs. I was seated at a table with about ten trustees. Someone congratulated me on the arrival of our son; the subsequent conversation made it clear to everyone that he was African American. A woman seated next to me asked in a stage whisper, "Is he very dark?" The conversation stopped. I smiled, said "yes," and continued talking. These are small but powerful acts of resistance. Our sons know that they can count on us to be forthright about who we are, and I believe that it has taught them to do the same about us and about themselves.

Our social activism through daily acts of resistance brings me to the final concept I discovered in reading the works of third wave feminists. Third wave feminists write about mothers and mothering from their standpoint as the daughters of second wave feminism. Adrienne Rich argues that daughters suffer from matrophobia, or the fear of "*becoming one's mother*" (italicized in original, 235). Matrophobia leads daughters to split from their mothers, to reject them and what they stand for. From the standpoint of third wave feminists, mothering has been viewed as a "taboo" subject. Mothers symbolize the inequities inherent in gender relations. Mothers are weak and oppressed by those who are more powerful. They care for their children but don't disturb the status quo. As daughters, many third wave feminists want to distance themselves from their mothers, to cut the ties that bind them, to create their own unique identity as daughters rather than as mothers (see, for example, essays in Hernández and Rehman).

I am writing from the standpoint of the mother, however, and my standpoint provides a different understanding of mothering. The mother is not a symbol of weakness and oppression. She is a symbol of possibilities. Through daily acts of resistance to social conventions, she creates new families and communities. From this standpoint, mothers are exemplars of bell hooks' definition of feminism: "a commitment to eradicating the ideology of domination that permeates western culture...and a commitment to reorganizing society...so that self-development of people can take precedence over imperialism, economic expansion, and material desire" (24). As a woman raised in second wave feminism who is now raising children in the third wave, I reclaim mothering as an instrument of resistance and mothers as individuals with the power to change the world for the better. I am proud to be a lesbian soccer mom.

Works Cited

Atkinson, Ti-Grace. *Amazon Odyssey*. New York: Links, 1974.

Anzaldúa, Gloria E. and Analouise Keating, eds. *This Bridge We Call Home: Radical Visions for Transformation*. New York: Routledge, 2002.

Belenky, Mary Field, Blythe McVicker Clinchy, Nancy Rule Goldberger, and Jill Mattuck Tarule. *Women's Ways of Knowing: The Development of Self, Voice, and Mind*. New York: Basic, 1986.

Brownmiller, Susan. *Against Our Will: Men, Women and Rape*. New York: Simon, 1975.

Collins, Patricia Hill. "Comment on Heckman's 'Truth and Method: Feminist Standpoint Theory Revisited': Where's the Power?" *Signs* 22 (1997): 375-381.

de Beauvoir, Simone. *The Second Sex*. New York: Bantam Books, 1965.

Fine, Marlene G. "New Voices in Organizational Communication: A Feminist Commentary and Critique." *Transforming Visions: Feminist Critiques in Communication Studies*. Ed. Patrice Buzzanell. Cresskill: Hampton, 1993. 125-166.

Frankenburg, Ruth. *White Women, Race Matters: The Social Construction of Whiteness*. Minneapolis: University of Minnesota Press, 1993.

Friedan, Betty. *The Feminine Mystique*. New York: Dell, 1963.

Gilligan, Carol. *In a Different Voice: Psychological Theory and Women's Development*. Cambridge: Harvard University Press, 1982.

Greer, Germaine. *The Female Eunuch*. New York: McGraw, 1971.

Harding, Sandra. "Comment on Hekman's 'Truth and Method: Feminist Standpoint Theory Revisited': Whose Standpoint Needs the Regimes of Truth and Reality?" *Signs* 22 (1997): 382-391.

Hartsock, Nancy. "The Feminist Standpoint: Developing the Ground for a Specifically Feminist Historical Materialism." *Feminism and Methodology*. Ed. Sandra Harding. Bloomington: Indiana University Press, 1987. 181-190.

Henry, Astrid. *Not My Mother's Sister: Generational Conflict and Third-Wave Feminism*. Bloomington: Indiana University Press, 2004.

Hernández, Daisy, and Bushra Rehman, eds. *Colonize This! Young Women of Color on Today's Feminism*. New York: Seal, 2002.

hooks, bell. *Feminist Theory: From Margin to Center*. Boston: South End, 1984.

Johnston, Jill. *Lesbian Nation: The Feminist Solution*. New York: Simon, 1973.

Jones, Lisa. *Bulletproof Diva: Tales of Race, Sex, and Hair*. New York: Anchor, 1995.

Keller, Evelyn Fox. *Reflections on Gender and Science*. New Haven: Yale University Press, 1985.

Labaton, Vivien, and Dawn Lundy Martin, eds. *The Fire This Time: Young Activists and The New Feminism*. New York: Anchor, 2004.

Litwin, Anne H., and D. Lynn O'Brien Hallstein. "Shadows and Silences: How Women's Standpoint and Unspoken Friendship Rules Cause Difficulties Among Many Women at Work." *Women's Studies in Communication* 30 (2007): 111-142.

Lopez, Adriana. "In Praise of Difficult Chicas: Feminism and Femininity." *Colonize This! Young Women of Color on Today's Feminism*. Eds. Daisy Hernández and Bushra Rehman. New York: Seal, 2002. 119-132.

Luke, Carmen. "White Women in Interracial Families: Reflections on Hybridization, Feminine Identities, and Racialized Othering." *Feminist Issues* 14.2 (1994): 49-72.

McIntosh, Peggy. "White Privilege and Male Privilege." *Race, Class and Gender*. Eds. A.L. Andersen and Patricia Hill Collins. Belmont: Wadsworth, 1992. 65-69.

Millett, Kate. *Sexual Politics*. Garden City: Doubleday, 1970.

Morgan, Joan. *When Chickenheads Come Home to Roost: A Hip-Hop Feminist Breaks It Down*. New York: Simon, 1999.

O'Brien Hallstein, D. Lynn. "A Postmodern Caring: Feminist Standpoint Theories, Revisioned Caring, and Communication Ethics." *Western Journal of Communication* 63 (1999): 32-56.

O'Brien Hallstein, D. Lynn. "Where Standpoint Stands Now: An Introduction and Commentary." *Women Studies in Communication* 60 (2000): 1-15.

Piepzna-Samarasinha, Leah Lakshmi. "browngirlworld: queergirlofcolor, organizing, sistahood, heartbreak." *Colonize This! Young Women of Color on Today's Feminism*. Eds. Daisy Hernández and Bushra Rehman. New York: Seal, 2002. 3-16.

Rich, Adrienne. *Of Woman Born: Motherhood as Experience and Institution*. New York: Norton, 1986.

Tzintzun, Cristina. "Colonize This!" *Colonize This! Young Women of Color on*

Today's Feminism. Eds. Daisy Hernández and Bushra Rehman. New York: Seal, 2002. 17-28.

Wood, Julia T. "Gender and Moral Voice: Moving from Women's Nature to Standpoint Epistemology." *Women Studies in Communication,* 15 (1997): 1-24.

Wood, Julia T. and Charles Conrad. "Paradox in the Experiences of Professional Women." *Western Journal of Communication* 47 (1983): 305-322.

7
Considerations

ANDREA FECHNER

I just want you to know that
there are women that choose to
parent without a mystical mother urge.

I just want you to know that
there are women who think they're going to make a dent
in the world's overpopulation problem.

I just want you to know that
there are women who think
their adoptive action was noble
then realize pride is not enough.

I just want you to know that
it's possible to hide behind the privileged wall of theory—
discourse on discourse
the subjectivity of subjectivity
the confluence of confluence.

I just want you to know that
white privilege shared in transracial adoption
may not transfer well.

I just want you to know that
there are women who stand before their students
trying to convince them that maternal essentialism
is a social mirage.

I just want you to know that
there are women feeling fraudulent

when they don't feel that
mother-glow thing.

I just want you to know that there are mothers staying up nights
surfing the web hoping they missed some incredible answer last night
when they searched then, too.

I just want you to know that
my children are weighted down by misfiring neurons, FAS induced fog, distract-
edness and their color in an East Tennessee world.

I just want you to know that
there are mothers trying to hand-off to their children
a life story concocted from
three sentences in a DHS report.

I just want you to know
that I am a mother who knows the final most powerful gift I can give
to my distracted, loosely bonded, neglected, drugged, assaulted, rejected, violated,
beautiful soul-in-the-eyes babies
is a cultural story they can hold in their hearts
to buffer the onslaught
even if I have to make it up.

I just want you to know
that the thing I can give myself is my sankofa
about mothering as a subversive act
to get in the face of the mini-moms with the mini-vans
whose intrusive questions require the script:

> Yes, they're adopted
> Yes, they're black
> Yes, they're special needs
> Yes, that's hard here
> Yes, I specifically asked for all this
> And Yes, I am their real mom.

Might I add—angry frequently, disillusioned frequently, at a loss frequently,
entering every day of mothering from a place of not knowing.

Fellow feminists, third wavers, second wavers, in between wavers, where are
you?

Jump into this morass with me
admit that mothering can feel like hell, sharing privilege can feel like hell, being
honest can feel like hell, thinking your children might read this someday—feels
like hell.

Keep moving on—check over your shoulder my Janus sisters—
see why you chose this motherhood—look forward and resolve to be truth tellers
about mothering—
The lies are keeping us apart—

In My Mother's House

Mothering, Othering, and Resisting Racism

AKOSUA ADOMAKO AMPOFO

The title of this chapter is a play on Kwame Appiah's *In My Father's House.* In his book, Kwame Anthony Appiah, son of a Ghanaian father, an Asante, and a British mother states, "I had decided to name this book for him: it was from him, after all, that I inherited the world and the problems with which this book is concerned. From him I inherited Africa, in general; Ghana, in particular; Asante and Kumasi, more particularly yet" (viii). I have often thought about the title of that book in relation to issues of my own identity. Like Appiah my father is an Asante, from Kumase, and my mother is European. I was born and raised in Ghana, and my siblings and I, especially my older sister and I, spent most of our holidays during our growing up years in Kumase, the capital of the Asante state,[1] at the home of my paternal grandparents. Unlike Appiah, however, who notes, "If my sisters and I were 'children of two worlds,' no one bothered to tell us this" (viii), in my own case my mother took pains to explain our "dual-cultural" heritage to us at some point in our childhood (even though I did not fully appreciate the uncommonness of this fact until I was well into my teens, and my memories today are of an effortless straddling of these worlds).[2]

As an adult I recognised that although I appreciated my German ancestry, at some point I had assumed an Asante/African identity.[3] Although, as far as I can recollect, my claims of an Asante identity were never contested, technically it is not quite accurate for me to claim to be an Asante. The Asante are a matrilineal people who trace their lineage through the maternal line. Thus, an Asante man's children belong to his wife's lineage and not his own. In my own case since my mother is not an Asante I cannot, strictly speaking, claim to be an Asante.[4] My father, and especially my paternal grandparents, taught my siblings and me about our Asante heritage and we were embraced into Asante traditions and ways of life; however, it seems to me that it was my mother's endorsement of our *Asante-ness,* and her lessons on identity politics that were particularly influential in my arriving at a place where I claim Asante and Ghana much more effortlessly than Wuppertal or Germany.[5] And so this chapter is not so much a dedication to my mother in the way that *In My Father's House* is Appiah's dedication to his father, although it is also that. More so, it is a recognition that my identity as an Asante, a Ghanaian, and, most importantly, an African and a person of colour, has been formed in large measure from growing up *in my mother's house*. This chapter is also a reflection on my own mothering politics as I raise my two daughters, and the recognition that, in many ways, they too are being raised in *my mother's house*. The data of course, are very much in my head. However, I also rely on a series of interviews conducted among non-Ghanaian women between 2000 and 2004, one of them being my mother, as well as journals that I kept between 1992 and 2004 (my most recent entry) about my daughters' growing-up experiences as seen through my eyes.[6]

Racialised Mothering

Western feminists have shifted along a spectrum of theorising on motherhood from attacks on motherhood as a patriarchal construct, to affirmations of it as a valuable identity that must be defended against male control and masculinist values. Third World feminists have sharply criticized what they regarded as the ethnocentricist and post-modernist radical reconstruction of much of this debate (Adomako Ampofo; Collins; Oyewùmí; Thenjiwe). Scholarship on interracial families and identity have generally come from psychology, social psychology, social work, or counseling perspectives. Work on "biracial" or "multicultural" children has focused primarily on issues pertaining to the children's personality adjustments and the conflicts said to derive from experiencing adjustments to two different cultures (for example, Brown; Poston; Root) with much of the research indicating the negative effects on identity, self-concept, and self-esteem (Adler; Johnson and Nagoshi; Overmeier). Although dominant groups are very influential in determining socialising norms and practices, "multi-cultural/ethnic and racial" families produce interesting variants in the practice. Mothers of "multi-racial," "multi-ethnic," and "multi-cultural" children may reproduce or contest and subvert racial politics in interesting ways. Nonetheless, while motherhood and the socialisation of children has been an important arena of theoretical enquiry in feminist analyses, very little attention has been given to trans-racial, trans-ethnic, and trans-cultural motherhood and its effects on transforming racialised and racist discourses and practices. France Winddance Twine argues that feminist theorising has assumed that mothering is practised primarily in "racially unified" families (29). What little work has been done in this area has come primarily from "white" mothers of "black" children in the US (Maureen Reddy's work is illustrative), the UK, (see France Twine's work), and to a lesser extent Western Europe (see for example Anna Rastas's work on Finland).

To date I have not come across any work on, or by, mothers of multiracial/ethnic/cultural background located in the global South. This is an important gap since location is very significant when it comes to experiences and responses to race, racialised spaces, and racism. "White" mothers of "non-white" children in Ghana can be expected to "do" motherhood in ways that differ not only from "black" mothers in Ghana, but also from "white" and "black" mothers in the global North.[7] Large-scale surveys carried out in the US indicate that allegiance to norms of exclusive motherhood, for example, may be racialised. "White" mothers show a much stronger preference for individualised forms of maternal care, especially during early childhood years, while "black" mothers are more likely to share mothering with "other-mothers" such as grandmothers, aunts, and other female relatives, as Akosua Adomako Ampofo, Patricia Hill Collins, and Katherine Newman have argued. Another interesting question is, what are the inter-generational relationships between women's politics of mothering? Analyses of the different ways of thinking about, and practising, mothering can open new ways of feminist analyzing and theorising.

In this chapter, I examine mothering that consciously seeks to destabilise race. I come to this work from the perspective of a "dual-raced" woman, daughter of a "white" European woman, Hanna Adomako, who moved to Ghana in 1959, and a "black" Ghanaian father, Joseph Adomako. It might seem obvious that a person born to a "minority" parent would be particularly sensitive to issues of race and identity. However, it has only been in the last decade and a half or so, as I have become more conscious of my relative positions of privilege here and disadvantage there as I live as an African, person of colour, or even an *Obroni* in Africa and the diaspora, that my interest in issues of race, identity, citizenship, and polity have become more consciously political.[8] My interest in the experiences of non-Africans, and later non-Ghanaians, living in Ghana culminated, in 1999, in my designing a research project on the lives of non-Ghanaian women living in Ghana. To date I have carried out focused conversations with 20 women aged between 36 and 80-something.[9] As a child of parents of two different "races," I observed that children from such "biracial" or multicultural families varied greatly in their racial identities and one of my interests became to understand the racial politics of non-Ghanaian mothers, how they transmit particular racial or cultural identities to their children, and how these children in turn develop racial politics. Ultimately, what do racial politics and culture have to do with mothering? My mother was one of my interviewees and the issues of race and mothering that I explore in this chapter link my analyses of her narrative, my own experiences of being mothered, and some reflections on my own mothering of my two daughters, Yaa Oparebea, (aged 13) and Akosua Asamoabea (aged 10) from a feminist, post-colonial perspective.

In My Mother's House: Learning Race and Antiracism

Feminism consciously informs my own notions of motherhood, mothering, and family. So do more African-centred notions of womanhood that provided women with many scripts, motherhood simply being one of them: roles as sisters, counselors, queens, chiefs, priestesses (see also Akosua Aidoo and Christine Oppong) even as "husbands" and "sons" (see Ife Amadiume). My mother, however, belongs to the generation of women for whom a woman's entire being was viewed as much more intimately tied to being a good wife and mother. Indeed, for many of the older women in my study, being a good mother, nurturing one's children, and serving one's husband was the ultimate destiny of a woman, so much so that some remained in unsatisfactory relationships to maintain this persona. While my mother clearly contested this construction in many ways as is obvious to me from her career goals for her daughters, and the fact that she worked outside the home until she retired at age 60, she certainly privileged the role of the home-maker and would not readily describe herself as a feminist.

Here my daughters and I differ from her somewhat. None of us feel particu-larly bound to biological motherhood (admittedly, for Akosua the thought of the physical pain of childbirth weighs heavy) nor can they conceive of a life without "work." "It would be boring," says Yaa, when I ask if she would consider being a homemaker if she were married to a wealthy man and he asked that she stay home to look after the children. "But the children will go to school!" quips Akosua, raising eyebrows to wonder, "so what would I be doing at home alone?"

Nonetheless my mother's anti-racist politics have always been much more conscious than her feminist politics even though prior to her move to Britain, where she met my father as well as several other African students, my mother had not been exposed to Negritude literature such as works by Fannon, Garvey, or Nkrumah. She had, however, been exposed to the science and popular literature that revealed Africans as inferior. Even before 400 BC, Herodotus (484-425 BC), hailed by some as the "father of modern history" was writing of Africa, "Here too are the dog-faced creatures, and the creatures without heads....and *also the wild men, and wild women, and many other less fabulous beasts*" (qtd. in Knopf 1997, emphasis mine). She would have been familiar with images of the undisciplined, untruthful, unreliable, and perhaps occasionally redeemable black man. Dr. Al-bert Schweitzer, renowned for having abandoned (or supposedly "sacrificed") the comfort of Western civilization for the dark continent of Africa noted of Africans in 1939, "I do not deny that they are undisciplined and in many ways unreliable... and that many of them give way to the temptation to appropriate other people's property and that all too often they are untruthful; nevertheless what a number of really faithful servants I have discovered in these years..." (132). My mother was also made aware that the African accepted the superiority of the white race as part of the order of nature (for example James Bryce in his impressions of South Africa, 1897). Hitler's own brand of racism did not escape her either. While only a child when Hitler came to power, she recollects her grandparents talking in hushed tones about how it was a "sin" and a "shame" what was being done to the people of the "yellow star," the Jewish people.

My mother's experiences of Ghana as a racialised society came from her interac-tions with other "white" people, but also from interactions with people of colour, and she continually had to confront individuals because of what she perceived as both covert and overt racism. Working with European-owned companies she constantly heard racist comments being made about Ghanaians that horrified her. She recounts an experience with one company during her early years when she did not yet have a car. The company was taking her to and from work in a company bus and she soon discovered that she was having to listen to conversations among the expatriate staff about Ghanaians, invariably referred to as "these people," that "appalled and disgusted" her. She took her colleagues on, complained to the boss, and soon thereafter left the company. White racism, while not to be accepted, was to be expected. Racism from other Third World people, towards Ghanaians, was particularly painful for her to deal with. She recounts an encounter with an Asian woman when she had gone swimming with my older sister and me. According to her, the woman took up our space outside the pool while we were swimming. Once we got out of the pool my mother informed her that we were the ones seated there, but the woman mumbled something and my mother took exception to her attitude. According to my mother the Asian woman was rude and treated my mother disrespectfully because she (my mother) was a white woman with "mixed race" children. I only remember the encounter vaguely: my mother confronting someone about inappropriate behaviour, as she herself explained, "I stood very firm with her." But for me it was an early lesson of many more that were to follow: my mother would not tolerate injustice of any kind, and when she felt that this injustice was bound up with notions of racial superiority, especially when it was her family that were at the receiving end, she could be ferocious. Generally, she had a mission: "I would fight for Ghanaians."

When I was younger I sometimes got embarrassed by my mother's bluntness. As an adult my daughters have sometimes been embarrassed by mine. A few years ago, when my daughters were about eleven and nine, we stopped for lunch at a popular, quaint restaurant en-route to our home in Accra from a weekend out of town. It was late, and except for a group of Britons seated at a table not far from us—chatting and laughing in, it seemed to me, relaxed after-dinner mode—the place was empty. The group seemed to consist of the usual study-abroad group including a couple of faculty members and several students. The buffet table was also almost devoid of food and the waiters advised us to wait for a few minutes while the dishes were being filled up. Several minutes later one of the waiters informed us that we could go ahead and eat, so Yaa, Akosua, and my husband got up to serve themselves. No sooner had they done this than a woman from the seated group accosted them. Her point was that the group had also been waiting for a long time and we were jumping the queue. All of this was said in a hostile manner with a few choice words thrown in to describe our uncouth behaviour. My family members were momentarily taken aback. While they were recovering from the shock I jumped up to inform her that we had no idea they were waiting to eat, that buffet tables normally do not operate on a first-come-to the restaurant-first-eat basis, that we had been advised by the restaurant staff to serve ourselves, and that in any case she could have expressed herself in more civil tones. Dissatisfied with my response and the fact that the four of us—who could not possibly have eaten enough to deprive her group of food—did not budge, she launched into a tirade: the restaurant was treating her unfairly, "these people" did not appreciate what people like her and the countries she represented did to help our societies, she complained about all the money she was spending in Ghana that supported our economy, and concluded that in future she would sow her seeds of kindness elsewhere. The waiters too were momentarily caught off guard. They made an attempt to placate me and calm her but this only incensed her all the more. She then got up, informed her somewhat bemused group of students that they would be leaving, and marched out. As she retreated I advised her that she might want to reconsider her motives and reflect on her seemingly missionary attitudes, and that it was attitudes like hers that caused so-called development assistance to fail. I also threw in, for good measure, my assessment that her expenditure in Ghana was probably too paltry to make an impression on our economy.

My daughters of course were embarrassed. We all felt bad that the restaurant lost its customers, especially since at that late hour not many people were likely to show up to do justice to the buffet table. For Yaa and Akosua this was their first encounter with racism, although Akosua did not recognise that this was about race, and, despite their embarrassment, they were offended. Of course our lunch was marred but we ended up having a discussion about respect, racism, social justice, and so forth. Today, Yaa, especially, has a much keener sense that "race" is about a lot more than colour. She is also much more conscious about issues of ethnicism within Ghana. Foreigners, and especially white foreigners, do not loom large on the Ghanaian landscape, nonetheless Ghana can be said to reveal racial diversity.[10] Indeed, as Emmanuel Akyeampong has explained, the Lebanese have long been a particularly economically important (if politically marginalised) category. The Akans (the larger group to which the Asante belong as do the Akuapems, my husband's matrikin) refer to white people, but also foreigners more generally as *abrofo* (singular *obroni*).[11] Long before I had ever discussed race with my daughters, when the older, Yaa, was three she would refer to me as "yellow" or *Obroni*, and her father as "dark brown." A few years later, when the younger, Akosua, was about four she too would refer to me as *Obroni*, herself and her sister as "brown" (sometimes "light brown"), and their father as "dark brown," "black," or on occasion, "purple." For Akosua, race is still very much about colour for even now, aged ten, she defines it as "the different colours of human beings," while Yaa says that "race" is tied up with "when one race feels superior to, and more important than, another and looks down on them."

In addition to whatever lessons I, as their mother, may have imparted, because both girls have had the privilege of traveling with me or their father in different parts of the world, they have been exposed to "difference" in different contexts early in life and are thus better able to pick up on some of the nuances. Both girls have complained about a Ghanaian teacher's favouritism towards a non-African student in Yaa's class. Having been a British colony, the official language in Ghana is English. However, the Ghana Education service curriculum requires students to study one Ghanaian language, which is one of six required subjects taken during the primary and Junior Secondary school.[12] This particular student was exempted by the teacher from expressing himself verbally in the Ghanaian language class, in this case *Twi*.[13] He was also exempted from taking the dictation exam, and was never reprimanded if he failed to do his *Twi* homework.[14] Both girls noted that other Ghanaian students from other ethnic groups, and who were non-*Twi* speakers, did not enjoy the same preferential treatment. My daughters concluded that this was because sometimes Ghanaians treat "white people" better. Yaa recognises that this is tied up with the complicity of some black people in racist agendas. Despite being able to articulate and recognise racism more readily than her younger sister, Yaa seems to have traversed this terrain with greater equanimity, while Akosua, generally more sensitive, has experienced her own "difference" more profoundly. During 2004-2005, for example, while I was on a year's sabbatical in the US, both daughters came with me. We lived in a small college town and the public schools were excellent—and also predominantly white. Akosua, my younger daughter, was in the 3rd grade at the time, and commented after her first or second day in school that it felt odd to be "different." "*How different?*" I asked. There was only one other child in her class who was "brown" she responded. Akosua recognises that more obvious differences between and among people based on phenotype often bring privileges or disadvantages, or unwanted attention, and she would much rather go through a more simple version of life. But perhaps so would we all.

My mother contested racist discourse and labels, and enacted an antiracist agenda in her plans for her children, especially her daughters. She reflected this in a variety of ways: her discourse, stories, dress, choice of food and schools, encouraging relationships with my father's family, encouraging us to speak *Twi*, although she never mastered it herself. As she herself says of her training of her children, "I taught them not to look down on anything to do with colour...to like Ghanaian food, to accept Ghanaian life, to accept Ghanaians; to accept that what makes them Ghana."

Not all white mothers of non-white children lead their children to develop a non-white identity; indeed some encourage them to construct a non-racialised identity. France Winddance Twine found that Asian and European-American mothers of daughters with African heritages played a critical role in providing daughters with experiences of racial neutrality ("Brown Skinned White Girls"). These daughters experienced class and gender identity as more primary than their African heritage in defining their identities. The mothers never specifically trained them for a racially marked identity, nor were they "racialised" or told that they belonged to a black racial category, so they were not conscious of having a racial identity as children. While most of the white women in my own study see their children as "black" or as children "of colour," a few reject these identities. One of the women in my study rejected the notion of racialising herself or her children. "I don't use *that* term," she responded vehemently when I asked what race she considered herself to be. Another, when I asked whether she thought of her son as any particular colour or race responded, "I don't see any colour." Normative whiteness thus goes unchallenged, exempting whiteness as a "non-race category."

My mother, on the other hand, while she taught us to think of our double heritage as special, that we were, in her words, "both Ghanaian and German," also encouraged us to be proud of a coloured identity. Like Ellen, a 40-something-year-old Irish woman in my research, who said that her children, like anyone "slightly darker than ivory" would be "black," my mother referred to us as "chocolate brown" or "black," distinguishing between phenotype and politics.

For my mother, having her children self-identify as persons of colour was about giving us a strong, proud, but also a "realistic" ethnic identity. After all, the white majority culture would never read us as white. She records an incident in the early 1960s, in Germany, when my elder sister Tina was about six, and she picked up that Tina was conscious of being "different." Tina did not want to go for a walk because, she complained, "people are looking at me." My mother responded, "They are looking at you because you are so pretty." To this my sister responded, "Yes, but I don't want to go." My mother persisted, "but they are looking at you because you have got such a lovely hairstyle." My mother now concedes, "I think she didn't trust me one hundred percent, but I tried to tell her." When they got to a café my mother made Tina go up and place her own order, despite the fact that my sister was conscious everyone would be staring at her. "I wanted to instill in her pride. Pride about her colour, pride that she was somebody, pride that she should stand up for herself and never mind what is around her," my mother notes. But it was also to make sure that in spite of recognising that we were "special," we would not develop any feelings of racial superiority over other "fully" black children in contexts where lighter skin was privileged. As Hanna Adomako tried to teach her children, "I wanted them to grow up to ignore colour, that the most important thing is character...be yourself and show your strength of character... let yourself be judged by wisdom, not by being superior."

Carmen Luke's US study of white women who were in relationships with black men found that the women, as a result of their family's rejection of them and their children and/or partners, all identified first and foremost with the culture of their black partners, even though their connection to that heritage was acquired, of shorter duration, and therefore, in many ways, weaker than the connections to the white culture into which they were born. In my own research, only a few of the white women I interviewed experienced such rejection on a long-term basis, thus they did not have the same reasons for identifying primarily with their partners' cultures. Like these women, my mother's love for her husband and her strong connection to Ghana did not seem to present a need to adopt a new racial identity herself. Thus, her transmitting a coloured identity to her children was not because she had adopted one for herself.

For mothers of my generation, we have many more "ethnic" symbols and paraphernalia to share with our children. Further, even though in today's neo-liberal, globalised world we are inundated with symbols of "whiteness" and "white" culture, and white culture continues to be privileged,[15] promoting a cultural education that valorises "blackness" is less difficult to achieve.

I, too, experience challenges around the colour of identity in the bringing up of my daughters. Whenever my daughters have referred to me as *obroni*, or, on rare occasions have narrated incidents when they themselves have been referred to as *obroni*, I have been quick to remind them that neither I nor they are *obroni*. When they were younger and insisted on an explanation of why they were one thing and not another I even resorted to mathematical explanations—since they had only one white grandparent and three black grandparents they were *more* black than white. Of course with such constructions I end up adopting the very racist-borne and racialised constructions that my mother and I try so hard to contest. The challenge remains as to how to refute race as real while acknowledging the significance of race in daily social intercourse.

Closing Reflections

My mother, my daughters, and I have inherited "race" and racialised discourses, but we can also transgress the discourses and locales that "racialise" us, and Motherhood, as it turns out, can be a powerful institution, if you like, but also experience, in which this transformative agenda can be located. As I have tried to show, mothers who classify themselves as members of a social category that is presumed to be distinct from that of their children can contest and disrupt hierarchies of inequality by challenging racist ideologies and constructions. While the racial issues confronting persons located in the global North are not the same as for those of us who spend most of our lives in the global South, our stories suggest that race is still recognised as an important variable of stratification, and even in a relatively less racialised society like Ghana's, resistances to mothering and racism can still occur and do occur effectively. The different status accorded motherhood, and the particular ways in which gender arrangements are constructed in Ghana, as in many parts of Africa, also make possible "radical" incursions into the dominant practices. Patricia Hill Collins refers to "motherwork" to show that mothering is work, constitutes an economic contribution, has to be learned, and, particularly with reference to "racial and ethnic women's motherwork," contributes to destabilising the dominant power and identity nexus (61).

[1]Kumasi (or Kumase) is also the capital of the Ashanti (administrative) Region of Ghana.

[2]This would seem to be supported from my interview with Peggy Appiah, the accomplished writer, artist, wife of veteran Ghanaian politician Joe Appiah, and mother of Kwame Appiah, when she indicated that she had never consciously thought of people as "different" because she had been brought up to regard every-body "of every nationality as the *same*" (emphasis mine). Interestingly, however, she noted that she met her husband when she was working for an organisation in London called "Racial Unity."

[3]This did not imply a rejection of a Euro-identity. For example, while in graduate school in the United States, I was most irritated that after I refused to check any of the racial boxes on some form or other from the graduate school (since they

made no provision for me to choose *both* an African and an European heritage) someone had, without even bothering to consult me, determined to categorise me as African/African descent.

[4]This notwithstanding the Asante (often written Ashanti), like many African ethnic groups, make allowances for people, such as slaves, foundlings, and even migrants to be "adopted" into Asante citizenship. Hence, for example, the term *Asante Kramo* (literally, "Asante Muslim") to describe settlers, typically from what is today Northern Ghana or other countries in the Sahel regions of West Africa, who came with their new religion, Islam.

[5]My mother's hometown is Wuppertal in the Ruhr area of central Germany.

[6]The study on the lives of non-Ghanaian women in Ghana was supported with a research grant from the University of Ghana in 2000.

[7]Although race, like gender, is a social and not a natural category, it still holds deep meaning and significance for most people. In his work Ratele (see for example 2004) uses the term thus: "race" (i.e with the word struck through) to problematise and complicate race. I have tended to parenthesise it and its derivatives: "race." Elsewhere I detail the importance of race for people "of colour" (Adomako Ampofo 2006). Suffice it to say here that people of colour do not usually have the option to choose our race or to "do" or "not do" race.

[8]Ghana does not collect data on "race," however, according to the 2000 Population and Housing census 92% of the population were "Ghanaian by birth" (Ghana Statistical Services 2002).

[9]Most of the interviews occurred between 2000 and 2004 but the study is on-going.

[10]See note 8.

[11]The term *Obroni*, like equivalents in many cultures, encompasses much more of a mixed bag than the English words "white," "black," "Caucasian," "nigger," etc. connote. Professor Mary Esther Kropp-Dakubu, a linguist at the University of Ghana, suggests that historically the term comes from the word for "white" ("blanc") in the trade Portuguese that was spoken on the West coast throughout the slave trade years. Kropp-Dakubu notes that Roemer (a Danish trader at Christiansborg, Gold Coast, in the mid-eighteenth century) went back to Denmark and in his memoirs said the natives on the gold coast referred to Europeans as "Blankes." Romer cites a couple of other expressions that make it reasonable to accept that however the word was pronounced then, it later became "bro," with a normal Akan prefix and the suffix -ni "person" added. The Ga word *blofonyo* had an open o, even more like "blanc," also with suffixes meaning "person" (Kropp-Dakubu, May 2006; personal communication).

[12]The others are core math, core English, core science, French, and social studies.

[13]In my daughter's school, as in many schools, a shortage of language teachers meant that only two Ghanaian languages were offered, *Twi* and *Ga*.

[14]Twi is the language spoken by most of the Akan groups.

[15]For example western technology as in the use of modern computers, and white-

ness as reflected in the privileging of the English language and the promotion of skin-lightening creams.

Works Cited

Adler, A. J. "Children and Biracial Identity." *Children's needs: Psychological Perspectives.* Ed. A. Thomas and J. Grimes. Washington, DC: National Association of School Psychologists, 1987. 55-66.

Adomako Ampofo, Akosua, "Mothering among Black and White non-Ghanaian Women in Ghana." *Jenda* 5 (2004).

Adomako Ampofo, Akosua. "White women have more sex; Race, Othering and Gender and Sexual Identities of Foreign Women in Ghana." Paper presented to the Nordic Africa Institute, Uppsala, June 8, 2006.

Aidoo, Agnes Akosua. "Women in the History and Culture of Ghana." *Research Review,* NS. 1:1. (1985).

Akyeampong, Emmanuel. "Race, Indenity and Citizenship in Black Africa: The Case of the Lebanse in Ghana." *Africa* 76.3 (2006): 297-323.

Amadiume, Ife. *Male Daughters, Female Husbands: Gender and Sex in an African Society.* London: Zed, 1987.

Appiah, Kwame Anthony. *In My Father's House.* New York: Oxford University Press, 1993.

Brown, Philip M. "Biracial Identity and Social Marginality." *Child and Adolescent Social Work* 7.4 (1990): 319-337.

Chodorow, Nancy. *The Reproduction of Mothering.* Berkeley: University of California Press, 1978.

Collins, Patricia Hill. *Black Feminist Thought.* New York: Routledge, 1990.

Collins, Patricia Hill. "Shifting the Center: Race, Class and Feminist Theorizing about Motherhood." *Mothering, Ideology, Experience and Agency.* Ed. Glenn Evelyn Nakano, Grace Chang, and Linda Rennie Forcey. New York: Routledge, 1994.

DeAnda, Diane, and Valerie Anne Riddle. "Ethnic Identity, Self-Esteem, and Interpersonal Relationships among Multiethnic Adolescents." *Journal of Multicultural Social Work* 1.2 (1991): 83-98.

Ghana Statistical Services. *2000 Population and Housing Census.* Accra: Government of Ghana, 2002.

Johnson, R. C., and C. T. Nagoshi. "The Adjustment of Offspring within Group and Interracial/Intercultural Marriages: A Comparison of Personality Factor Scores." *Journal of Marriage and the Family* 48 (1986): 279-284.

Kerwin, C. J. Ponterotto, B. Jackson, and A. Harris. "Racial Identity in Biracial Children: A Qualitative Investigation." *Journal of Counselling Psychology* 40.2 (1993): 221-231.

Knopf, Alfred. *The Histories.* New York: Everyman's Library, 1997. (Originally published fifth century BC by Herodotus).

Luke, Carmen. "White Women in Interracial Families: Reflections in Hybridization, Feminine Identities, and Racialised Othering." *Feminist Issues* 14.2 (1994): 49-72.

Magwaza, Thenjiwe. "Perceptions and Experiences of Motherhood: A Study of Black and White Mothers of Durban, South Africa." Presented at the Conference on *Images of Motherhood – African and Nordic Perspectives*. Dakar, February 15-19, 2003.

Newman, Katherine. *Declining Fortunes*. New York: Basic, 1993.

Oppong, Christine and Katherine Abu. "Seven Roles of Women." *Impact of Education, Migration and Employment on Ghanaian Mothers*. Geneva: ILO, 1987.

Overmeier, K. "Biracial adolescents: Areas of Conflict in Identity Formation." *Journal of Applied Social Sciences* 14.2 (1990): 157-176.

Oyewùmí, Oyérònké. *The Invention of Women. Making an African Sense of Western Gender Discourses*. Minneapolis, London: University of Minnesota Press, 1997.

Poston, W. S. "Biracial Identity Development Model: A Needed Addition." *Journal of Counselling and Development* 69 (1990): 152-155.

Rastas, Anna. "Am I Still 'White'? Dealing with the Colour Trouble." *Balayi: Culture, Law and Colonialism* 6 (forthcoming): 94-106.

Ratele, Kopano. "Kinky Politics." Ed. Signe Arnfred. *Re-thinking Sexualities in Africa*. Uppsala: Nordic Africa Institute, 2004. 139-156.

Reddy, Maureen. *Crossing the Color Line. Race, Parenting and Culture*. New Brunswick: Rutgers University Press, 1997.

Root, Maria. "Resolving "Other" Status: Identity Development of Biracial Individuals." *Diversity and Complexity in Feminist Therapy*. Ed. LL. S. Brown, and M. Root. Harrington Park, CA: Hawthorn, 1990. 185-205.

Schweitzer, Albert. *African Notebook*. New York: Holt, 1939.

Thenjiwe, Magwaza. "Perceptions and Experiences of Motherhood: A Study of Black and White Mothers of Durban, South Africa." Paper presented at the Conference on *Images of Motherhood – African and Nodic Perspectives*, Dakar, Senegal, February 2003. 15-19.

Twine, France Winddance. "Brown Skinned White Girls: Class, Culture and the Construction of White Identity in Suburban Communities." *Gender, Place and Culture* 3.2 (1996): 205-224.

Twine, France Winddance. "Managing Everyday Racisms: The Anti-racist Practices of White Mothers of African-Descent Children in Britain." *Everyday Inequalities: Critical Inquiries*. Ed. Jodi O'Brien and Judith Howard. Malden, MA: Blackwell, 1998. 237-252.

Part III
Mothering Contradictions

9
Second Wave Silences and Third Wave Intensive Mothering

D. LYNN O'BRIEN HALLSTEIN

Every day feminist mothers must negotiate the complex struggle between intensive and empowered mothering. This struggle is as much about mothering as it is about feminism because it is also a struggle for women to resist the discourse of intensive mothering in favor of an empowered mothering that allows for maternal agency. Indeed, feminist academics such as Susan Douglas and Meredith Michaels, Sharon Hays, and Andrea O'Reilly argue that the ideology of intensive mothering is deeply problematic for women because, within the United States context, it rests on at least three core beliefs: 1) children need and require constant and ongoing nurturing by their biological mothers who are single-handedly responsible for meeting these needs; 2) in meeting those needs, mothers must rely on experts to guide them, and 3) mothers must lavish enormous amounts of time and energy on their children. In short, mothers should always put their children's needs before their own. Thus, even though not all women practice intensive mothering, as Hays argues, it is the ideology of contemporary mothering that all women are disciplined into, across race and class lines, even if not all women actually practice it.

Feminist scholars (Douglas and Michaels; Hays; O'Reilly) suggest, then, that this *proper* ideology is a backlash against second wave feminist gains, particularly in terms of gains in education and the workplace. Like the beauty myth that Naomi Wolf argues regulates women by demanding impossible-for-most-women-to-meet standards of beauty and slenderness, the ideology of intensive mothering is a "counterattack" against second wave feminist successes for women. The intensive ideology works to regulate women by demanding impossible-for-most-women-to-meet standards of mothering. In short, as Andrea O'Reilly argues, drawing on Adrienne Rich's work, intensive mothering gives women "powerless responsibility;"[1] it assigns mothers all the responsibility for mothering but denies them the power to define and determine their own experiences of mothering. It defines how women are to mother and how they should feel about mothering. Finally, it also isolates women from each other and ultimately denies women "personhood": a sense of self outside of mothering. Thus, in their daily interactions with and decisions about their children, as O'Reilly suggests, a feminist or empowered mother has to resist intensive mothering and instead mother in ways that emphasize maternal power and agency in everyday mothering practices.

Doing so, however, raises important questions. How does a feminist or empowered mother resist the pervasive force of intensive mothering? How does she mother in ways that emphasize maternal power and agency: the ability to define one's own standards and definitions of good mothering and to resist the always-present pitfalls of intensive mothering? These questions suggest that this complex struggle between empowered and intensive mothering is also a uniquely "postfeminist," third wave feminist mothering tension for contemporary mothers. As a feminist academic with a Ph.D. in Communication and Gender Studies, one would think that I might be good at managing the complex struggle between intensive and empowered mothering. Moreover, my family-of-origin and upbringing also make it even more likely that I would be immune from the pitfalls of intensive mothering. Unlike many feminist scholars who "discover" feminism in graduate school, I was raised a feminist (both of my parents were committed to feminism in the 1960s, but it was my mother who actively raised her children as feminists and saw doing so as one of her most important jobs as a mother). From the time we were old enough to lick League-of-Women-Voters-pass-the-ERA-N.O.W. envelopes, ride on the buses to ERA marches, and jointly carry signs in those marches, my twin sister and I were raised as card-carrying feminists. When we were in middle school and told "girls cannot play soccer," both my mother and father initiated and won a before-it-went-to-court Title IX lawsuit on our behalf so we could play on the boys' soccer team. In short, everything about my way of thinking and being is infused with feminism and a commitment to living an outside-the-norm life; hence, one would think that being a feminist mother who resists intensive mothering should have been easy, more "natural" for me than my later-to-feminism mothering peers and, most importantly, should have made me better able to manage the struggle between intensive and empowered mothering.

My feminist mothering has evolved such that I now understand that the relationship between feminism and intensive mothering is much more complex than simply "my feminism saved me" from the intensive ideology. Indeed, my feminist upbringing and intellectual training in some important ways confused me and made me *less* immune to intensive mothering. Moreover, a difficult yet life-changing experience of living within a traditional culture in Switzerland as a feminist mother taught me as much, if not more, about the possibilities for empowered mothering. And, at the same time, my upbringing and intellectual training were what gave me the strength to manage and learn from my difficult Swiss experience so that I could become less confused and more certain about what empowered mothering means to me. While my journey has been unique, I hope that telling my story about how I have both engaged in intensive mothering and resisted it in favor of empowered mothering can reveal some insights into how to manage the struggle between intensive and empowered mothering.

My story also resides within a framework of privilege because the struggle to resist intensive mothering for empowered mothering is, ultimately, a struggle of privilege. Although women are disciplined into intensive mothering across race and class lines, feminist scholars (Collins; Douglas and Michaels; Hays; James; Thomas) have decisively shown that the intensive ideology supports and privileges white, heterosexual mothers. Moreover, as a white woman whose mother found and practiced feminism within the context of the US middle class, my story only provides what many feminist academics (Harding; Hartsock; O'Brien Hallstein, "Postmodern") would call "situated knowledge,"[2] and what many third wave feminists (Findlen; Hernández and Rehman; Walker) rightly point out has driven much second wave feminist theorizing. By this I mean that both my experiences and knowledge are situated within a very specific context of privilege and advantaged cultural currency. That this is where I began my narrative is important for two reasons. First, I do not want to dishonor others' knowledge by claiming that my own is in any way universal and not fundamentally within the context of privilege. Second, as I will show shortly, losing much of that privilege is what transformed my understanding of how empowered mothers can resist intensive mothering. How I lost my privilege and transformed my thinking will come shortly. For now, I need to start my story at the beginning of my feminist-mothering journey: my first pregnancy at 35.

My first pregnancy was a delightful surprise; it was unplanned and did not fit into my "schedule." Like many women today, after completing my education, I deferred even thinking about children until I had reached a key milestone in my career. While I was in a serious relationship and knew that I wanted to have children, it never crossed my mind that I would do so until I achieved academic tenure. Indeed, I had no doubt that this was the "best way" to proceed. However, to my initial great shock and soon delight two years away from tenure, I discovered I was pregnant. It was and still is a great mystery how I got pregnant (the mechanics, of course, I understand but the actual failure of birth control is the mystery!). I re-adjusted my plan, and my oldest son was born.

In retrospect, I now understand how lucky I am that I did get pregnant when I did. I watched so many of my women friends who delayed pregnancy for a career then struggle with just getting pregnant because of age-related infertility. Had I stuck with the plan, it might have been much harder for me to actually get pregnant when I wanted. Recognizing this potential problem is especially poignant to my story because three years later, I briefly encountered some infertility issues when I wanted to have my second child (Fortunately, everything resolved itself and I was able to get pregnant that second time.). What all this brings to the forefront for me, however, is the first very real issue that my feminist background failed to prepare me for: the possibility that desiring to have children—both the psychological desire and physical possibilities—and actually having them might not be as easy as I was led to believe.

That I was led to believe otherwise is intimately related to my feminist mother's primary strategy in terms of how she addressed motherhood with me. She was mainly silent on the topic. As a result, in my growing up, the only issue we discussed in terms of my desire to have children was *not having children until I wanted to do so*. This silence about desiring children or the difficulties one might have in planning when to have a child or in just conceiving a child, then, were a direct consequence of my mother genuinely trying to help me see myself as a person and a woman first rather than "only" a mother. In all fairness, I understand that there was no way that my mother (and other second wave feminists of the time) could have known what we are now finding out about age-related infertility. We are learning as we live with the successes of feminism. Still, silence about motherhood as a strategy, in a strange sort of way, is deeply embedded in an unstated feminist assumption about women and motherhood: as long as it is a "choice," motherhood will "naturally" occur for most women. This assumption played a central role in second wave white feminisms, continues to pervade much third wave feminist thinking,[3] and is proving to be a somewhat erroneous and complex assumption for many contemporary women.

Intellectually, I also have come to understand that my mother's silence on motherhood was part and parcel of a form of second wave feminism that feminist scholars (Hirsch; O'Brien Hallstein "Conceiving, "'Demon' Texts") argue was organized around the notion of sisterhood rather than motherhood. Early white, middle-class, second wave feminists organized as sisters rather than as mothers because they, rightly, found 1950s motherhood and the associated social roles and responsibilities confining and constraining patriarchal traps for women. Consequently, as Hirsch suggests, organizing as sisters provided white middle-class second wave feminism[4] the possibility of a life and set of relations outside of the paradigm of motherhood and freed women, as many second wave feminists were fond of saying, to give birth to themselves. Feminist maternal scholars such as Marianne Hirsch, Sara Ruddick, Diana Taylor, and Judith Stadtman Tucker have shown that the sisterly focus led many early second wave feminists to either abandon motherhood entirely[5] or, at best, made motherhood secondary, even for women who actually had children (including my mother).

Clearly, then, my mother primarily raised me to be a sister rather than a mother, an approach that was also encouraged in my intellectual training. As a result, she focused all of her attention on encouraging me to "give birth" to myself as a woman who is athletic, independent, strong-willed, educated, and a professional. So, by the time I actually got pregnant, I had no sense of myself as a mother. I found myself, in fact, afraid of my impending motherhood in ways that I believe go beyond the normal first-time-mother fear. Simultaneously feeling unprepared and being a good academic, my first response to my pregnancy was to read every book that I could find about birthing, childrearing, parenting, etc. While I understand now that this move on my part was deeply encouraged by the ideology of intensive mothering and probably emerged in part by my being caught up in it, the reason *why* I sought out so much "expert" advice was that I felt like I had no idea how to be a mother. What I am trying to suggest here is that my early inability to see myself as a mother is a direct result of my feminist intellectual training and upbringing. As a good feminist who believed deeply in the idea that gender roles are socially created and that mothering was neither "natural" nor my expected role in life, I had no sense of myself as a woman who could mother.

In all fairness, I need to clearly state that I am not trying to engage in mother-blame here, neither against my biological mother nor the second wave feminists who laid the groundwork for my ability to take advantage of their hard-fought battles. Rather, I am simply trying to point out that in both my intellectual training and in my own family upbringing there was a silence on mothering that ultimately confused me in important though not devastating ways when I became a mother and, ironically, seems to have pushed me toward rather than away from intensive mothering. We can understand this without being evaluative. Given the historical time and context it makes sense to me that this basic approach was taken at the time. One impact of it, however, is that I believe many third wave era feminist mothers have ended up in the same place as I did: in some ways feeling ill-equipped or totally unprepared for mothering. When you couple this with a strong sense of self, educationally and professionally, it does not surprise me that I, and many of the well-educated women I know, felt ill-prepared for mothering and looked for help from others—advice manuals out there about pregnancy, childbirth, and parenting. In short, in a complicated and ironic way, I am suggesting that in the service of helping women see themselves as more than "just" mothers, the very silences within which many early second wave feminist intellectuals (my own mother included) participated inadvertently supported the ideology of intensive mothering. The legacy of that silence positions women like me to feel simultaneously empowered and in need of help. This, in turn, can fuel a key tenet of intensive mothering: the suggestion that women on their own are ill-prepared for mothering and need expert help as a result.

This knotty dynamic of feeling empowered as a woman but less sure as a mother also played into a complex set of personal and professional circumstances that culminated in my choosing to live in Switzerland when my oldest son was three and I was pregnant with my second son. While I was on a post-tenure sabbatical in Switzerland, my Swiss husband was offered an incredible, career-enhancing job. We decided to stay, even though it was a difficult decision for me personally and professionally. It was one of those dual-career-couple-with-young-children decisions that contemporary feminists face regularly: the ongoing complexity of juggling two people's ambitions and professional opportunities within the context of what is best for the family. In my own case, having turned down other opportunities to support my tenure pursuit, it was my husband's turn to privilege his career; it also seemed like an incredible opportunity for our son (and future second child) to become fully bi-lingual and to experience living in his "other" culture of origin. In short, my husband and I were faced with a complicated decision that required us to try to balance both of our professional ambitions in light of what we believed was best for our family. In retrospect, it is clear to me that part of my decision-making in that situation was deeply influenced by my own mixed feelings about being a mother and a person with her own professional life. Still lacking clarity about the relationship between my personhood and motherhood, I allowed myself to downplay all that hard-fought-for personhood that was a gift to me from both my mother and second wave feminism. Moreover, in terms of feminism and mothering, the Swiss cultural context within which I made that decision was and is very different. At every step, I was encouraged by Swiss culture to forgo personhood for motherhood.

As a consequence, I found myself a US feminist mother living in Zurich, Switzerland. The best way to describe how I was there is to use an old expression: I was like a fish out of water. Indeed, I often believed that it was some sort of cosmic joke that someone with my feminist history and intellectual commitment ended up living in a country that is so different in terms of its culturally understood beliefs about women. It is difficult for me to describe these different-from-mine gender beliefs without comparing it in negative ways to the American context. The best way I can think to describe the situation without sounding ethnocentric is to suggest that I experienced the culture expectations of women as being like the American 1950s ideal for women. Women are taught, and those whom I met believe, that their primary job as a woman is to become a mother and everything about the society supports this view. Thus, even though there is not a one-to-one match with the US intensive mothering ideology, three similar beliefs prevail: children need and require constant and ongoing nurturing by their biological mothers, biological mothers are single-handedly responsible for meeting these needs, and mothers should always put their children's needs before their own.

These beliefs are deeply supported both at the ideological and structural level of the culture. An example from the education system will make this clear. From the time that children enter kindergarten until they graduate from high school, they come home for lunch, every day without exception. Of course, this system fundamentally assumes that there is someone at home every day to make and serve that lunch and there is: the mother. Even if a woman works, she takes a job that allows her to be home for lunch. As a result, given that the professional norms are no different from the US in terms of assuming that "real" professionals are available all day, every day, women are tracked into lesser-paying, lower-status, part-time, non-professional jobs. When this is coupled with the fact that there is almost no daycare available across class lines, these structural barriers and assumptions about gender roles make it virtually impossible for any two-career couples with children to exist. I did not know or meet one family like this in the four years that I lived there. In short, after becoming mothers, women are primarily responsible for raising their own children and, at every turn, are encouraged to forgo their personhood for motherhood.

Fortunately, I was able to create a part-time academic position and a consulting practice that allowed me to work around this system, but neither was satisfying professionally; they were, in the end, just jobs. And, more importantly, my desire to work and to have a professional life—to feel like both a person *and* a mother —were not only unsupported at the structural level; it was unthinkable for many in the culture. After trying to articulate my dual desires within the hurricane force of disapproval about them, I quickly quit talking about my desires and struggle outside the Expatriate ("Expat") community of women (those living abroad, away from their home country) whom I befriended.

In addition to being my feminist-struggle safe haven, the pull toward my Expat community was also fueled by two complicating issues that, in the end, fundamentally influenced my understanding of empowered mothering. For the first time in my life, I found myself on the receiving end of ethnocentric thinking, and I found myself unable to communicate fully. In terms of the ethnocentrism, I was living in a culture that is particularly disinclined to accept "foreign" others or those from a different culture. In short, I found myself in the position of the disliked "foreign" other for simply being born an American (and being American at the start of the very unpopular Iraq war). This was layered with a second level of powerlessness because my own weak German skills seriously impaired my ability to speak the language with fluency. As a result, in many instances, I simply could not speak. For someone with a Ph.D. in Communication, this was particularly devastating. Thus, I was also pulled toward my Expat community of women because I had lost so much of my previously unearned privilege in the US I found myself turning toward this group of women for support, comfort, and fortitude as a way to manage my previously unknown marginalization.

In addition to the sustenance the community provided, another pleasure of this group was its cultural diversity. Even though we were all English-speaking, we were a diverse group: one woman was from India, one from Australia, two were British, one was Canadian, and two were American. While the American women and I were all still caught up in the intensive ideology, another joy of the connection for me was to watch and learn from mothers who did not buy into it. Even more interesting, only two of the women explicitly identified as feminist mothers; the others were simply good women trying to be good mothers within a context that marginalized them as women. They were also women who were not raised with the kind of silences on mothering that had permeated my intellectual and family-of-origin upbringings. As a result, their struggle against the confining roles for women was not also a struggle *against mothering* in any way; their struggle was how to resist the cultural barriers *and* mother well.

In being with and talking with these women, I learned how much I had actually bought into the intensive mothering ideology, in part because I felt so empowered as a woman. While this statement seems counter-intuitive, I came to recognize that I had, like many professional women I knew before moving to Switzerland, adopted the intensive mothering tenets in a uniquely educated-professional-woman manner. While I did work and my child attended daycare, because of my white privilege, class status and good luck, I made sure that when I was not with my son, he was in the "best," developmentally focused daycare. Moreover, when I was with him, I was totally and completely devoted to meeting his needs for nurture and support.

Of course, any child in daycare deserves to be in a quality daycare and nurturing children is important. There is no disputing these points. What I am trying to convey, however, is that out of both my own uncertainty about my ability to mother and my own internalized guilt I still felt about my working, when I was with my son, I tried to "make up" for my absence by being the culturally accepted "good mother." In my particular case, the way I did this was by continuing to work a full-time schedule but only having my son in daycare three days a week. So, on the three days I was on campus, I worked furiously while, on the two days I was home with him and on the weekends, I got up early, worked late, took turns working with my partner, and generally exhausted myself trying to be both a good mother and good professional.

Simultaneously, I still was in the mode of thinking that putting my son's needs in front of my own was absolutely essential to good mothering. Again, I do not mean that I never put my needs in front of his. What I am suggesting is that my perception of the balancing of my needs and his needs—balancing my need for personhood and mothering—always worked to privilege his needs first as often as possible. In short, I had, in an odd and uniquely professional and privileged way, internalized intensive mothering without even really understanding it. I did it because I had no clear sense within myself about what I thought good mothering ought to entail and no clear understanding *in advance of having children* about how I could and should try to balance both roles.

Fortunately, my experience being within an Expat community of mothers on a daily basis also transformed both my experience of and thinking about these issues and, as a result, my understanding of empowered mothering. My recognition of how caught up I was in the intensive ideology and my transformation from that ideology began in a seemingly simple interaction with one of the British women in the community. I will never forget the first time my friend Linda called early in our getting to know one another and said, "My children are making me crazy. Can I bring them by for an hour or two so I can take a run and have a break?" I was shocked. First, to publicly admit that her children were making her crazy, then, to leave them with a not-known-deeply friend and to so clearly put her needs above her children (even if only for an hour) totally stunned me. Of course, I said yes and began to quickly emulate the practice myself.

Moreover, because our Expat community was so marginalized from the culture and there was so little daycare, we had to rely on one another to help in times of illness, stress, and if we actually did work in some capacity. A week did not go by without me having someone else's children for some time during the week, and the same was true of my own children. The freedom emotionally and physically that this gave me was quite profound. In the Northeast community where I first began to mother, mothering was done completely in isolation, without any sense of community effort. There, I never once cared for someone else's children and, in fact, would have been afraid to do so because of my own insecurity about my mothering ability.

My Expat experience, then, "resituated" my knowledge about intensive mothering and helped me recognize the power and importance of what many Black feminist scholars, including Patricia Hill Collins, Arlene Edwards, Stanlie James, and Trudelle Thomas, suggest has driven much of black women's mothering: othermothering—the practice of accepting responsibility for a child that is not one's own, in an arrangement that may or may not be formal, and community mothering—the practice of supporting and sustaining the larger community. Othermothering, which emerged initially from Africa, continued to be necessary in America because of the brutal practices under slavery that often separated children and mothers. Black feminist scholars (Collins; Edwards; James; Thomas) all argue that contemporary American racism and classism also "encourage" other and community mothering today by excluding non-white and working-class women from domesticated, stay-at-home mothering. Simultaneously and ironically, however, the practices of other and community mothering are viewed as deviant within the intensive mothering ideology because these practices challenge and resist the belief that only bloodmothers can care for children, refuse the practice of mothering only in isolation, and defy the notion that mothers must lavish all their attention on their children at their own expense. As such, other and community mothering also challenge both the Swiss gender and the American intensive mothering ideologies.

I have come to understand, then, that my own marginalization, while still deeply intertwined with race and class privilege, is in some ways analogous to but not the same as African-American women's marginalization. Having an Expat circle of women friends gave me the opportunity to practice community mothering and othermothering and challenged the three core beliefs that drive both the Swiss gender ideology and the American intensive mothering ideology. In addition, I came to understand that the community of mothers who sustained me also helped me return to the strong sense of self that was second wave feminism's and my mother's gift to me. In other words, the focus on personhood that initially confused me in my early experiences of mothering was the very thing that saved me when I found myself so marginalized, such a "fish out of water."

As a result of my community of Expat mothers, I was able to "rebirth" myself a second time. The powerful sense of self that I was raised with rose up from some place deep inside me such that I could find the voice to say, "I cannot do this anymore; I cannot live within a culture that cannot recognize my right to both personhood and motherhood. I want both." And so, because I could not find a way to have both recognized in Switzerland, my family and I left so that I could return to a full-time position in a university in the US.

In returning to the Northeast, I am back in a community of highly educated professional women who are struggling with the push-pull between empowered and intensive mothering. While my personal struggle between empowered and intensive mothering—between personhood and powerless responsibility—is unique, I believe this push-pull is a central struggle for all women mothering in the third wave, including those with whom I am reconnecting. Indeed, a recent cover story in *Newsweek* begins with the following question: "What happened when the girls who had it all became mothers?"[6] While the *Newsweek* cover story is neither specifically feminist nor sensitive to race and class privilege, it does address the complex struggle contemporary mothers engage in every day in making sense of living as empowered feminist maternal subjects (as women who have benefited from feminist gains) who simultaneously experience the pressure to conform to a maternal subject position that has powerless responsibility within the "proper" ideology of intensive mothering. Both the *Newsweek* exploration and those found in this volume, then, are vital to help contemporary mothers make sense of the push-pull between empowered and intensive mothering that defines mothering in the third wave. In the end, my own personal journey has taught me that negotiating that push-pull is best managed within a community of mothers who are inclined toward practices similar to community mothering and othermothering.

[1]Adrienne Rich, in her landmark book *Of Woman Born*, was the first feminist scholar to note that mothering entails powerless responsibility. In her own more contemporary work, Andrea O'Reilly decisively shows just how much the intensive ideology continues to position women as primarily responsible for raising children without cultural power.

[2]Here, I am thinking about the work of feminist standpoint scholars who argue that all knowledge and experience are situated within race, class, gender, and sexual privilege.

[3]Consider, for example, recent writing (Hayden, Hirshman, and Solinger) that explores the role choice has played historically and in contemporary thinking within feminisms and contemporary women's lives.

[4]bell hooks suggests that feminist analyses in the early second wave reflected the white middle-class biases of early participants. Moreover, she argues "had black women voiced their views on Motherhood, it would not have been named a serious obstacle to our freedom as women. Racism, availability of jobs, lack of skills or education … would have been at the top of the list—but not motherhood" (133).

[5]Claiming that feminists abandoned or rejected motherhood in the early second wave is somewhat contentious among some feminist scholars. Umansky, for example, argues that feminists have attended to motherhood, even in the early second wave. She notes, however, that much of the rhetoric surrounding that attention was inflammatory and/or misunderstood within 1960s leftist politics. Moreover, Snitow argues that early second wave feminists did not reject motherhood; rather, they were just mostly silent about it. Feminist scholars noted here

(Ruddick; Taylor; Tucker), however, continue to argue that feminists have ignored motherhood almost entirely. While feminist scholars may never resolve this dispute, it has arisen because all would agree that the relationship between feminism and motherhood has long been and continues to be complicated.
[6]February 21, 2005, pg. 42.

Works Cited

Collins, Patricia Hill. "The Meaning of Motherhood in Black Culture and Black Mother-Daughter Relationships." *Double Stitch: Black Women Write about Mothers and Daughters.* Eds. Patricia Bell-Scott, Beverly Guy-Sheftall, Jacqueline Jones Royster, Janet Sims-Wood, Miriam DeCosta-Willis and Lucie Fultz. Boston: Beacon, 1991. 42-60.

Douglas, Susan J., and Meredith Michaels. *The Mommy Myth: The Idealization of Motherhood and How It Has Undermined Women.* New York: Free Press, 2004.

Edwards, Arlene. "Community Mothering: The Relationship between Mothering and the Community Work of Black Women." *Mother Outlaws: Theories and Practices of Empowered Mothering.* Ed. Andrea O'Reilly. Toronto: Women's Press, 2004. 203-214.

Findlen, Barbara. Introduction. *Listen Up: Voices from the Next Feminist Generation.* Ed. Barbara Findlen. Seattle: Seal, 1995. xi-xvi.

Harding, Sandra. "Comment on Hekman's 'Truth and Method: Feminist Standpoint Theory Revisited': Whose Standpoint Needs the Regimes of Truth and Reality?" *Signs* 22.2 (1997): 382-391.

Hartsock, Nancy. "Standpoint Theory for the Next Century." *Women and Politics* 18.3 (1997): 93-102.

Hayden, Sara. "The March for Women's Lives: Reanimating the Debate between <Life> and <Choice.>" Paper presented at the Western States Communication Association meeting, Feb. 18-21, 2006.

Hays, Sharon. *The Cultural Contradictions of Motherhood.* New Haven: Yale University Press, 1996.

Hernández, Daisy, and Bushra Rehman. Eds. *Colonize This! Young Women of Color on Today's Feminism.* New York: Seal, 2002.

Hirsch, Marianne. "Feminism at the Maternal Divide: A Diary." *The Politics of Motherhood: Activist Voices from Left to Right.* Eds. Alexis Jetter, Annelise Orleck, and Diana Taylor. Hanover: University Press of New England, 1997: 352-368.

Hirshman, Linda R. *Get to Work: And Get a Life Before It's Too Late.* New York: Penguin, 2006.

hooks, bell. "Revolutionary Parenting." *Feminist Theory: From Margin to Center.* Boston: South End, 1984. 133-147.

James, Stanlie M. "Introduction." *Theorizing Black Feminisms: The Visionary Pragmatism of Black Women.* Eds. Stanlie M. James and Abena P.A. Busia. New York: Routledge, 1993. 1-12.

O'Brien Hallstein, D. Lynn. "'Demon' Texts and "Sisterly' Subjectivity: Rereading Rhetorically *Of Woman Born* and Early White Second Wave Feminism." Paper Presented at the National Communication Association Annual Conference, November 16-19, 2006, San Antonio, Texas.

O'Brien Hallstein, D. Lynn. "Conceiving Intensive Mothering: The Mommy Myth, Maternal Desire and the Lingering Vestiges of Feminist Matrophobia." *Journal of the Association for Research on Mothering 8.1 (2006): 96-108.*

O'Brien Hallstein, D. Lynn. "A Postmodern Caring: Feminist Standpoint Theories, Revisioned Caring and Communication Ethics." *Western Journal of Communication,* 63.1 (1999): 32-56.

O'Reilly, Andrea. "Introduction." *Mother Outlaws: Theories and Practices of Empowered Mothering.* Ed. Andrea O'Reilly. Toronto: Women's Press, 2004. 1-30.

Rich, Adrienne. *Of Woman Born: Motherhood as Experience and Institution.* 2nd ed. New York: Norton, 1986.

Ruddick, Sara. *Maternal Thinking: Toward a Politics of Peace.* Boston: Beacon, 1989.

Snitow, Ann. "Feminism and Motherhood: An American Reading." *Feminist Review,* 40 (Spring 1992): 30-51.

Solinger, Rickie. *Beggers and Choosers: How the Politics of Choice Shapes* Adoption, Abortion, and Welfare in the United States. New York: Hill and Wang, 2001.

Taylor, Diana. "Overview: The Uneasy Relationship Between Motherhood and Feminism." *The Politics of Motherhood: Activist Voices From Left to Right.* Eds. Alexis Jetter, Annelise Orleck, and Diana Taylor. Hanover: University Press of New England, 1997. 349-351.

Thomas, Trudelle. "'You'll Become a Lioness': African-American Women Talk About Mothering." *Mother Outlaws: Theories and Practices of Empowered Mothering.* Ed. Andrea O'Reilly. Toronto: Women's Press, 2004. 215-228.

Tucker, Judith Stadtman. "Care as a Cause: Framing the Twenty-First Century Mothers' Movement." *Socializing Care: Feminist Ethics and Public Issues.* Eds. Maurice Hamington and Dorothy C. Miller. Lanham, MD: Rowan and Littlefield, 2006. 183-203.

Umansky, Lauri. *Motherhood Reconceived: Feminism and the Legacies of the Sixties.* New York: New York University Press, 1996.

Walker, Rebecca. Being Real: An Introduction. *To Be Real: Telling the Truth and Changing the Face of Feminism.* Ed. Rebecca Walker. New York: Anchor, 1995. xxxx-xi.

Wolf, Naomi. *The Beauty Myth: How Images of Beauty are Used Against Women.* New York: Morrow, 1991.

10
Embracing the Tensions of a Maternal Erotic

AMBER E. KINSER

Most of what I know about feminist living I learned from second wave thought and struggle, yet it is probably third wave sensibilities that help me process my day-to-day confusions and chaos about feminist mothering. This both/and space among the "waves" functions as fertile ground for me, because it is here where I remain rooted by feminisms that are second-wave-born, before the choking weeds of "postfeminism" in this third wave era began to overgrow and try to force out the thinking that was thriving there. It also is from this ground that I am nourished and strengthened by third wave era feminisms and their renewing attention to contradictions, tensions, paradoxes, ambivalences. For me, third wave thinking invites even more examinations of the messiness of feminist living than we have heretofore been situated to explore, partly because of the strong second wave ground on which we stand, and partly because the current political, global, technological, postfeminist, sociocultural milieu creates messier living. From this second/third wave ground I am able, like the perennial Black-eyed Susan, to stay rooted, to keep coming back and to keep pushing back the weeds that have tried to choke out my liberation, and to spread and spread until that prickly postfeminism, which promises to flower but never does, finally dies. The struggles here are marked by complex feminism that does not provide precise answers or resolutions but in fact resists same, in an effort to escape monologic and even dualistic thinking that can thwart growth.

The comfort I feel in these spaces, though, should not be misunderstood to mean the warm, relaxed, peaceful kind, but rather the same kind that seems to have prompted my childhood cat, Snowflake, to birth her kittens on top of the toys in my toybox when I was little girl. Somehow, in the middle of the mess in that bedroom closet on 34th Terrace, Snowflake managed to mother her kittens, without the need to set everything aright first, or disconnect from the rest of her family/community and their interdependent chaoses and disorder(s), or find a place that would lend itself to some sort of pure mothering uncomplicated by her larger world. She found a way to embrace the imprecision and disarray of it all. This is the image that helps to illuminate the chaotic feminism that guides my mothering, the chaotic mothering that guides my feminism.

There are many points of tension in the struggle toward feminist mothering, enough to fill a multi-volume work. I want domestic duties shared between my partner and me, and also can't seem to weaken my preference to call all the shots on that front. I want to restrict the media messages my children are exposed to, and also I want them to exercise their own agency and make their own choices. I feel that empowered mothering should focus on the mother (O'Reilly), and also I think my own mothering rarely does. I could spend days adding to this list, years writing about these tensions and the question of their reconciliation. Dominant ideology imposes itself further into my already oppositional thinking, further complicating my capacity to make up my feminist mind. Among the many sources of my feminist confusion are the intensely passionate feelings I have toward my children, by which I mean not only physical connection, emotional attachment, and spiritual union, but also the darker dimensions of passion: feelings of rejection, betrayal, repulsion.

In this chapter, I examine some complexities of the eros of motherhood, confirming the location of intensely intimate mother-child relationships on a sexuality continuum. I discuss the necessity and messy complexities of a maternal erotic in an effort to dislodge what Susan Chase and Mary Rogers call the "cultural wedge commonly driven between motherhood and sexuality" (119). My effort here is directed both at evoking the intense emotional/spiritual connection emergent from the sensorial depth and abundance of my motherwork, and at confronting the discomfort that such an evocation invites.

I mother in tension with "the pervasive supposition that eros has nothing to do with motherhood" (de Marneffe 302). Marla Arvay and Patrice Keats have argued that discourses of popular culture, for example, and the myths and norms emerging therefrom, "continue to pathologize the integration of women as both mothers and sexual beings" and, drawing from Suzanna Walters, they explain that mothers are confronted by a double bind discourse: "a woman must identify herself as either a mother or a sexual being—each identity being outside the realm of the other" (78). Despite cultural efforts to separate our mother selves from our sexual selves, and despite how willing we may be to talk and live as if this split existed, we persist in mothering as sexual beings. We persist in mothering from some place on a spectrum of sensuality that implicates bodies and desires and the erotic. And to the extent that we have been indoctrinated to deny the maternal erotic and its power, we have been denied the ability to embody mothering, and the rest of our lives, in their fullness, in wholly abundant and integrated ways. As Audre Lorde has argued:

> The erotic is a resource within each of us that lies in a deeply female and spiritual plane, firmly rooted in the power of our unexpressed or unrecognized feeling. In order to perpetuate itself, every oppression must corrupt or distort those various sources of power within the culture of the oppressed that can provide energy for change. (53)

The erotics of maternal life—not only a woman's sexuality, but sensuality, the body, physical and spiritual intimacy, sensual intensity, creativity, and how all of these are embodied, talked about, resisted, framed in the family—is a significant source of both power and vulnerability. A maternal erotic is the depth of spiritual and bodily feeling and knowledge and groundedness that is rooted in the embodied mother sustaining and nurturing the embodied child. It is:

a measure between the beginnings of our sense of self and the chaos of our strongest feelings. It is an internal sense of satisfaction to which, once we have experienced it, we know we can aspire. For having experienced the fullness of this depth of feeling and recognizing its power in honor and self-respect we can require no less of ourselves. (Lorde 54)

Dorothy Dinnerstein and Noelle Oxenhandler have written of the erotic in parenthood, as Daphne de Marneffe notes (299-301), and Tuula Gordon, Lynda Marín, and Fiona Giles have explored a sexuality/sensuality fusion in motherhood. But out of a clear and justifiable concern for transgressing children's boundaries in ways that are, as de Marneffe articulates, "redolent of potential exploitation" (302), and in response to the patriarchal split of the sexual from the maternal and its consequent madonna/whore dichotomy, writers on mothering have largely stayed away from the maternal erotic, unable to locate their intensely sensual experience of mothering on a sexual continuum or to even conceptualize a maternal erotic. The consequences in any case have been the denial of a lifeforce in mothering, an impoverished theorizing of the embodied maternal—yet another severing of woman from her body, another way of keeping mothers from narrating their own lives.

If we are to understand subjectivities of mothering, what it is like to mother from the mother's point of view (O'Reilly), we must rescue the erotic from "the silent margins that delimit the discourses of mothering" (Marín 134). We must give ourselves permission to honor the erotic bond between mothers and children (143). Embracing the maternal erotic is a way that we, as mothers, interpret ourselves *to ourselves* as needing to be intimately and spiritually nourished by the bodies our bodies have nourished. And I am speaking here not of a biological imperative to mothering—of pregnancy, birth, breastfeeding, though these can't be excluded—but of a broader, deeper, more complex imagining of nourishing: holding and patting; singing and chanting; wiping and bandaging; smelling and stroking; using my lips and tongue to test the taste and heat of food my children will take in with their lips and tongues; choosing clothing fabrics that will caress them in my absence; kissing the blood of their knee scrapes; putting my cheek to a forehead to check for fever and following that with a kiss in the same way my mother did; pushing a hand between the car seats to touch an ankle in the backseat, or a knee, or fingers outstretched; pouring a cupped handful of water over their heads as they lay back in the tub, full bodies exposed and trusting. I speak also of the smell of a grown son, the sweat and breath of this "man child" (Lorde); the feel of his shoulders and width of his back in an embrace; his cheekbones pushing his masculinity through the contours of his face; the desire to fondle the hair at his neck and the wavering ability to resist, or not; being able to admit that he's always had the greatest butt and that you might give anything to lay with him, even now, with his head on your chest while you stroke his hair and kiss his forehead, this baby of yours. I speak of talks with a daughter about the pain of youthful, developing nipples; and how to wash out underpants and put in tampons; of what erections mean, and don't; of kisses from men and kisses from women and mucous plugs and sexy perfume; and what cleavage means, and doesn't. I speak of the smile at her lingering after-shower smell; the conclusions you draw about her body in that bathing suit; the feel of her female form against yours in an embrace.

If, in several of the above examples, we were referring to lovers rather than daughters and sons, the images would have decidedly erotic components, and comfortably so. Yet such experiences have erotic components across relationships. "Motherly affection" and "female passion" are not, as it turns out, easily distin-guishable and this is, for some reason, "one of the best kept secrets," Lynda Marín writes, because "no one likes the idea that a mother enjoys the boundarylessness of relation with her child" (13). I can readily admit the awkwardness of writing now about a "maternal erotic," given what Fiona Giles refers to as our "moral panic about paedophilia, and the fashion for policing parent-child intimacy" (12). The language of eros has been made to feel like it doesn't belong to me in my mother-hood, like I should have permission before I use it and, barring that, I should find another. It is by no accident that we lack a language for talking about a sexual realm that doesn't hold men at its center. It is by no accident that I sheepishly look over my shoulder as I write this, that I remain nervous that as this chapter is published I will be misconstrued. The conceptual excision of the erotic from the maternal is one of many reasons why feminist writers must continue to expand our understandings of the sexual, to create an "enlarged definition of the erotic," as Susan Chase and Mary Rogers argue, "if we are to resist the maternal guilt and shame that so often impinge on women's relationships with their children" (121). And such a celebration, as Giles suggests, "of the body and its functions within the family need not inspire incest, and may in time be shown to thwart it" (12).

That there are times when I want to pull my 16-year-old daughter and other times my ten-year-old son and still other times my 66-year-old partner to my long-since dry breast, to soothe and ground them, is not something I can say to anyone but my partner. But the desire to find in my bareness a source of quietude for the people I love and let that flow to them is sometimes palpable. This desire indicates how both maternal erotics and adult sexual longing, though not the same, pull from what de Marneffe calls "the same kind of integrating delight" (302). That I want my daughter to *truly* understand *precisely* how weak the connection is between her ability to orgasm and penile penetration, is not finally something I can do anything about other than perhaps to simply tell her, though that won't provide the precision I seek here. That each of my children still feels compelled to embrace me fully when we swim in the pool, legs and arms wrapped round me, skin against skin nearly nude in our bathing suits, faces touching, sharing breath, in this kind of sexual union, is not surprising, or unsettling, nor wholly unlike the sexual intimacy I share with my partner. That my son communicates, however subtly, a concern over my bra showing around the straps of my tank top, or more so, over more cleavage showing than usual, is not something I can negotiate easily. And while I have seen evidence of Oedipal conflict in both my children, a more extensive conceptualizing of eroticism would bring us farther than Freud and Chodorow. The Oedipal is hardly the only conflict emergent from a maternal erotic or even a primary one much of the time. Jocasta had her own things to say but she was given no real voice, as Marín points out (135).

I found no discomfort laying on my side and breastfeeding my infant while my body was cupped by my partner's as I pulled him inside of me; these seemed all so utterly consistent, connected, consummate, a way of "inviting [him] in for a taste of the art of motherlove" (Giles 11). I admire the buttocks at my house—all of them—clothed or zipping naked between their bathrooms and bedrooms. I appreciate the work and body discipline implied by the smell of sweat, as well as the tenderness and softness implied by freshly bathed bodies. I take in the smell of their morning breath as I kiss them all awake, trying to appreciate it as proof that they are still breathing with me another day. I still relish the feel of their bodies leaning against me, when I can convince them, at 10 and 16 years, to sit in quietude on my lap. I am fed by the sensually charged energy in our home.

I also feel sharply betrayed, given our therefore intense physical/spiritual connection, at being ignored, or treated flippantly, or having my intimate gestures being as good as forgotten, or worse, rejected. And neither is this sense of betrayal wholly unlike that I might feel, and have felt, with my partner. What does she *mean* she doesn't want to go to dinner with me, given the intimate time and space we have shared? Why is he still expecting me to scratch his back tonight when he just stroked my hand in empathy for my difficult day? I thought we were one, she and I, he and I. After all I've given of myself. There I go, making myself vulnerable again. Oh the "torments of an unrequited love," Oxenhandler notes, "for a child is the flower, the fruit, of a parent's life in the way a parent never is for the child" (114). And still there are other times when I feel like screaming at my children's touch, repelled by the thought of giving still more; my body feeling mauled by the incessant needs of other bodies; their bodies blissfully unaware of reciprocity in erotic bonding. There are times when, frustrated with them for one thing or distracted from them by another, their slow tender kiss to my cheek makes me shudder. I can no more "go there" in these frustrated/distracted moments than I can kiss my partner just after a fight. But he rarely asks me to, and they rarely fail to. And, as with a lover, I begin to resent their inability or refusal to anticipate my needs, when I so assiduously anticipate theirs. How can they know me so little, after all we have meant to each other, that they cannot see I have nothing left to give in this moment? Locating mother-child intimacy on a sexuality continuum means acknowledging the darkness that also is part of erotic connection—betrayal, vulnerability, broken heartedness. It means remembering that passion has a grim side, too.

This line, this sometimes nearly imperceptible line separating adult sexuality from the maternal erotic, germinated for me in my relationship with my own mother. I felt no bodily shame about things sexual, no fear of asking probing questions even at 5 years old, or about orgasms somewhere between 5 and 10, or of asking "Mom, can you look at this red spot on my inner thigh?" "What is this mark on my butt?" "Why do my nipples hurt so much?" and having her never once flinch or hesitate to talk to me about my body. I realize now, when I talk with my students and colleagues, that this was a unique gift that few families offer, this plainness and clarity of body talk. I suppose my parents, and especially my mother, started formulating this gift, as I have recounted in other writings, in their comfort with their own sexuality, no matter their conservative and religious politics (Kinser). Their barely disguised sexual winks and touches, smooching sounds and giggles, the closed door of their bedroom for an hour or so in the middle of a weekend day, my mother streaking across the house to her bedroom from the laundry room, where she had just peeled off her clothes to add them to the washer. I was fed then, as I am now, by the sensually charged energy in our home.

Despite my comfort in talking about the body, our groundedness in things sexual, I still never understood before I had children, like Heather (one of the women Tuula Gordon interviewed for her book), "what it meant to have sexual feelings towards a child…just very intense feelings of possessiveness and all those things that previously I had associated with a sexual relationship with somebody my own age" (121). I certainly never understood the "fusion and separateness," the "excitement and response" of the maternal erotic evoked by Oxenhandler (qtd. in de Marneffe 300). But I do know now, and, like Sari (also from Gordon's study), I can say that "living with children has enlarged my notion of what sexuality is" (121).

Certainly, everyday life offers up moments that ask for boundaries, as Chase and Rogers argue. And mothering in particular offers up innumerable moments like these, across multiple contexts. Yet acknowledging and taking on one's responsibilities to clarify boundaries is "completely compatible with embracing the pleasure, delight, and transcendence that belong to eros in the mother-child relationship" (Chase and Rogers 123). In healthy, respectful, intimate relations there is a "both/and" dimension to their intense sensuality thus emerging. Even the oft recited "Oh I could eat you!" uttered by mothers as they fascinate over their children, as Oxenhandler points out, captures both the "'too-muchness' that a parent feels, and the restraint" (209). Understanding contradiction in feminist living means embracing "both/and" tensions in parent-child simultaneous connectedness and separateness. It includes recognizing that these children who are mine also are not *mine*; that I want them at some level to remain at my breast, and also I let my milk dry; that I am wounded a little that their privacy means my exclusion, and also I do not invade it.

Feminist mothering in the third wave invites ever more pointed attention to paradoxes and oppositional tendencies. A postfeminist ideology would have us be thrown by feminist confusions, would have us lose faith in a liberatory practice (hooks) whose principles are not clear-cut, would drive us instead into the constricting arms of monolithic thinking. But we could refuse to be thrown, refuse to lose faith, refuse to be driven out and away. We could learn to find comfort in the disarray of it all. We could find ways to embrace the passions of motherhood, light and dark. We could locate mothering on a sexuality continuum (among other continua) to help us make sense of and work through its emotional intensity, *and* offer safe haven to our children.

Works Cited

Arvay, Marla J. and Patrice A. Keats. "Opening Pandora's Box: Examining the Implications of Mothers' Adolescent Sexuality Narratives on Mother-Daughter Relationships." *Journal of the Association for Research on Mothering* 4.1 (2002): 77-86.

Chase, Susan E., and Mary F. Rogers. *Mothers and Children: Feminist Analyses and Personal Narratives.* New Brunswick: Rutgers University Press, 2001.

Chodorow, Nancy J. *The Reproduction of Mothering.* 1978. Berkeley: University of California Press, 1999.

de Marneffe, Daphne. *Maternal Desire: On Children, Love, and the Inner Life.* New York: Little, 2004.

Dinnerstein, Dorothy. *The Mermaid and the Minotaur: Sexual Arrangements and Human Malaise.* New York: Harper, 1976.

Freud, Sigmund. *The Interpretation of Dreams: 1856-1939.* Cutchogue, New York: Buccaneer, 1985.

Giles, Fiona. "Fountains of Love and Loveliness: In Praise of the Dripping Wet Breast." *Journal of the Association for Research on Mothering* 4.1 (2002): 7-18.

Gordon, Tuula. *Feminist Mothers.* Washington Square: New York University Press, 1990.

hooks, bell. *Teaching to Transgress: Education as the Practice of Freedom.* New York: Routledge, 1994.

Kinser, A. E. "Family Sex Communication." *Family Communication: Theory and Research.* Ed. Lorin Basden Arnold. New York: Allyn, 2007. 298-306.

Lorde, Audre. *Sister Outsider: Essays and Speeches by Audre Lorde.* Freedom: Crossing Press, 1984.

Marín, Lynda. "Mother and Child: The Erotic Bond." *Mother Journeys: Feminists Write about Mothering.* Ed. Maureen T. Reddy, Martha Roth, and Amy Sheldon. Minneapolis: Spinsters Ink, 1994. 9-21.

O'Reilly, Andrea. *Rocking the Cradle: Thoughts on Motherhood, Feminism, and the Possibility of Empowered Mothering.* Toronto: Demeter, 2006.

Oxenhandler, Noelle. *The Eros of Parenthood: Explorations in Light and Dark.* New York: St. Martin's, 2001.

Walters, Suzanna Danuta. *Lives Together/Worlds Apart: Mothers and Daughters in Popular Culture.* Berkely: University of California Press, 1992.

11
Mothering Sons in Japan

WENDY JONES NAKANISHI

As an American who is a long-term resident of Japan, as an academic who happens to be female, inhabiting a culture which automatically relegates her sex to a second-class citizenship, as an older woman whose children sometimes are mistaken for her grandchildren, I find that issues related to nationality, gender, and age can preoccupy my life.

One morning I find myself saying, "I hate men. I hate men."

My husband, a Japanese farmer, is drinking his coffee and reading the newspaper. Ethan, our youngest child, looks at me anxiously. "Are you okay, Mommy?"

I don't want to blight the future of my three sons: Peter, aged 17, Simon, 15, and Ethan, 11. I adore them. They are men in the making. Can I make them the men I want inhabiting my own future? Perhaps if I can write this piece as a cathartic exercise, expressing my feelings of being, on occasion, less than enamored with the male sex, I'll be less inclined to voice my complaints out loud, in a moment of exasperation. Someday my sons are bound to make the connection: if Mommy hates men, does that mean she hates me?

Experience has taught me the expediency of biting back any words of protest or irritation at demands and challenges posed by life in Japan, but tiredness had made me careless. Although I am a tenured, full-time member of staff at a university where my husband boosts his farm income with salaried employment as a part-time teacher of Swahili—a combination of work ensuring a far more flexible schedule than mine—it "naturally" devolves upon me, as the wife and mother, to shoulder most of the household chores.

There are both cultural and historical reasons for the woman's primary assumption of domestic duties and childcare in Japan. The feudal concept of woman's natural role as being one of homemaker and mother holds sway even in modern Japan, coupled with an equally ancient principle of "danson johi," which stipulates that men must be respected, and women scorned. With the feudal family's dependence on the eldest son, daughters were seen as "gokutsubushi" or "grain wasters," and cases of female infanticide were common, justified as a necessary measure for economic survival.

Modern Japan is a society characterized by the notion of a "father-absent system":

in 1991 "the average Japanese worker put in 2,044 hours of work—about 200 more than the average American or British worker and 500 hours more compared to a German or French worker" (Fujimura-Faneslow, Kameda 229). Given the inflexible exigencies of the traditional Japanese workplace, requiring long hours, dedication to the "company," and providing little in the way of holidays or provision for maternal leave, the Japanese full-time employee is usually male. As Sonya Salamon observes in her article on "'Male Chauvinism' as a Manifestation of Love in Marriage," this situation at least partially explains why Japanese "employers are not favorably disposed toward married women, let alone mothers" (135). Becoming a mother forces a working wife into unemployment or into a poorly-paid, part-time job lacking the benefits and security of a full-time position. According to Salamon, "Japanese middle-class motherhood is characterized as 'being nailed in the house,' cut off from social contacts, and occupied with the drudgery of household routine" (134).

After graduating from university, my husband, Kenji, worked in Kenya for three years in the Japanese equivalent of the American Peace Corps. His learning Swahili there had proved unexpectedly beneficial for us, securing his job at my college. I attribute much of the success of our marriage to the fact that, unlike most Japanese, he has actually had considerable experience of the world outside the insular—both metaphorically and literally—environs of these islands.

I think my husband's friends sometimes pity him, imagining him to be under the thumb of a domineering western woman. To his mother's horror, he is expected to wash the dishes and occasionally, even to cook supper. His own father typifies the traditional Japanese male, scarcely knowing how to boil water and only entering the kitchen to partake of meals prepared by my mother-in-law. I know few Japanese men would do as much as my own husband. A 1995 survey held by the Prime Minister's office found that 90 percent of those polled said that cleaning, washing, cooking, and cleaning up after meals are women's responsibilities; 80 percent described household finances and shopping as the "wife's chores," and 70 percent identified child care as a "female activity" (White 91). Because the husband/father is conspicuous in the Japanese household by his absence, the mother occupies a primary role and enjoys an almost iconic status. The Japanese mother traditionally has been idealized as a self-sacrificing, angelic soul "devoted to her children, [who] always shows them affection, and is willing to sacrifice her own plans and desires on their behalf" (Ohinata 205). Masami Ohinata likens this idealization of the mother figure who represents the bedrock of Japanese society to a kind of "religious faith" (205).

The heavy weight of expectation placed upon the Japanese mother is seen as partially responsible for the severely plummeting birthrate in Japanese society. The mother must participate in a strenuous schedule of activities related to her children's education, for example. Success in life in Japan often depends, both for boys and for girls, on perceived academic achievement. Whereas children in the United States tend to be able to enter the high school nearest their home, the Japanese child is subjected to a series of exams at junior high school which will determine whether he or she may enter one of the area's public high schools, which are segregated hierarchically by test scores and whose places are fiercely competed for, or a private high school, which is easier to enter but which requires roughly five times the amount of school fees as a public school. The Japanese mother must instill in her child the habit of unremitting study and be willing to pay heavy fees for extracurricular "cram" schools. Some 42 percent of Japan's pre-school children attend such schools, a number increasing to 69 percent for children in their early teens (Morley 60).

I am grateful that it is my husband rather than myself who participates in the many and diverse events organized by the parent-teacher associations at the primary, junior high, and high schools our children attend. E. W. F. Tomlin believes that in Japan, these "parent-teachers' organizations are becoming increasingly powerful" and that "a mother who absents herself from the meetings ... may lose face in the neighbourhood" (43). Given my poor command of spoken, let alone written, Japanese, it is my husband who liaises with school officials and who assists Ethan with the daily homework given him by his primary school teacher.

I know that some of my American and European friends think I spoil my kids. But I think that they fail to comprehend the context of my behavior. Like most Japanese mothers, I am reluctant to adopt a strict or authoritarian role in the household, knowing that my children, in attending the local schools—and particularly my elder two boys, enrolled in junior high and high school—are immersed in an educational system characterized by "bureaucratic control and regulation," by austerity and regimentation, and knowing that they are expected to complete a daily amount of studying and homework almost inconceivable by western standards (Kameda 114). While Japanese schoolchildren may seem to lead pampered, sheltered lives in their home environments compared to their counterparts in western countries, it is a phenomenon counterbalanced by the strict treatment meted out to them within their schools. In a country which highly values academic achievement, the Japanese household is focused upon facilitating the children's scholastic success (Lebra, *Japanese Women* 192-3).

My sons' exacting position outside the home ensures their privileged role within it. Peter is required only to manage the family bedding—laying out the futon mattresses each evening and positioning them for an airing each morning—and Simon and Ethan must dry the dinner dishes. I feel I can ask no more of them. In the past, Japanese children, and especially those inhabiting rural areas such as our own, were expected to couple schoolwork with hard manual labor at home. Now it seems enough if the children can accomplish the required goals of entering reasonably "good" high schools and universities. I am always anxious to provide an easygoing atmosphere in our own home to alleviate stress my children may feel outside it, focusing in particular on providing nurturing comfort to Peter and Simon. I am haunted by the phenomenon of the "popularity" of teenage suicide in Japan, often attributed to the pressures a Japanese child encounters at junior high or high school, which the child may perceive as unbearable.

Takie Sugiyama Lebra describes as "noteworthy ... the extent of suicides by young Japanese facing an actual or anticipated failure in schoolwork, especially in entrance examinations" (*Japanese Patterns* 199). She argues that the self-destructive tendency rooted in "status-role commitment" is only aggravated in such a society as Japan's, "where everyone is under pressure to elevate his [sic] status through academic and occupational achievements" (*Japanese Patterns* 199).

My husband helps me to cope with this pressure-cooker environment not only by assuming some domestic chores within the household but also by acting as the family chauffeur. He ferries the children to Sunday piano lessons and Simon, in his final year of junior high school and thus plunged into the depths of what is popularly known as "examination hell," to twice-weekly sessions at a cram school located in the heart of the city nearest our family farm. As noted above, these cram schools are a familiar component of most Japanese children's lives, with many boys and girls enrolled as toddlers whose parents are determined that they are able to pass exams required by some private "good" kindergartens. Graduation from high school does not ensure an end to the torment of a childhood spent toiling at academic tasks—the typical long school day's labors compounded by a further two or three hours spent at a cram school. If a child is unable to gain admittance to a "good" university, his parents may advise him to continue as a full-time student at a cram school until that university entrance examination can be passed—a process which can take several further years of intensive study. Christie W. Kiefer believes the competition for places at good schools and "prestigious universities" in Japan requires an "inhuman" study schedule on the part of applicants (343).

With Ethan's primary school located nearly two kilometers from our home—and no school buses provided and we parents actively discouraged from driving our offspring there—he must leave shortly after seven, clad in his uniform of black shorts, a black tunic, and a yellow cap, with a black school satchel bulging with textbooks strapped to his back. Simon is more fortunate. His junior high is only a ten minutes' brisk walk away, but Peter must jump on his bicycle at a little after eight to navigate three kilometers of heavy city traffic to reach his high school.

I can't linger to see Peter on his way. I have to prepare for my first class. With my university situated a good hour's drive away, my breakfast for the past twenty years of full-time employment has tended to be an apple consumed in the car as I hurry to work. As I arrive at the campus, through long years of practice, I find I can easily adopt my work persona and banish all thoughts of being either a wife or mother. This deliberate abandonment of what I might term my "private self" is a tacit requirement of my job. My university colleagues rarely discuss their families; at work, we are "workers" first and foremost. I have few female colleagues, and most of them are single and childless. Until very recently, Japanese women were forced to choose between marriage and parenthood or a career. With mothers rather than fathers viewed as the lynchpin of the family, it was viewed as an impermissible self-indulgence for a woman to try to "have it all," the rationale being that a person juggling two such huge areas of responsibility would devote insufficient energy and concentration to both.

Despite the enactment of the Equal Employment Opportunity Law in April

1986, women still routinely suffer from sexism in Japanese society in general and in the Japanese workplace in particular, earning lower wages and expected to resign from full-time employment upon marriage. There are strikingly few Japanese women to be found in the higher reaches of Japanese companies or institutions. In the educational system, for example, while over sixty percent of Japanese primary school teachers are women, in the Japanese university, there are fewer than ten percent (Kameda 117). On taking up my position at Shikoku Gakuin University, I knew of only one female colleague similarly circumstanced—married, with young children. She was Korean. Our nationalities, our being non-Japanese, provided us with an exemption to the rule tacitly governing Japanese women.

I know I was also treated with unusual indulgence because I was the mother of three boys, mirroring the view traditional in Japan that "the essential worth of a bride lies in her fertility, especially in producing a male child" (Lebra, *Japanese Women* 159). I had paid my dues as a Japanese wife. I had had my sons in the local hospital, each childbirth unassisted by the slightest pain relief. The custom of "natural" or un-medicated delivery is not only a product of the Japanese "child-centered" focus on childbirth, reflecting the commonly-held idea that any drug or medical intervention should be avoided as it might damage the baby, but it is also a product of the opinion that the pain of the experience is a means by which the mother and the child form an indissoluble bond (Jolivet 82-3). According to Takie Sugiyama Lebra, a Japanese mother will forego what she sees as "artificial parturition" involving any form of medical intervention in favor of "natural parturition" because of a belief in "learning and understanding through bodily experience, particularly suffering" (*Japanese Women* 168-9). Too, the Japanese place great value on the mental and physical will-power to endure pain without complaint; a mother's stoicism in childbirth is traditionally viewed as the "ultimate test of feminine discipline" (*Japanese Women* 169).

When the doctor administering an ultrasound examination during the course of my third pregnancy inadvertently let it slip that the fetus showed unmistakable signs of being male, he expected disappointment, assuming that, as the mother of two sons, I must have wanted a daughter. This was not the case. Not only did my husband and I feel that a third son would be desirable as a boy might be more easily accepted by our two elder children—three boys growing up together, shar-ing, probably, the same toys and interests and, providentially, clothes and school uniforms—but I was reluctant to raise a girl in a society which I perceived then and continue to view as inherently sexist. My being American and my educational achievements have won me exemptions from many of the challenges facing women in this society, but I wouldn't care to expose a child of my own to them.

When I was becoming romantically involved with Kenji, I asked a girlfriend—a fellow American and a long-term resident of Japan married to a Japanese—her opinion of him.

"Listen to how he talks to his mother," she suggested. "That's how he'd talk to you, if you got married."

"But," she airily continued, "there's no chance of that. He's a *chonan* and not only the eldest boy in his family but, from what you tell me, he's apparently the eldest son of the main branch of a traditional rural farming family. He'll never marry you, however much he might want to. His parents would never agree."

My friend was wrong, as it transpired. Kenji was then in his mid-thirties. His parents may have been desperate. In any case, they accepted our marriage. Since our wedding, however, I have been able to understand my friend's opinion more fully. It is still the custom in our area for the eldest son of a farming family to continue to inhabit the family home, to which he will bring his bride, and where they will raise their children. It is his wife's duty to look after her mother and father-in-law as they grow older and to nurse them through any illness. It is a farmer's wife's responsibility to assist her husband with the farm work. No wonder my husband remained single for so long! Few Japanese women, nowadays, would relish such a prospect (Dore 157-71).

I suspect I have only found it bearable because, again, as a foreigner and one who holds what is considered a high position in society as a university professor, I have been exempted from some of these expectations. I rarely help with the farm work, and my husband and I have been able to construct our own home, albeit one within a five minutes' walk from what my husband invariably describes as the "family compound": the traditional one-story squat black farmhouse inhabited by his parents, topped by a heavy tile roof, surrounded by storehouses and gardens, all encircled by a high stone wall. Still, we are expected to join in memorial services for Kenji's ancestors, to pray at the family graves during Japan's three-day "O-Bon" period or "Festival for the Dead," and to participate in a wide range of neighborhood activities, such as the cleaning of the area's drainage ditches. Too, my husband is required to assist his parents on a nearly daily basis. Since childhood, he has helped them with the farm work and recently, with the onset of an illness suffered by my father-in-law, he has assumed sole responsibility for it. He also often ferries his parents to doctors' appointments or to shops and undertakes any minor repair work required in their house or for their car.

In fact, although some of my husband's friends may pity him for his marriage to a westerner, I suspect he is also the object of some envy. Although it is his wife who is a university professor rather than himself, it is a position which carries considerably more social cachet in Japan than it does in the west, and it is well-paid employment with considerable benefits. This may be one reason why Kenji rarely complains about me in the way many Japanese husbands do with their wives.

A curious paradox lies at the heart of the typical Japanese household. On the one hand, the wife is not only in charge of managing the household—supervising the children and their education, and entrusted with the family finances—but she also becomes a kind of parent to her own husband, doling out, for example, a monthly allowance from his salary for his "fun" and welcoming him home, undressing him, and putting him to bed when he returns in a drunken stupor after "entertaining clients" or socializing with colleagues. Thus, many Japanese men revert to an "infantile role within the confines of marriage, acting as the wife's son rather than her husband" (Salamon 136). On the other hand, the typical Japanese husband makes himself "problematic by calling into question [his] wife's competence, by being critical of how she manages the house, or by denigrating her" (Salamon 136). Joy Paulson quotes what she describes as a belief still common in Japan: "A woman's thinking is shallow," yet, despite her "extreme 'stupidity,'" the wife is given the responsibility for the household (11). This uneasy relationship between wife and husband may account at least in part for what Ronald P. Dore characterizes as a "truism" of Japanese society, that the strongest tie within the Japanese family is between the mother and son: "Many Japanese women find relief from the emotional aridity of an arranged marriage relationship with an insensitive or domineering husband in a passionate fondness for their eldest son" (145).

Sexism is endemic in Japanese schools as well as in Japanese society. Atsuko Kameda argues that although the "formal setting of schools and classrooms is co-educational ... daily exposure to ... [the] kinds of gender bias practiced in schools is likely to instill in many youngsters a consciousness of gender differences and male superiority" (114-5). In checking attendance, teachers routinely call out the boys' names first; girls and boys are usually seated separately within the classroom and placed separately in sports teams and within a variety of other activities. The subtle differentiation of the sexes is reinforced on a more obvious level: traditional Japanese uniform codes permit girls only to wear skirts and dresses to school; boys carry black satchels to primary schools and girls, red ones. In my classrooms at Shikoku Gakuin I am amused by the invariable voluntary segregation of the sexes; the boys and girls always sit in their separate groupings and manifest embarrassment when my seating charts require them to sit beside a member of the opposite sex.

However, in recent years, reversing a trend dating from time immemorial, most Japanese parents are no longer concerned with the production of a son to carry on the family line. In an article penned for *The Los Angeles Times* in 1999, staff writer Sonni Efron describes the finding that up to seventy-five percent of young Japanese parents now prefer baby girls as a "stunning repudiation of the traditional Asian values that for centuries have put a premium on producing male heirs" (A1). In her article Efron cites the National Institute of Population and Social Security Research in Tokyo which, she observes, has

> systematically documented the growing preference for girls by asking the same questions of married couples every five years. In 1982, the survey found that of those families who wanted only one child, 51.5% wanted a boy. But by 1987, only 37.1% wanted a boy, and by 1997, it was just 25%. (A1)

Efron attributes this phenomenon to a "national pension scheme that makes male offspring less essential in financially supporting their elderly parents, a weakening of the ancestral male-dominated family system, increasing individualism and the much-improved socioeconomic status of women" (A1). The couples questioned as to their preference for a daughter also advanced the opinions that "life is no longer sweet for Japanese boys" and that daughters are more likely to be obedient and to maintain a lifelong bond with their parents (A1). The common perception is that the privileges which once were attached to being male in Japanese society have vanished, and now only the responsibilities remain.

Japan is a country which not only countenances but demands polite fabrications to ensure the smooth workings of its complex social structure. I am able to lie to protect my children without experiencing the smallest pang of compunction, and when my mother-in-law suddenly appears in my kitchen, as she does on a disturbingly regular basis, I am usually able to conceal irritation at what I view as an invasion of my privacy and to attempt a feeble hospitality. My husband's mother only occasionally bothers to knock before entering our house. In the area of rural Japan we inhabit, it is considered impolite to lock the front door. Relatives, friends, and neighbors still are expected to be able to enter each other's homes unreservedly. Yet a certain formality always holds sway in Japanese society. When I am upset by what I think of as my husband's "emotional stupidity," his inability to empathize or sympathize with my feelings, I can usually regain equanimity by the memory of Kenji's once confessing that he cannot remember ever having been kissed or held by his own mother. And his case is far from unusual in Japan. Social countenancing of physical demonstrativeness is a recent phenomenon in this country.

I suspect that my mother-in-law sometimes worries that I am making her grandsons "girlish" with my own extravagant displays of affection. I attribute the high incidence of hugging within my own family to two reasons: the fact that, as an American, I expect and even insist upon it but, secondly, my children's very limited English ability and my own limited capacity to converse in anything but simple Japanese mean that our communication must adopt forms other than that afforded by spoken language. Gestures, actions, and looks constitute a large part of our "conversations." But perhaps this is not so unusual. Sociologists estimate that the larger portion of humans' ability to communicate their feelings and thoughts is non-verbal, and this may be especially the case between men and women, whatever their relationship to each other. Angela Phillips observes that "physical affection is a good substitute for understanding, and mothers will use it with their sons just as they do with their lovers" (103).

There are several reasons for my sons' inability to speak English with any fluency. As the family's principal breadwinner and as an individual holding a full-time, tenured position at a private Japanese university, I was required to return to work two months after each of my babies was born. My sons were entrusted to the care of my husband's mother until they reached their first birthdays, when they were enrolled in a local nursery school. I was, and continue to be, the only native-English speaker my boys are in contact with on a regular basis. Because my husband is a taciturn individual, and because I often returned from my job too exhausted, in any case, to hold lively conversations with him at the supper table, my sons have had limited exposure to English, despite my having taken them on a number of occasions to both Britain and America. Too, whereas a French speaker might easily be able to pick up Italian or Spanish because of the similarities of those languages to her/his own, Japanese and English differ significantly in nearly every respect: in syntax, in grammar, in pronunciation, and in their writing systems. I console myself with such reflections when I think of my own limited Japanese ability. I speak to my sons in English; they reply in Japanese.

Earlier, I anticipated that the composition of this chapter would represent a kind of "cathartic" exercise. On completing it, I would like to revise that analysis. A sociologist named George De Vos once described the typical Japanese mother as a parent who has "perfected the technique of inducing guilt in her children by silent suffering" (84). I know the type, encountered far too often in this society—the kind of individual I once would have dismissed as suffering from a maternal "martyr's complex."

I hope that my boys will remember me rather differently. Perhaps it is through writing this that I can confirm that what I most want to have bequeathed them is what I consider a parent's most valuable gift to his child: the realization that he or she has been loved unconditionally. I long for my sons to experience what Phillips wonderfully describes as the "intoxicating pleasure of the passionate devotion of someone who thinks they are the bees' knees, the cat's pajamas, or the best thing since sliced bread" (171). This chapter is also intended as an apology to my boys that my appallingly poor linguistic abilities, coupled with my coming from a country which only represents a holiday destination for them, have left us unable to communicate with the offhand easy casualness common between most mothers and sons, who share the same language and culture. I can only hope that the old adage is true, that "actions do speak louder than words."

Works Cited

De Vos, George. "The Relation of Guilt toward Parents to Achievement and Arranged Marriage among the Japanese." *Japanese Culture and Behavior: Selected Readings*. Rev. ed. Eds. Takie Sugiyama Lebra and William P. Lebra. Honolulu: University of Hawaii Press, 1986. 80-101.

Dore, Ronald P. *Shinohata: A Portrait of a Japanese Village*. New York: Pantheon, 1978.

Efron, Sonni. "Japanese Couples Think Pink." *The Los Angeles Times* 15 Nov. 1999: A1.

Fujimura-Faneslow, Kumiko, and Atsuko Kameda. "The Changing Portrait of Japanese Men: A Dialogue Conducted Between Charles Douglas Lummis and Satomi Nakajima." *Japanese Women: New Feminist Perspectives on the Past, Present, and Future*. Ed. Kumiko Fujimura-Faneslow and Atsuko Kameda. New York: Feminist Press, 1995.

Jolivet, Muriel. *Japan: The Childless Society?* London: Routledge, 1997.

Kameda, Atsuko. "Sexism and Gender Stereotyping in Schools." *Japanese Women:*

New Feminist Perspectives on the Past, Present, and Future. Eds. Kumiko Fujimura-Faneslow and Atsuko Kameda. New York: Feminist, 1995.

Kiefer, Christie W. "The Psychological Interdependence of Family, School, and Bureaucracy in Japan." *Japanese Culture and Behavior: Selected Readings.* Eds. Takie Sugiyama Lebra and William P. Lebra. Honolulu: University of Hawaii Press, 1974. 342-356.

Lebra, Takie Sugiyama. *Japanese Patterns of Behavior.* Honolulu: University of Hawaii Press, 1976.

Lebra, Takie Sugiyama. *Japanese Women: Constraint and Fulfillment.* Honolulu: University of Hawaii Press, 1984.

Lebra, Takie Sugiyama, and William P. Lebra, eds. *Japanese Culture and Behavior: Selected Readings.* 1974. Honolulu: University of Hawaii Press, 1986.

Morley, Patricia. *The Mountain is Moving: Japanese Women's Lives.* Vancouver: University of British Columbia, 1999.

Ohinata, Masami. "The Mystique of Motherhood: A Key to Understanding Social Change and Family Problems in Japan." *Japanese Women: New Feminist Perspectives on the Past, Present, and Future.* Ed. Kumiko Fujimura-Faneslow, Atsuko Kameda. New York: Feminist Press, 1995.

Paulson, Joy. "Evolution of the Feminine Ideal." *Women in Changing Japan.* Eds. Joyce Lebra, Joy Paulson and Elizabeth Powers. Boulder: Westview, 1977.

Phillips, Angela. *The Trouble with Boys.* London: Basic, 1994.

Salamon, Sonya. "'Male Chauvinism' as a Manifestation of Love in Marriage." *Japanese Culture and Behavior: Selected Readings.* Rev. ed. Eds. Takie Sugiyama Lebra and William P. Lebra. Honolulu: University of Hawaii Press, 1986. 130-141.

Tomlin, E. W. F. *The Last Country: My Years in Japan.* London: Faber, 1974.

White, Merry Isaacs. *Perfectly Japanese; Making Families in an Era of Upheaval.* Los Angeles: University of California Press, 2002.

12
Empowered Self

LORIN BASDEN ARNOLD

Empowered

I discovered the power of controlling food at 12,
The failing of hunger proving my success.

I discovered the power of feminism at 25,
The writings of Daly feeding my soul.

My second power arrived after
The first was well-formed and well-nurtured.

The power of motherhood arrived unexpected
During a time when my feminism was newly born.

I struggled to gain comfort with these new ways of being,
In the space of a body of knowledge I had lived with for years.

Though I understood the reality of pregnancy, birth, and parenting,
I ached to escape the weight gaining, body changing, food providing.

My knowledge, and intellectual acceptance, of my mothering role
Did not prevent my increasing revulsion at the centrality of food.

We, and by this I mean you, feminists of whatever wave,
View feminist knowledge as change inducing power.

If women know and truly understand a feminist perspective,
They will be better caretakers of self—more empowered.

Empowered

The pregnant self developed a predictable schedule
Of feeding and fasting leading up to the inevitable public weighing.

It wasn't that I didn't know what I weighed in every moment;
I know every fluctuation in my weight over days, and hours.

The depression and discomfort of the medical weighing
Lay in the admission that I could not prevent the creeping increase.

Eat for the baby (but not too much), the baby needs the nutrients,
But, be sure to fast the last two days before the weighing happens.

The months that I gained, I smiled motherhood and cried later alone;
The best/worst months were when the doctor scolded me for weight loss.

What kind of a mother was I, even before I became a mother,
To despise the weight gain that represented the life I was creating?

A baby born, and then another, and on and on through six pregnancies;
And the gaining never got easier, and the shame never became less.

After the pregnancies ended, the mothering continued,
With babies hungry for the breast and the breast that must be fed.

And through the years the patterns developed and overdetermined,
Mothering through food, in an anxious state of semi-disgust.

Empowered

I wake up every morning a feminist, in a body that I experience
As something to fight, and manage, so that its failings are not exposed.

Each day becomes a struggle between my need to avoid eating
And the constant presence of food in the life of mothering.

As I turn down meals ("Oh, I had a big lunch"), I understand
I am setting the very example that my theoretical convictions rail against.

The children look at me with surprise when I fill a (small) plate at dinner,
The six year old says with surprise, "Mommy, you're going to eat?"

I suspect my younger children think this is how "Moms" eat.
I hope they don't know how I panic about their weight.

Dinner conversations with a prepubescent daughter
Include the motherly and feminist platitudes of healthy eating (and power).

While inside I cry "No second helpings! Have some self-control!"
What a fine feminist mother I am.

I tell my children that media images of women are false, unrepresentative,
And cause women to see themselves in self-destroying ways.

All the while, I stand as a representation
Of exactly what I speak against.

Empowered

I wonder what kind of mother I am (who finds herself annoyed by child hunger)
What kind of feminist I am (who measures worth by scale numbers)

Feminism and motherhood have both taught me to be strong,
Yet, I remain conflicted about what it means to be powerful.

I struggle every day over whether it is truly stronger to be
"Above" my body's desire for food or "beyond" societal ideals of body.

I experience every holiday, birthday, and family dinner
As an intrusion into my personal battle.

Going to the mall on vacation, just to find a scale to weigh myself,
Turning this into a joke for the amusement of the family.

A trip for ice cream becomes a site of struggle and anger,
My only choices seeming a rejection of family or surrender to calories.

I resent the need to buy groceries, bake cookies, get the Halloween candy
(Do I need that temptation?) And I abhor that resentment.

As I continue in this obsession/repression after over 25 years,
I listen for my experience in the voices of scholars, feminists, other mothers.

I note only absence; where am I?
No hollow cheeked Olsen twin, my experience is voided.

Empowered

In my home and in my classes,

I teach about the power of patriarchal visions of women.

In gender class, we read Clifton;
We sing her embrace of ample hips.

We write the feminist standpoint,
While I eat hypocrisy in lieu of food.

Talking about music videos, I assure my daughter,
"Those girls are too thin," while I long for their bodies.

I quiz my son on the food pyramid, preparing for school
And on the inside, I think what a ridiculous amount of food it is.

Leading these conversations, waves of shame, guilt, and anger
Are never exposed to the "children".

The children must be protected
(I must be protected) from any denial of the "truth".

Of course, adults, mothers, feminists
Don't have eating disorders.

Adult feminist mothers
Are empowered.

Empowered

13
All Hail the Militant Mom

Love and War in the Foster-to-Adopt Home

KELLY A. DORGAN

When I first started writing this essay, I set about comparing my mothering style to a tough drill sergeant or a powerful commander. I had a single vivid image in mind: A hardened military officer in a meticulously kept uniform, confidently leading her son through chaos, confidently tending his profound wounds. But that image has mutated the deeper I push into the world of Motherhood. At times, I still feel like that self-assured commander, but more often, the unrelenting warfare involved in mothering has created other mental icons: The haggard soldier, suspicious eyes shifting, forever trying to penetrate the unknown, and the stereotypical self-sacrificing Appalachian mother in the United States, waving the white flag but never giving up on "her boy." In part, this split in my identity has resulted from the act of writing my personal narrative; in doing so, I have had to simultaneously be the judgmental "self-doing-the-talking" and the sinful "self-being-talked-about" (Terry 210).

Most days now, I am an ambivalent militant. All I know is that I can be a bad-ass mom, but secretly I am terrified about my mothering decisions and abilities. I want to be this empowered mother that Andrea O'Reilly describes, one who "practices mothering from a position of agency, authority, authenticity, and autonomy" (45), but I have surprised myself: I don't know how to live up to any of the existing mothering models, and I haven't learned how to gracefully create my own unique model. For example, even my ability to be authentic, to honestly narrate my mothering experience, is constrained by my son's foster-care status. First, I have signed confidentiality agreements with our state children services agency, thereby limiting my ability to confess in my *confessional writing*. Second, I am constrained by my desire to avoid disclosing anything that may embarrass or hurt Austin further. Though I have struggled mightily as I have constructed my personal mothering experience, I want to protect him from further absorbing the struggles of adults.

Yet, I also yearn! I yearn that my narration may yield validation. I yearn both to change who I am and to remain steadfast in my ways. I yearn to defend myself—from every stranger or acquaintance who silently judges my mothering style, as well as from that internal judge whose whispers are wicked and unremitting.

Simply put, I am at war with my mothering narrative just as much as I am at war with the culture of Motherhood.

From Childfree Woman to Foster-to-Adopt Mom

The adopted child. Magnificent to behold. One of a kind ... Intricate roots that need to be healed.   —Sherrie Eldridge (5)

Austin entered our lives when I was 37 years old and he was six. My husband and I were matched with him nearly a year into our attempt to adopt through the foster care system and nearly eleven years into our childfree marriage. He is blonde, blue-eyed, and as Sherrie Eldridge writes, his biological features do not match mine. He is also intelligent, charming, ready to help with chores, and all of these characteristics are delightful—until you realize he is quite capable of using them for nefarious reasons. Understandably, because he spent a number of years in foster care (we are his fifth family), he has developed survival skills: He can be sneaky, controlling, manipulative, deceitful, and bullying. Adults may initially fail to see these survival skills because he can be exceedingly polite. And it is that politeness I distrust, even fear.

This politeness is one of his survival skills, helping him hide his losses, just as Sherrie Eldridge explains in her book, *Twenty Things Adopted Kids Wish Their Adoptive Parents Knew.* I am only beginning to understand Eldridge's warning: "If left unresolved ... grief can and often does sabotage the strongest of families and the deepest potential within the adopted child" (5). So when people practically squeal with delight, "He's so polite!" my fears and concerns are not assuaged. Many adults are enamored with his civility ... how he introduces himself with a dainty handshake, coy smile, and flirty eyelashes. They remark about how impressed they are when he kindly asks other kids, "Please, may I play with you?" But few have seen the darkness peeking between his fused cracks. If he is rejected, for example, Austin has been known to knock over toys, tear up books, call names, and even punch other kids.

Honestly, I think sometimes that I am at war with him too. Perhaps like the soldier in a war-torn world, the foster-to-adopt mother may not be able to relax during the still moments or fully enjoy the good times. I, for one, wait for the explosions; I know they will come. They may be unpredictable, but they're also relentless.

Venturing into Hostile Territory: Militant Mom in Motherhood

Culture hides much more than it reveals, and strangely enough what it hides, it hides most effectively from its own participants.   —Edward Hall (29)

This quote by anthropologist and scholar Edward Hall has special meaning for me: Until I became a mother, I never knew how hidden the culture of Motherhood was to me. I only became conscious of this culture when my emerging mothering style violated some well entrenched values and norms. Like anyone visiting a new land or people, I'm shocked by what I am discovering about Motherhood, its inhabitants, and especially myself. For example, I never fully realized how mothers are expected to provide a plush, velvety place on which to fall. And I never realized how UN-velvety I am. When he first joined our family, Austin wanted hugs for every reason: because he was greeting me; because he was happy; because I was angry with him; because I was busy; because his father and I were hugging; because I was petting the cat; because I was working at the computer; because I was cleaning the toilet. What I soon concluded was that he wanted hugs to validate his *place* in his new family, and perhaps to make up for his years of abandonment. Yet, I am generally sparing with my physical affection; some might say stingy. All I know is that in some profound ways, Austin and I were mismatched in the ways that we love.

In this essay, I discuss the negotiation and renegotiation of my Militant Mom status within my foster-to-adopt family. Similar to Deanna Chester's work on examining her identity within the context of her infertility, my "personal storied look" is also not intended to fix or teach (775). It is simply an exploration of who I became, who I am becoming, and how I teach my son to live in a world that is both orderly and chaotic. By writing, I, like bell hooks, "am pushing myself to work with ideas in a way that strips them down" (40). This essay is simply a declaration: I am a Militant Mom, often invisible, at times reviled, and seldom a hero, neither in the culture of Motherhood nor in my own mind.

Militant Mom: At War with Motherhood

I am at war with the symbols of Motherhood and how those symbols are created and sustained by us mothers and our larger culture. As with most of its members, I too have been enculturated into Motherhood. Through my own Appalachian childhood, as well as in magazines, television programs, and books, I have absorbed the culturally defined version of the "good" mother. And she does not look like me. She does not act like me.

Sharon Hays contends in *The Cultural Contradictions of Motherhood* that "images of children, child rearing, and motherhood do not spring from nature.... They are socially constructed" (19). Subsequently, *mother-love* (the behavioral and emotional practices associated with loving one's child) is socially constructed as well. I find truth in Hays' argument because my mother-love contradicts the prolific images I see, especially in Appalachia. When I drop off Austin at school in the morning, I watch the other mothers in the car-lane, their beaming faces leaning in for a kiss from their cherub-like children; these are the images that match my enculturation: the glowing mom, adoring children, and quick and pleasant "good-byes."

I live in contrast to the dominant "ideology of good motherhood" (O'Reilly 40). In the school car-lane, I sternly warn Austin against stealing, lying, or bullying.

In a store parking lot, I admonish him for trying to steal candy, and then I march him into the manager's office to scare him about the consequences of shoplifting (all the while, I watch the feverish darting of the assistant managers' eyes as they appear to assess my *unique* mothering style). Even within our white middle-class family, I must guard against the dominant culture's attempts to control Austin's ideas of mothering. For example, he has already been told by other children that I am not his mother, simply because I did not carry him inside me or give birth to him. On top of navigating the special needs associated with his foster-care history, he must also attempt to mesh my militant mother-love with the images he devours. I cringe at the soft-spoken and doe-eyed mothers in the cartoons he watches. Is that longing I see, a longing for some fantastic fantasy birth mom that I will never be, one with velvety snuggles, girlish giggles, and delightful coos? I recognize that he needs "positive fantasies" (Eldridge 76), including those about his biological mother; however, I also feel compelled to protect him from cultural *fantasies* about mothers—both good ones and bad ones. For instance, one time he came home from school with *My Working Mom*, a not entirely flattering depiction of a career woman who, when angry, sends her husband and child scurrying. As I read this book to him, I wondered if Austin was already signaling his resentment for all my meetings, lack of frivolity, and banal efforts at cooking. I wondered if his pain from his "dual heritage," both biological and adoptive (Eldridge 39), was mixing with his pain over having a mother who can be so *different*.

Militant Mom: Standing Her Ground in Appalachia, but Does She Stand a Chance?

Growing up in southern Appalachia, I have been surrounded by deeply en-trenched expectations about mothering. Generations of Appalachian families have generally followed "traditional gender roles," consisting of the "provider father" and "caretaker mother" (Bush and Lash, 170). But I did not consciously wrestle with these expectations until I actually entered Motherhood. I have always known strong Appalachian women and mothers, but I was blind to the cultural expectations they have endured. It was not uncommon, for example, in weddings, church sermons, and funerals for preachers to celebrate the dutiful wife or the glorious mother who martyrs herself for her husband and children. I would sit on those hostile wooden pews and wonder why a woman had to sacrifice herself so thoroughly before her community praised her. During those sermons and eulogies, I would silently scream, knowing that some of the women they praised had long endured alcoholic and/or violent husbands. This example reminds me of Edward Hall's elaborated arguments that many people fail to see how deeply culture controls our behaviors.

For years, I too failed to see how my culture had controlled my perceptions of mothering and mother-love, but now I am having a thoughtful *mothergiving* experience—in place of a "birthgiving experience" (Ruddick 38): I am giving birth to new strategies for loving my son. Assuming the role of Militant Mom, I have ordered Austin to stand at attention, his eyes wide, pupils swollen, body slightly trembling; I have commanded him to run suicides in our driveway, scrub the tub, and one time, brush the bathroom floor with a toothbrush. Afterward, I point to his successes, like the sparkling tub or freshly scrubbed floor, and say, "This is what I want people to know you for. For being a hard worker and a caretaker, not for lying, stealing, and bullying." All the while, haggard soldier and weary Appalachian mother haunt me; in fact, these archetypes are emboldened by my exhaustion and fear: I fear both that I am being too tough or not tough enough; I fear that I am deepening his wounds, not healing them; and above all, I fear that he will continue to lie, steal, hit, name-call, and that he will never be surrounded by people who love him—other than his Militant Mom who may be too wounded herself to help lead him to safety.

Militant Mom Joins a Snuggling Club

One day Austin came home with an amethyst-colored folder that contained sheets for tracking his reading. Written boldly at the top of *each* sheet was, "Snuggle Up & Read Club." More damning was the image that adorned *each* page: A photocopied drawing of a smiling woman tightly nestled against her enthralled, literate child. When Austin first "joined" the Snuggle Up & Read Club (he joined by having the teacher hand him the folder), I told him to sit in a chair across from me so I could watch him as he read aloud. He quickly protested, "But mom, it says to 'snuggle up and read.' We have to snuggle and read."

Dread scurried across my skin like a jungle creature trapped under camo. I was still getting to know Austin; however, I was suddenly expected to live up to the quiet perfection of this pencil-drawn mother. Of course, I relented and allowed him to crawl onto the couch beside me, but since then, I have repeatedly faced demands by the culture of Motherhood that I should automatically and instinctively be a hugger or cuddler. In fact, my foster-to-adopt experiences appear to underscore what Andrea O'Reilly points out: "our culture regards mothering as natural to mothers" (36).

Consider, for example, that Austin's counselor has told me multiple times that I—not his father—need to wrap my son in a blanket, hold him close, and cradle him in my arms. All the while, I am supposed to tenderly whisper about how I would have nurtured him *if only* he had been born to me. Let me be disturbingly frank about my reaction: I nearly wretched the first time the counselor advised me to do this. Apparently, my antipathy was so obvious that she, a bright and experienced professional, added the second time that she suggested this technique, "I know this isn't your style, but … ." Then, she vividly described this horrific blanket scenario once more.

Nearly daily, I experience the culturally defined rules of mother-love. I am to spend endless amounts of "quality time" and great amounts of resources on him (Reilly 40; Hays). Never am I to punish him, raise my voice, or say, "I don't feel like hugging because I'm really mad at you right now!" These are not acceptable forms of mother-love. In fact, others have corrected my mother-love in front of Austin. Once, my son was confessing to a family acquaintance that his lying, stealing, and sneaking made "mom mad." The woman quickly interrupted him with, "No, it doesn't make her mad. She's disappointed." Apparently, showing anger toward a child who has just lied, stolen, or vandalized is an unacceptable form of love. In the end, the culture of Motherhood ignores the complexities of authentic mothering, instead promoting images of "Disappointed Mom," "Sad Mom," or "No-I'm-Not-Mad-At-You-But-I-Am-So-Hurt-Mom."

Honestly, I want Austin to learn that people get angry when they are violated and that if he continues to act certain ways, there will be *nonviolent* but still powerful relational consequences. For example, the *first time* I discovered that Austin had punched another student, there was no hugging or kissing away his frustrations that the boy had refused to say, "Hi" (the reason my son had hit the student). Instead, I marched into his bedroom, made him stand at attention, look me straight in the eye, and account in detail what he had done. He stood before me for quite some time until I was satisfied that I had been told the entire story (which ended up being more half-truths and lies by omission). The next day, I accompanied him to school to make sure he apologized to the boy. As I was discussing the incident with his teacher and telling her that he had been grounded, she surprised me. She disclosed that she thought I was going to yell at her for not taking my son's side in the conflict. Unfortunately, I have had several encounters with childcare professionals who are amazed that I am "realistic" about my son. My question then is: How many mothers are UNrealistic about their children?

In facing my son's behavioral challenges, I have begun desperately searching for other mothering models. My experiences underscore what Donna Bassin and her co-authors have described: women are compelled to "appropriate, resist, and create a multiplicity of meanings about motherhood" (8). Just as feminist theorizing about motherhood has to be shifted to account for the "ideas and experiences of women of color" (Collins 60), we must also account for the experiences of those mothering children with special needs. We must open ourselves to what Sharon Hays argues: "Mothers are as unique as the children they raise" (76). We must recognize that current representations of mother-love may not apply to the moms of children with attachment, attention, and defiance disorders. For these moms, "snuggling up" may be a luxury. Rather, they may have to love their children in different, even militant, ways. By embracing the breadth and depth of femaleness, we may come to see ALL that is within the Mother: anger, disappointment, kindness, rage, sacrifice, vulnerability, and even militancy. Until we realize this, I will remain at war with Motherhood.

Militant Mom: At War with Other Mothers

I am fighting on multiple fronts. Not only do I feel like I am fighting Motherhood, but I also feel I am at war with other mothers. *And that is not a war I want!* Frankly, sometimes I dread interacting with some moms because of what Patricia Hill Collins claims: "Other mothers become unwitting conduits of the dominant ideology" (69). When I am with moms, I become painfully aware of the core cultural assumption that mothers are "naturally loving" (Ruddick, 30). I feel eyes on me when I am "too demanding" or "too stern." I have had moms give me unsolicited advice about how Austin will rebel against me for being "too strict." Sadly, his rebellion was going on long before he joined our family, but many adults often fail to see how Neglect and Abuse taught him to interpret kindness as weakness and conversation as debate.

I worry for Austin's present and future because I see how he pushes boundaries, as well as the people who erect those boundaries. Yes, he is rebelling—He *has* become a rebel. And his favorite allies are other moms. One time, for instance, I took hold of his arm in a busy school parking lot. Yes, I was angry for a yet another lie he had told me, so I was holding his arm instead of lovingly cradling his hand in mine as we headed to our car. The *very moment* another mother approached, he jerked his arm away and began wailing loudly, "You're hurting me." I spun him around, and with the other mom as a witness, I said unflinchingly, "I will put my hands on you. I am your mother and I will make sure you don't get run over by a car." Not surprisingly, he immediately stopped crying as soon as we were alone in the car and away from the other mom. "I'm sorry, mom," he said, adding, "you can put your hands on me." He actually said those words, calmly, without dramatics. And that's exactly what scares me: that he can pull on politeness as quickly as a pair of pristine white socks over soiled feet.

Lios Ruskai Melina helps me understand what might be underlying his behaviors when she writes, "Neglect, abuse, failure to set appropriate limits, frequent moves, and failure to form attachments affect a child and are likely to continue to affect her to some degree after she is placed in an adoptive family" (157). I have grown to see my son's survival techniques with new eyes: his manipulation is his beloved teddy-bear, and his need for control is his soothing blanket. These techniques have been with him longer and done more for him than any adult, toy, or household ever has. Unfortunately, being manipulative and controlling may have helped him survive Neglect and Abuse, but those behaviors will not help him create a warm, loving family or healthy, loyal friendships.

In their personal wars, moms of children with special needs must remain vigilant, always prepared to fight for their unique mothering ways and for their unique children's futures. Ultimately, though, we must also acknowledge that the persistently vigilant mom can become so exhausted in her fight that she transforms from confident commander into faded warrior.

"Just Love Him!" and Other Invaluable Advice

Some days I feel my resilience and power fading. I want to surrender at times. I dream about how easy my life would be if I went AWOL by ignoring the red flags on his report cards or the sabotaged gifts hidden in his bedroom. In my first year of being a parent I already agree with Sharon Hays' characterization of our culture's current model of mothering, a model that depicts child-rearing as labor-intensive and costly. Mothering is emotionally costly as well. Somehow moms—even new ones—are supposed to naturally want to spend endless amounts of emotional currency on their sons and daughters, even when the children are acting in unlovable ways. Personally, I have experienced—repeatedly—others' expectations that I should have automatically, deeply, and completely fallen in love with my son the moment I saw him. In those first months when Austin joined our family, I intentionally sought out allies: Other parents. I confessed to them my disbelief, anger, and fear, and I received in return: "You've just got to love him" and "Give him plenty of love." Eventually, I concluded from this advice:

- Even when he purposefully tears the bedding I spent so much time and money buying, I should just love him;
- Even when he repeatedly draws on walls and carpeting instead of in the coloring and art books I gave him, I should just love him;
- Even when he shreds the cardinal-red shirt I just bought him, I should just love him;
- Even when he lies, steals, then lies to cover up his lying and stealing, I should just love him.

For the Militant Mom, the real problem is not the ripped shirt, the torn bedding, or the freshly graffitied walls. No, the real problem is that these actions are vivid metaphors for a child's despair, disdain, and defiance. Eldridge tells me that I must grant Austin permission to "feel the pain, scream the anger, cry the tears" that adoptees experience (5). Even this wounded and exhausted Militant Mom would welcome the screams and tears, but they rarely come. Like the soldier longing for hand-to-hand combat, I want to face his pain straight on. More frequently, though, he takes his pain and loss to school and unleashes them on young girls; he takes his pain out on his friends, clothes, and meager possessions. Each one of his actions are like small, but soul-shaking explosions that seem to come out of nowhere, and each one damages everyone around him, particularly his allies and himself.

Militant Mom: At War with My Selves

The fiercest battle I face, though, is with myself. As mentioned throughout this essay, I have several dominant archetypes fighting for control in my head: the commanding Militant Mom; the battle-worn soldier; and a gentler but still resilient Appalachian mom. Militant Mom wants me to be tougher, to not question my decisions and tactics. My fatigued soldier wants me to remain distrustful, especially during the cease-fires, or maybe even retreat altogether. And Appalachian mom suffocates me with guilt. As my talking-self writes this, she forces the talked-about-self to confess: I am terrified that instead of reinventing mother-love, I am simply reinforcing existing models of hierarchy and dominance, and instead of teaching him not to bully I am, in fact, teaching him that his mom is a big ol' bully.

In this essay, I have attempted to contribute to "identifying, interrupting, and deconstructing the patriarchal discourse of motherhood" (O'Reilly 9). It is my maternal quest to nurture Austin in meaningful and authentic ways, by providing him with opportunities to learn experientially and grow into a problem-solver; I want him to know how to manage freedom and navigate chaos. Yet, as my narrative reflects, I must always remain alert about my son's past since he has only recently been introduced to the concepts of *consistent consequences* and *safety rules*. This is a kid whose years in foster care engendered in him a *Lord of the Flies*-like compartmentalization of life: There are rules to live by when adults are around and other rules to live by when they are not (see Golding).

As I attempt to put forth a "maternal narrative" that runs counter to existing patriarchal narratives (O'Reilly 9), I seek to re-define what a mother's love should look like. In my first year of mothering, I have quickly discovered that Abuse and Neglect, like cruel and domineering parents, had already taught Austin to equate softness with weakness, and attention (of any sort!) with love. Having lived in foster care, a system that can encourage self-absorption out of necessity, Austin had to be concerned about his own desires, especially since no one else seemed to be. Therefore, the moment he joined a safe and relatively functional family, his self-absorption actually damaged himself, his father, and me.

Instead of attending to my son's immediate desires, I see myself as an instrument to reshape them. Rather than desiring to control girls, I want him to learn how to respect them. Rather than desiring his school-mates' possessions, I want him to learn to steal their hearts. Rather than desiring a fantastic fantasy family, I want him to learn to *create* family. Rather than acting happy, I want him to be happy. Until all these objectives are achieved, I will have to resign myself to the long-term war inside my head.

Mutually Assured Destruction

In my war with Motherhood, other moms, and myself, I have developed unique approaches to addressing Austin's behaviors. I call one of these approaches M.A.D., or Mutually Assured Destruction. Yes, I use this term tongue-in-cheek; yet, my motives for using this tactic are quite serious: Deterrence of negative behavior by promising reciprocity.

The first *and only* time I employed M.A.D. was the afternoon my son came home from school with a note explaining that he had called a girl "gay." I would like to believe that he had not used "gay" as a *weapon word*, a word designed to hurt someone and negate or spoil their identity; however, I knew otherwise. In fact, Austin later admitted that he had called her "gay" because he was jealous of having to share her with another girl. Since becoming a family, my son and I have had many open discussions about weapon words, because I knew that as a white, male Appalachian, he would be exposed to them, even encouraged to use them. So when he actually used one of those words, it was simply one more time that he chose to ignore his parents' rules and requests; hence, I took drastic measures: M.A.D.

As soon as he came home, he first had to sit in silence at the table, copying down long definitions of "homophobia," "bigotry," and "homosexuality." Then,

I explained in a hand-written note how I was going to behave towards him for the rest of the day: Because he had repeatedly ignored my values and requests, he had made me feel invisible, so I was going to reciprocate. That afternoon and through bedtime, I refused to answer his questions, look at him, or talk to him, even to say, "Goodnight." This was my way of reminding him that his behaviors—negative or positive—provoke reciprocal behaviors from others. I wanted him to understand that if he continued to ignore the requests of teachers and peers, they would ignore him; I wanted him to consciously examine the pain of being disregarded and discarded so he didn't have to continue learning these lessons in more dramatic and less safe ways.

Up to this point, his father and I had tried all the traditional non-violent punishments. We'd grounded him, taken away privileges, required him do tedious chores, and made him give up his favorite toys, but none of these worked. Let's be honest! Austin is already used to having his freedom restricted and his things taken away ... like toys, homes, parents. So, I took away what he craved the most: control over people and attention from people. Yes, I chose a dramatic way to show him that he could not ignore our family's values without consequences, but I would rather do that than let his homophobic statements, misogynist actions, and controlling behaviors continue to frighten away his potential allies.

Still, I am ambivalent about my decision to take such drastic measures. That night, I kept thinking, "A mother can't treat her son like this. You're a mom now. Act like one." I had seen my own mom turn the other cheek so many times that I felt guilty that I wasn't offering Austin the other side of my face. Especially when he ran into his room, threw himself on the bed, and cried himself to sleep, I felt the rightness in Sara Ruddick's words: "During most of the years that I was actively taking care of my children, mothering was said to be love and feminine duty rather than a thoughtful project" (29). Even though I had *thoughtfully* examined my actions and strategies, I still felt myself directly contradicting Motherhood's expectations. A mother is supposed to take her son in her arms and protect him in some idealized feminine way. A mother is supposed to hug away her son's possessiveness of girls and kiss away his cruelty. A mother is supposed to see her son's most dastardly behavior in the most innocent way. That night, though, I hoped by my choosing to protect the girls that he has repeatedly hit, name-called, and bullied, I also chose to protect him and his future. Militant Mom won the battle that night, but she is weary and the war isn't over.

All Hail: The Rise (and Fall?) of Militant Mom

There are times that Austin seems to thrive under the consistency and order I provide. He talks about the importance of being a "caretaker" and creating a "safe family." Family, friends, and teachers claim they see improvement. But once again, I fear the seething darkness that underlies our shared moments of peace. He is capable of displaying love that is softer than any silk. His small hands delicately caress our cats. He kindly helps clean the bathroom, dry and put away dishes, and take out the garbage. And still I wait for the explosions. Particularly when picking him up from school, I study his face, trying to determine if he has been ally or saboteur today. Will I find some stolen prize or demolished shirt stuffed in his backpack? Will I have to respond to yet another note about him calling girls *honey*, *gay*, or *fat*? Will I have to cancel family plans yet again because he will be grounded for lying or hitting? These questions explode around me like invisible grenades, while I stand amidst the cheerful moms and their seemingly predictable, adoring children.

I doubt. I doubt. I doubt! Then, I examine and re-examine my maternal expectations and narratives. I try to view the stealing as his way of capturing the pleasure that was stolen from him. I try to view the demolished shirt as his manifested desire to strike out against those who abused and neglected him. I try to view his bullying of girls as his way of controlling all the moms—birth and foster—that he couldn't control. Still, my son and I must move beyond simply *understanding* his metaphoric behaviors; we must create new behaviors to help him thrive, not just survive.

So, I resign myself to being the confident commander one day, the haggard soldier the next, and the self-sacrificing Appalachian mom the day after that. I resign myself to the war that I am fighting on many fronts: within me, with other moms, with Austin, and with Motherhood itself.

Works Cited

Bassin, Donna, Honey, Margaret and Kaplan, Meryle Mahrer. "Introduction." *Representations of Motherhood.* Ed. Donna Bassin, Margaret Honey and Meryle Mahrer Kaplan. New Haven: Yale University Press, 1994. 1-25.

Bush, Kevin Ray and Lash, Sheryl Beaty. "Family Relationships and Gender Roles." *Encyclopedia of Appalachia.* Ed. Rudy Ambramson and Jean Haskell. Knoxville: University of Tennessee Press, 2006. 170-171.

Chester, Deanna. "Mother. Unmother: A Storied Look at Infertility, Identity, and Transformation." *Qualitative Inquiry* 9.5 (2003): 774-784.

Collins, Patricia Hill. "Shifting the Center: Race, Class, and Feminist Theorizing about Motherhood." *Representations of Motherhood.* Eds. Donna Bassin, Margaret Honey and Meryle Mahrer Kaplan. New Haven: Yale University Press, 1994. 58-74.

Eldridge, Sherrie. *Twenty Things Adopted Kids Wish Their Adoptive Parents Knew.* New York: Delta, 1999.

Glassman, Peter. *My Working Mom.* Singapore: HarperCollins, 1994.

Golding, William. *Lord of the Flies.* New York: Putnam, 1954.

Hall, Edward. *The Silent Language.* New York: Doubleday, 1959.

Hays, Sharon. *The Cultural Contradictions of Motherhood.* New Haven: Yale University Press, 1996.

hooks, bell. *Remembered Rapture: The Writer at Work.* New York: Henry Holt, 1999.

Melina, Lois Ruskai. *Raising Adopted Children: Practical Reassuring Advice for Every Adoptive Parent.* New York: Quill, 2002.

O'Reilly, Andrea. *Rocking the Cradle: Thoughts on Motherhood, Feminism and the Possibility of Empowered Mothering.* Toronto: Demeter Press, 2006.

Ruddick, Sara. "Thinking Mothers/Conceiving Birth." *Representations of Motherhood.* Ed. Donna Bassin, Margaret Honey and Meryle Mahrer Kaplan. New Haven: Yale University Press, 1994. 29-45.

Terry, David P. "Once Blind, Now Seeing: Problematics of Confessional Performance." *Text and Performance Quarterly* 26.3 (2006) 209-228.

Part IV
Representing Motherhood

14
Cherríe Morraga's Queer Transformations

Becoming a Butch Mother

SUSAN DRIVER

I read Cherríe Moraga's *Waiting in the Wings: Portrait of a Queer Motherhood* almost a decade ago, when I was a young graduate student in the midst of a research project focused on "queering maternal desires" that would inspire my emotional and intellectual curiosity for years to come. Moraga's book puts into practice what I had been struggling to conceptualize: non-binary relations of mothering tuned into corporeal and historical specificities. This book continues to grab my attention as one of the few attempts to write about butch maternal subjectivity in ways that challenge heteronormative assumptions while producing innovative styles of representation. Whereas so much feminist analysis of motherhood remains detached from the vulnerable edges of the desiring body, Moraga writes about her experiences of pregnancy, birth and mothering with a candid and ambivalent exploration of queer gender and sexuality. Moraga's book transgresses institutional divisions separating queer, feminist, and postcolonial modes of understanding while also bridging theoretical inquiry and experiential writing.

Situating My Reading

My reading of *Waiting in the Wings* is not an abstract scholarly exercise; for me it is a profoundly moving process of remembering and rethinking the very status of maternal differences. Against the tide of a dominant culture fixated on hierarchical and normalizing ways of naming and differentiating "good" and "bad" mothers, Moraga's book disrupts concepts through which motherhood is generalized. This approach speaks to me on many levels. Raised by a white, working-class, single mother, whose embodied intelligence and passion never ceased to inspire my dreams, I have never believed in the static notion of "family values" or ideals of maternal "goodness." Beyond media images of perfect moms in nuclear families, I learned about diverse maternal experiences through intimate teachings within an urban social housing project where I grew up amidst mothers whose familial, working, and romantic lives defied the terms of middle-class ideologies. I have always imagined mothering to be a practice of love, care, and desire that has the potential to shatter normative paradigms and reinvent new ways of living. From my social standpoint, the transgressive qualities of mothering are not rooted in any single text or identity but emerge out of volatile convergences of race, class, and sexuality happening daily in the life-worlds of economically and socially marginalized women.

As a queer daughter who wants to become a queer mother, Moraga's book provides me with languages through which to recognize variant and uneasy passages into motherhood. Moraga's book does not speak my experience but it does open up spaces in which to signify female masculinity and maternal nurturance together, which is an invaluable gift as I envision parenting with my butch lover. The deep awareness that my lover and I share about the challenges and possibilities of raising a child together finds resonance in Moraga's text. As a femme I recognize my butch lovers' potential to become an amazing parent. Yet there are virtually no public languages to confirm or value these feelings. In this gap, Moraga's text narrates the fears and pleasures of a queer maternal self in process, Moraga refuses to polish over or close off the emotional and social uncertainties that come with forging alternative family relations. Such public representations of personal ambivalence, that do not diminish the intense joys of queer mothering, are a vital force that help to dislodge reliance on demonizing or romantic images. In the raw flux of her thinking body, Moraga shares with others the stakes of mothering against the grain of heteronormativity.

I approach Moraga's text between reflexive closeness and a respectful distance. My close reading of Moraga's text is dialogical insofar as I pick up on words and ideas that resonate with my own desires while attending to our distinct social locations. I try to attune myself as a reader into the specific contexts that shape Moraga's experiences that touch me while reminding me that my history as a white queer woman marks the process through which I interpret this text. In many ways I feel that such attentive reading is crucial for overcoming either sweeping generalization or insular personalization. In between individual and political texts, confession and theory, intimate reflection and cultural description, Moraga's book crosses boundaries that inspire new ways of reading and writing maternal experiences. I have learned so much from this book, and while it is impossible to recount its richness in a short essay, I attempt to reread select fragments as openings for further reflection.

Reinventing Familia

Cherríe Moraga's *Waiting in the Wings: Portrait of a Queer Motherhood* purposefully replays the joys and fears of her experience of queer maternal beginnings that are always already continuations and disruptions of what has come before. Moraga shows the importance of reconstructing queer maternity in the now by recovering and transforming historical elements of Chicana identity and kinship. Reinvention of maternal symbols and practices emerge in the flux of bridging aspects of her life as a butch Chicana lesbian going through insemination, pregnancy, birth, and the first stages of parenting. Moraga writes through a desiring self, oscillating between remembering past lives and imagining future ones.[1]

It is crucial to contextualize Moraga's life writing as a queer mother in relation to critical and creative fields of Chicana discourses. In a similar vein to Gloria Anzaldúa, Moraga avoids mutually exclusive identity categories and politics between her queer and maternal affiliations, writing through intimate experiences throwing into question essentialist ideals of motherhood.[2] Whereas Anzaldúa reconstructs a queer maternal vision by working over symbolic traditions from her contemporary position as a Chicana daughter, Moraga begins with the everyday details of her experience of becoming a mother. Moraga combines journal entries[3] and dream texts as well as political commentary of the events surrounding her conception, pregnancy, and early years of mothering as "a kind of poet's memoir," a "personal fiction." The time frame is contemporary as Moraga inscribes her feelings and responses in the moment, speaking very close to her newly lived conflicts and pleasures. Moraga becomes a mother within a lesbian relationship through alternative insemination by a young gay man, a relationship she refers to as "a queer contract." In *Waiting in the Wings*, Moraga reconfigures her family relations in ways that do not divide or curtail her identifications as a Chicana, writer, lesbian, mother, but allow for an expansion of desire across spaces and relations struggling for their coexistence. In her words:

> So, the search for a *we* that could embrace all the parts of myself took me far beyond the confines of heterosexual family ties. I soon found myself spinning outside the orbit of that familial embrace, separated by thousands of miles of geography and experience. Still, the need for familia, the knowledge of familia, the capacity to create familia remained and has always informed my relationships and my work as an artist, cultural activist, and teacher. (Moraga 17-18)

Moraga's complex experiences of familia involving her mother, father, siblings, and extended relations are elaborated throughout her plays, poetry, and prose. Her familia offers loving social relations through which the transmission of Mexican-American-Indian cultural and linguistic ties become formative parts of her life writing. She transfers stories passed down through lines of kinship from her position as a lesbian who experiences marginalization and conflict with her blood relations because of her gender and sexual differences. Leaving her parents' home in an attempt to separate from patriarchal and heterosexist restraints imposed upon her, Moraga tells of her struggle to create new familia and community relations as a Chicana lesbian who remains linked to her birth place and the cultural practices and values she learned growing up.

Moraga's reconstruction of familia involves her efforts at writing "stories to agitate, stories to remind us what has been forgotten" (47). As a site through which narratives and myths are passed across generations, familia gains even more significance at the point in Moraga's life when she becomes a mother: "*Somehow my giving birth involves me in this trajectory, this continuing history of conquests and culture clashes, of the regeneration of raza and the creation of new razas"* (38). She establishes connections between elements of her maternal genealogy and her present relations with lovers and friends, choosing a Mexican-American gay father as a way of queerly reforging ties with her mother's ancestral blood-lines. She reads her baby's body as a *"map of generations revisited"* (68), preserving and integrating Chicana identifications into her life as a lesbian mother. But while blood relations signify the value of maintaining kinship ties in the wake of racial genocide and cultural violence against Moraga's ancestors, her vision of familia is not delimited by blood ties, but includes permeable social networks and cultural fictions: "making familia from scratch each time all over again" (69). It is within such complex reinscriptions of familia that mothering comes to signify many possibilities for Moraga, becoming part of intergenerational acts of resistance and survival, and also configuring an interracial "queer" family following a double movement toward recuperation and reinvention.

Moraga's account resonates with the unfolding of my own story of becoming a mother. The convolutions of interracial queer family making have profoundly shaped how my partner and I pursue our dreams to become parents. As we plan our insemination we think through the best ways to embody my partner Carrie's genealogical ties to her mother's birthplace of Granada. We want our child to have living connections to Caribbean culture and more concretely to have physical traces of Carrie's beautiful brown skin. The importance of establishing physical and symbolic ties that link both of us through the child's unique embodiment are part of a more expansive attempt to create our family through the terms of our specific histories and familial legacies. Having to make compromises within medicalized systems of anonymous sperm donations makes this difficult, but it is an attempt not so much to pin down biological certainties of bloodlines as to create possibilities for complex connections through which we both feel intimately part of the ongoing invention of our family across our cultural and racial differences. Moraga's writing forges ways of understanding the process through which queer kinship criss-crosses multiple lines of generational experience, embodiment, and unpredictable invention that defies the expectations of normalizing family ideologies.

Mothering as Movements and Transitions

Moraga speaks about becoming a mother through metaphors of movement, change and transition, going so far as to proclaim that *"travel seems more possible now thinking of this life"* (29). Mothering is understood as generating desire through interactions with others rather than establishing a stable gender identity and domestic security. Instead of being an identity to be taken for granted, mothering is portrayed as the effect of a creative yet uncertain process of alteration: "Mother: the term assumes the shape of my being very gradually" (92). Moraga details a continual unfolding of her maternal subjectivity in relation to others:

"as family—Ella, Pablo and I work out our evolving roles and our evolving consciousness in the midst of an evolving child" (38). Even in those moments of her text where she focuses on her encounters with her child as an intensely emotional interdependency, she stages a dialogue between the two of them as they both grow and learn together as part of wider and overlapping cultural relations. Moraga displaces norms of maternal insularity and authority, preferring instead to position herself as undergoing transition through the lessons offered by her son (as her teacher) as well as others around her. She reveals herself to be a maternal subject in process rather than any finalized and fixed identity: "I had come to my motherhood along the long hard path. Nothing has been a given for me, not even my womanhood" (17).

Waiting in the Wings explores how Moraga's self-identification as a butch lesbian complicates her relation to hegemonic feminine-maternal expectations, articulating the ways sexual desire propels her bodily experiences and her retrospective interpretations of them. At several points she describes her gender/sexual dissonance as a mother: "*I go to sleep wallowing in my queer sense of isolation/alienation even from my lesbian lover. She's a femme, I think. She really doesn't understand*" (45). Yet her narrative does not uphold clear-cut boundaries, as her lover Ella is shown as inhabiting a complex position as a co-mother within a butch/femme dynamic. It is Moraga, not Ella, who expresses and fulfills her desire for motherhood at the age of 40, refusing to accept mutually exclusive categories that would foreclose her queer butch maternity. Not only does she speak affirmatively about her gender contradictions, but turns attention onto butch women as sources of identification and nurturance for children. She opens her book by telling a parenting story revolving around another woman's gender subversion:

> A brilliant butch woman told me years ago about a boy she had raised with his mother for many years. One night her heart broke when, tucking in the bespectacled boy of ten, he wrapped his arms around her neck and called her daddy, with everything he had in him. When I finally met the boy, I saw that he shared Maria's poor eyesight, wit and brainy humor. Most of all, he learned how to be a boy from Maria. He learned masculinity from Maria and she was a wonderful male role model: the best of fathers with a woman's compassion. (15)

Moraga uses this story as a departure point for destabilizing and reorienting gender assumptions of lesbian mothering. She contests biological and complementary models of parenting, turning away from fixed forms to innovative and situational practices of caring for her child with her partner. Moraga writes about the paradox of gaining public recognition as a mother because of her biological function ("even though she is the 'dyke'") and Ella's lack of recognition because of her non-biological status. Institutional powers relegated to biological mothers are questioned as Moraga interweaves complex gender, race, and sexual identifications into her narrative as a butch Chicana lesbian.

Moraga's touching memory of a butch caring for a child who in return calls her "daddy" grips my imagination with undeniable force. My partner Carrie's tenderness is deeply marked by her butch daddy gestures and actions which are so immediately recognized by both of us, yet so difficult to communicate in a world where mother and father roles are divided along rigidly biological norms of sex and gender difference. I know very deeply how nurturing Carrie will be as a queer daddy, blending gender in ways that give rise to new modes of masculinity in the daily practices and emotional interactions of protecting, loving, and educating a child. Thinking and talking about female masculinity as a central locus of queer child-raising becomes vital in our discussions of becoming parents. Yet what we come to believe is possible in the creation of new queer formations of mommy-daddy love hits a wall of symbolic and social invisibility and ridicule. So little has been represented to affirm queer daddy relations that we often feel our dreams will be expressed and lived out in a cultural void. It is precisely in the public articulation and circulation of experiences through which butch daddies become intelligible and valued that Moraga's text unfolds a collective horizon of empowering alternatives.

Moraga's narrative emphasizes a sense of pleasurable ambiguity, elicits readers' desires for variant and unexpected experiences. Unexpected and subtle shifts in Moraga's psychic and bodily perceptions provide new understandings of the interrelationships between her maternity and sexuality. Moraga writes about her increasing sensual awareness of her body, paying close attention to her heightened sensitivity to touch and smell: "*a lesbian sex-smell. A mother-smell. A mother-lover, a mother-fucked smell. It is life*" (68). Moraga's textualization of her changing body is focused around the emergence of surprising contradictions:

> *Ella tells me daily how much more feminine I look. I see it, too—my hair longer than it's been in fifteen years, my hips and thighs and breasts rounding from this pregnancy, the softening taking place throughout my body, the tears. I like it and yet in bed feel a strong urge to reassert my butchness, my self as a love-maker.* (45)

Moraga writes and interprets her desires and pleasures throughout her experiences of insemination, pregnancy and birth in ways that focus on the malleability of her embodiment and psychic life. Her dreams are written as loose associative images and narrative fragments which trace the shifts of her affective and unconscious life, enabling her to explore imaginary relations to her body through a language that can be shared with others. Becoming a mother works to expand her self-perceptions, erotic languages, and corporeality.

While Moraga does textualize her sensual transformations she does not romanticize her maternal body as an isolated and blissful process detached from the messy everyday world of poverty, racism, and illness that surrounds her. During her pregnancy, Moraga speaks about mothering as an act of life which derives its meaning and sense of responsibility in relation to the world around her. This situates her child as a source of future possibilities interconnected with socio-cultural and political conditions restricting the futures of many people. She writes:

> *I know the life I carry within me causes me to imagine a future....Driving home, the radio announces the Senate passage of a bill outlawing the entrance of HIV-infected immigrants. One reporter speaks of 270 Haitians imprisoned in camps, "a living hell," he calls it. And a prayer rises up to my lips. "We all deserve a future."* (29)

The significance of being pregnant becomes connected to rethinking social injustices, inadequate living conditions, oppression, and suffering. It is by continually situating herself in relation with others that Moraga's own experiences of the life and death struggle of her sick, premature son Rafael become contextualized. Moraga writes that "Rafael Angel is a messenger of death" (40) through which she gains a "knowledge of impermanence," and an understanding of her own ephemerality and limits. Writing through her psychic anxieties and fears of having to live daily with the threat that her son may not live, Moraga transforms private grief into a deeper understanding of surrounding communities. Many of her self-reflections on mortality take place in the midst of collective experiences of illness which call for responsible acts of narration and political coalition. Moraga makes sense of her private pain through her links with those who have died or are dying of AIDS and cancer, using her writing to encompass relations of empathy and caring across differences rather than identity and sameness. Audre Lorde's death after a long struggle with breast cancer becomes another point of remembrance and alliance for strengthening cultural and political bonds which enables Moraga to situate her activity of giving birth within an interconnected process of history. When Moraga speaks in memory of Lorde she refers to her as part of a chain of strong and creative women: "*June and Pat and Merle ... sister-poets gone and surviving with cancer*" (35). Moraga remembers those who have died as part of an attempt to construct non-biological intergenerational bonds at the same time that she is engaged in a flesh and blood relation with her yet to be born son:

> *Hearing that Tede had AIDS so close to the news of Rafael's boyhood/maleness. Is there a kind of queer balance to this birthing and dying...lesbians giving life to sons, or brothers passing? He is the child of queers, our queer and blessed family, laughing with Pablo and Ella after the insemination, sitting on the bed next to me. We just laughed and laughed.* (62)

Moraga's words are performatively reparative "to recover loss by reliving those moments of first motherhood" (99). Her writing exceeds individualizing languages of mothering by asserting her desires for collectively meaningful and creative work. Moraga makes it clear that her need for art is not lessened by the satisfaction derived from her relations with her child, which impels her to negotiate her life as a writer. Journal writing becomes one aspect of Moraga's attempt to forge a passage between motherhood and her artistic imagination, allowing her to document her maternal experiences but also to textually rework them through fictional and poetic acts of rewriting. Limitations of time and energy are explored in her journal writing as a material fact of her daily existence as a mother, compelling her to immerse herself in fictional acts which detach her momentarily from demands of caring for others. Writing and mothering are configured as conflictual yet not oppositional relations, they produce tensions throughout Moraga's text as signs of ambivalence located and transgressed within the social conditions that circumscribe her choices as a writer and mother. Refusing binary frameworks which separate motherhood from creative desire, Moraga suggests that her maternal experience is itself a signifying activity, offering new incentives to write and imagine otherwise. Moraga textualizes her ongoing internal dialogues with her child while she is pregnant and her intersubjective conversations with her son once he is born as a challenging inspirational force within life. She also replays her communications with her son and considers the stylistic innovations constituted through her maternal perspective. The personal and cultural significance of Moraga's bilingualism takes on new meaning as she passes languages onto her child in the emotional immediacy of her speech and desire to connect with and teach Rafael. This leads her to reconsider how her written texts configure future possibilities for generations to come. Moraga's maternal and writing subjectivity are shown to be mutually shaped without becoming simplistically merged:

> *Rafaelito watches me write. He is not interested in the baby gym set dangling over his head. He is interested in the movement of my hand across this page. Black strokes against the soft beige grain of the paper. He watches me. And for the first time it occurs to me that he may have something to learn from me, by my example. "This is my work, hijo. I am a writer." I am trying to be a mother who writes well. I am trying to be a writer who mothers well. Somewhere inside me, I feel the forces rise up to stop me.* (95-96)

Moraga's words unleash my own longing to be both an independent creative subject and a mother. I realize how anxious my generation is in the face of having to sacrifice individual autonomy for the vulnerable dependencies of taking care of a child. Much of my own hesitations and ambivalence around becoming a mother revolve around my fears that I will not have time to think or act outside predictable codes, fears that I might lose spaces in which to reflect and write about the world where I can explore daring ideas on my own. Creativity is bound up with queerness for me insofar as it is driven by an urgent need to question, challenge and broach new ways of desiring, interpreting, and acting. The refusal to give this up is inscribed and enacted throughout Moraga's book, where the enactment of a queer maternal voice calls upon creative desires to go beyond conventions and invent new beginnings. What I begin to grasp is that the everyday inventiveness of queer mothering demands that imaginative autonomy be fostered in conjunction with relational empathy. The mutual exclusivity of intellectual creative work and mothering is overcome within Moraga's narrative, as she negotiates both with equal passion. I am struck by the ways she frames her own mothering as inextricable from her political and artistic commitments. It is Moraga's pursuits as a creative and critical writer that become integral to her self-perception as a good mother, able to teach and guide her child responsibly. She bridges these dimensions of herself, and it is such active and conscious attempts to forgo either/or logics that compel me as a reader, as a writer, and as a potential mother.

Moraga's text performs her ongoing trials and discoveries as a Chicana writer, mother, lesbian lover as part of her reinvention of familia and community. She refuses to forego the complexities of her desires even as she attempts to construct a home for herself and her child, challenging attempts to mold sexuality into monogamous conjugal forms: "Keep your marriages...I want the freedom of this unpredictable desire" (111). Showing how crucial it is to experiment with non-conventional kinship relations and living arrangements rather than conform to an external definition of domestic happiness, Moraga establishes bonds with the father and co-mother of her child without relying on the illusory permanence of a nuclear family structure. Affirming her friendship with Rafael's father, Pablo, and appreciating the "colored queerboy contingent" he belongs to, she exclaims after participating in a pride day celebration: "How glad I am to be in their company, to bring my son into their circle of fine and critical minds, smart mouths, and indignant dignity" (97). Similarly she affirms the complexity of her ties to her lover Ella as they negotiate their lives together as parents. Moraga and Ella choose to live in separate households without undermining their dedications to caring for each other along with their son. What emerges out of their mutual decision to live independently is an intensification of sexual attraction and spontaneity in their relationship outside the boundaries of cohabitation. The reinvention of home and familia are reworked out of an ethics of care and sexual desire. Ending *Waiting in the Wings* by addressing her lover with a declaration of her "delight of lesbianism" and the importance of "savoring the 'style' we generate from each other," Moraga insists upon the value of embracing the unpredictable tenacity of her erotic life, willing to take risks and acknowledge the urgency of her desires which include other women and other occasions of desire and attraction. She provocatively writes:

> *Maybe "lover" has been replaced with "mother" these days, but it does not satiate. At times I miss la pasion, fear how remote it has become between Ella and me. Worse, fear it no longer matters to me, which I know is a lie, a camouflage waiting in the bushes to jump out and fall on some other woman's bones.* (109)

Conclusion: Reading Queer Maternal Life-Writings

I came upon *Waiting in the Wings* at a time when I was searching for maternal voices to address the complexities of queer desires. Beyond the formal and abstract languages of queer theory, what I craved were queer articulations in the flesh and blood, textual translations of how it feels to engage in the most intimate acts of love in ways that exceed heteronormative frameworks. I realize now that I am older how crucial it is for young queer women to access personal stories of mothering that defy normalizing appeals to sameness and uniformity, without forsaking meaningful family connections and community belonging. Moraga's text articulates longing for both familia and sexual passion between women, against the either/or logics of hegemonic family discourses. Yet in forging a life that embraces inventive forms of inclusion, Moraga elaborates struggles and ambivalence along the way. Nothing can be taken for granted or guaranteed, and it is her willingness to avow the contingencies of mothering outside conventional structures that passes on a valuable lesson to the next generation.

Reading Moraga's experiential narratives as a site of cross-cultural and cross-generational learning, I come to understand queer mothering in terms of contested practices and knowledge that call for receptive modes of understanding and response. It is precisely Moraga's naming of her differences while reaching out to others to name their own, that enables her text to be partial and changing and also collectively empowering. Moraga interweaves many strands of political commitment, personal loss, erotic pleasure, and maternal devotion into a story of becoming a queer Chicana mother that is always already more than merely a mother's tale. Drawing upon the richness of Moraga's stories that detail the daily work of shaping queer relationships with lovers, friends, and children, I am spurred on to think through the concrete possibilities of my own queer maternal storylines. As such Moraga's writings enlist me to pay close attention to the textures of her unique experience out of respect and hope for queer maternal futures.

[1]The revision of historical and textual maternal figures is common in Chicana writings (see for example the visual art and writings byYolanda Lopez, Gloria Anzaldúa and Ana Castillo). Norma Alarcon traces the complex ways in which Malintzin has been reinterpreted: "Because Malintzin's neosymbolic existence in the masculine imagination has affected the actual experience of so many Mexicanas and Chicanas, it became necessary for 'her daughters' to revise her scanty biography. Through revisions, many undertaken in isolation, contemporary Chicana writers have helped to lay bare Malintzin's double etymology which until recently appeared illusory and hallucinative: one privileges the sociosymbolic possibilities for signification; the second, the existential and historical implications." ("Traddutora, Traditora: A Paradigmatic Figure of Chicana Feminism," *Cultural Critique*, 13, Fall 1989, 83)

[2]*Borderlands/La Frontera* was written just prior to the historical moment when "queer" notions came to have broad academic and political currency, and as such Anzaldúa makes use of this word loosely as signifier of her culturally based gender non-conformity and sexual defiance. "Queer" marks a located yet expansive term

in Anzaldúa' text which metonymically associates many instances of resistance to binary logics rather than pinpointing a discrete identity or collective movement. Anzalúda's writes about her ambivalence toward queer theory in :"Queer is used as a false unifying umbrella which all 'queers' of all races, ethnicities and classes are shoved under. At times we need this umbrella to solidify our ranks against outsiders. But even when we seek shelter under it we must not forget that it homogenizes, erases our differences" ["To(o) Queer the Writer—Loca, escritora y chicana,"*Inversions: Writings by Dykes, Queers and Lesbians,* ed. Betsy Warland, (Vancouver: Press Gang Publishers, 1991, 250]. Even though both Anzaldúa and Moraga use the word "queer" throughout their writings, they contest its universalizing ahistorical tendencies, adopting it with critical intentions, denouncing queer theoretical tendencies toward abstraction from working class and colonial histories.

[3]Moraga italicizes her journal entries and my quotations of them will also be italicized.

Works Cited

Anzaldúa, Gloria. *Borderlands/La Frontera The New Mestiza.* San Francisco: Aunt Lute, 1987.

Moraga, Cherríe. *Waiting in the Wings: Portrait of a Queer Motherhood.* New York: Firebrand, 1997.

15
Going Down for the Third Time

S. ALEASE FERGUSON AND TONI C. KING

I'm not the average girl in your video…
My mama said a lady ain't what she wears, but what she knows
But, I've drawn a conclusion, it's all an illusion, confusions the name of
the game
A misconception, a vast deception
Something's gotta change.[1]

—India Arie, 2001

Battling the Deep

The war between the generations is by no means new. Across the ages elders have always wondered just why it is that youth rebel. "Why can't young people behave and make a smooth transition into adulthood?" we ask. Why can't they settle down and stay rooted to their cultural core? Wouldn't it be easier for them to glide into maturity by profiting from our mistakes and benefiting from our hard won victories? Especially those victories that brought social advancements, open doors, and opportunities for generations once denied entrance? These are inter-generational questions of the ages. However, as evolution would have it, young people do mature; they do find their way to adulthood and often do ultimately capitulate to mainstream social values. We have seen this time and again. From the bobbie-soxers, to Beatlemania, to flower power—yesterday's teen rebel becomes tomorrow's productive citizen. After lamenting the flagrant rebellion of their offspring, most parents have had the satisfaction of seeing their sons and daughters recover and eventually claim their adult status in the world.

At this juncture of the twenty-first century, however, we see a major change. At this time, at least for African American children, the cycles of young adult rebellion followed by resuming adult roles, sensibilities, and lifestyles has been ruptured. Today some of our youth, born and bred in what scholars refer to as the Hip-Hop culture, have come of age and are lost to us. And this generation, embedded in Hip-Hop values, has now begun its own parenting cycle, with some of their children already lost or in grave danger of being lost to us as well. In reading the works of scholars, educators, and leaders within the Black community who critique the social effects of Hip Hop, such as Johnnetta Betsch Cole, Beverly Guy-Sheftall, Michael Eric Dyson, and Bakari Kitwana, we have learned the context and history of Hip Hop. Ironically, the origins of Hip Hop were admirable—in that this form of cultural expression served as a voice for the marginalized. As such it passionately expressed the lived experience of youth growing up in a turbulent and oppressive world. Hip Hop, in both form and function, mixed entertainment with a radical critique by the young regarding the increasingly virulent and inescapable effects of institutionalized oppression. And for the Hip Hop cultural expressions that have remained true to this original spirit, the contribution of this form of cultural expression continues to provide a much needed source of socio-political resistance to the hegemonic global machinery.

Historically, Hip-Hop music came into existence in the United States during the mid 1970s and became a large part of modern popular culture in the 1980s. By definition, Hip Hop is dynamic and ever changing in its uses by youth in the expression of their lives. Thus it has transcended the music that gave birth to it and is now a global cultural movement inspired by the evolving cultural expressions of inner city African American youth. It cannot be glossed over that African American youth, in their struggle to be heard, taught a new form of self and cultural expression to the world. The resulting art forms, such as break dancing and its derivatives, urban-inspired art, graffiti, and slang, have now been exported due to intercultural contact and the worldwide access we have to each other because of technology (e.g. television, the internet).

In the 1990s, a variant of Hip Hop evolved. Or perhaps we should say that, as with any cultural artifact that has widespread appeal, a variant of Hip Hop was commodified and made available on a mass marketing scale. This form emphasized all things "gangsta"—that is, it was accompanied by values that glamorized the gangsta' or thug life style. With its emphasis on commercialization, this lifestyle manifested in the music, fashions, personas, language and mindsets of the youth who identified with it. Most egregious and harmful to youth was the wholesale and uncritical introjection of hegemony's emphasis on gross materialism—in which people are expendable commodities equated solely with the materialism they can tout—reflected in the slang terminology of "bling bling."

The lyrics of this form of Hip Hop (which we will, from this point on, refer to as Gangsta' Rap Hip Hop) have created major controversy between the status quo and stable adult communities across race because the lyrics are perceived as promoting violence, terrorism, promiscuity, and misogyny. Whether causality between such lyrics and actual violence can be determined, cultural scholars who explore the implications of Gangsta' Rap Hip Hop attest to its valorization of a ruthless, anti-social, thug-life mentality, a rebellious relationship to society associated with living outside of the law, feeling entitled to doing whatever one can do to serve one's own ends, loyalty only to one's peers, and objectification of women, rivals, gays, or those who "cross" them. In this essay, it is the Gangsta' code of conduct that we address as being detrimental to youth, and particularly insidious in its acculturation of women and young mothers socialized in its grasp.

Paradoxically, the institutionalization of Hip Hop by the industries positioned to capitalize from its commercialization is diametrically opposed to the original, grassroots voice that is the foundation for Hip Hop cultural expression. We cannot emphasize enough the divergence of these two forms.[2] One form represents Hip Hop as cultural expression—a necessary voice of dissent, critique, self-determination, and unrest. The other form represents Hip Hop commodified as Gangsta' Rap and its accompanying set of values. Because our own critique is one among many, we want to be clear that we are speaking out about the cultural package that accompanies Gangsta' Rap Hip Hop. We see the cultural milieu and its values as problematic in the disproportionate impact that it has on some of the current generation—particularly girls. As therapists, we encounter those most wounded by this cultural milieu, those most unlikely to critically assess its messages.

Of course, the story of Hip Hop as a music and performance genre is itself dialectical, multi-layered, and divested with the multiple and sometimes conflicted or contradictory self expressions of its authors. Nowhere is this more true than with the women and girls who themselves engage in this form of cultural production. Scholars work to refract the kaleidoscopic facets of their voices. Some Black female MCs speak to the strengths of women of African descent, others signify motherline models and legends, some define and redefine girl to women identities, creating discourses that range from queens and divas to fly girls, sistas with attitudes, and lesbians (see Keyes).[3] Others fashion Black feminist messages of resistance and revolution against "isms" that affect women at the intersections of race, class, gender, and sexualities (see Morgan "Hip Hop Women Shredding the Veil").[4]

No template is or could be exhaustive of the evolving voices of Black female MCs as they do the work of producing culture on their own terms. As Hip-Hop feminist scholars continue to speak the realities of these socio-cultural trends, we become increasingly aware of the Black feminist/womanist girls and women negotiating identities, intimacy, sexual expression, and the politics of relaying their lived experience in this artistic genre. Hip Hop as artistic expression, and in the context of its grassroots character, is used in empowering ways by the women and girls who negotiate new spaces of testifying to their lived experience while contesting oppressive representations. We view with awe the multi-crafting of their spoken word on terms of their own making.

Our concerns remain conscious of the multi-plex sociocultural theatre in which current generations ply their craft. In contrast to this rich historical tradition of invoking radical voices of resistance, testimony, and triumph over dominant representations, we are gravely concerned with the shadow side of the Hip-Hop industry as produced, allowed, commercialized, and targeted to our youth. We are concerned with the inculcation of all things Gangsta' into everyday culture and the way that Gangsta' Rap Hip Hop culture functions to generate what scholar-theologian Emilie Townes calls the cultural production of evil (see Townes). We are solely concerned here with the effects of Gangsta' Rap Hip Hop on those who have been so adversely affected by modern day racism, sexism, classism, ableism, and heterosexism that they approach current cultural productions with uncritical introjection.

As Black feminist social scientists and clinicians, our work lies in clinically diagnosing the wounding within Black communities and the social trends and patterns that produce the likelihood of psychological distress. We are concerned with the ways in which institutionalized oppression functions to create structural and cultural arrangements that overwhelm healthy cognitive functioning. We see a morphing of colonization in the twenty-first century to re-inscribe the problem of the color line in the minds of our youth—by their very access to dominant ideologies of hegemony. We see these ideologies hidden (albeit in plain view) within the Trojan horse of Hip Hop Gangsta' Rap culture and other forms of commercialized racism, sexism and classism.

Pre-emininent scholar A. Leon Higginbotham, whose work bridges the twentieth and twenty-first centuries, frames Ten Precepts of American Slavery Jurisprudence. This framework conceptualizes the status of African Americans as: 1) inferior beings incapable of guiding their own destinies; 2) property or commodities that can be used as tools of manipulation in the commercial realm; 3) subjects that are powerless in the face of legal, social and market forces; 4) a group that can be divided in class action and unity on the basis of social positioning linked to the degrees of racial purity; 5) persons subject to manumission of Free Blacks; 6) a group to be disabled through the dismantling of the black family; 7) a group slated for denied access to educational and cultural knowledge critical to empowerment, social mobility, and integration into the mainstream society; 8) a group against whom religion is used as an opiate, or means of social control, to divide the group or prohibit realization of its aims; 9) a group where liberty and resistance are construed as destructive to the legal precepts originally established to control and delimit their particular freedoms; and 10) a group who must by any means possible be contained and subjected to a position of inferiority and social controls (see Higginbotham).

We read the deluge of Gangsta' Rap Hip Hop cultural production that is mass produced through the profit-making corporate complex as one of the most effective methods of re-inscribing Higginbotham's Ten Precepts of Slavery Jurisprudence in twenty-first century time. We view the Gangsta' Rap Hip Hop cultural stream that we are discussing as one very effective vehicle in the matrix of racism, classism, sexism, ableism, and heterosexism. Our voices seek to name this dynamic and to join those Black feminists throughout history, also known as "race women," who focused on the nexus of race, class, and gender in their work. We name this dynamic for those who are most vulnerable in our community, particularly those girls and young women who have not had adequate relational, social, communal, and structural factors in their lives to inoculate them against these institutionalized forces. In such cases, this artistic genre is mass marketed as an opiate of the masses. It requires substituting materialism for meaningful relations, reflection, and the struggle to resist the objectifications of oppression.

We speak from the place of struggle with girls who have succumbed on their journey to adulthood to the overwhelming presence of cultural factors arranged toward their demise.

Ostensibly, the values of the Gangsta' Rap Hip Hop cultural framework disparage the unity of Black families, and the primary function of the male and female partnership and co-parenting functions, as well as the range of co-female support and possibilities. The hegemonic dictates undergirding the proliferation of Gangsta' Rap Hip Hop cultural values simultaneously undermine co-female (eg. lesbian or bisexual) partnerships that might offer support structures for young women who have become mothers. The ability of "women who love other women sexually or non-sexually" (see Walker) might lend itself to woman-to-woman partnerships for the effective parenting of children. Yet Gangsta' Rap Hip Hop culture, like the patriarchal society it serves, prescribes strict adherence to heterosexual relations.

The impact of induction into Gangsta' Rap Hip Hop culture is tantamount to what Jungian psychologist and story teller Clarissa Pinkola Estés calls poison bait and leg iron traps. In her widely acclaimed *Women Who Run With the Wolves*, Clarissa Pinkola Estés uses these terms to refer to how trickery, guile, and seductive influences can derail a woman's instinctual capacity and self knowledge about what is safe, healing, and whole. Gangsta' Rap Hip Hop uses as one of its cornerstones a sexualized objectification of women in which they become another form of material goods to be acquired and used by men. In our discussion, we take particular issue with this desecration of the feminine. Yet the glamorization of women as worthy only to the extent to which they are desirable objects sends the message to girls that this is a valuable and esteemed path. Now the poison bait is set—and once these values are internalized, the leg iron traps have closed on their minds and spirits.

We are two mid-twentieth century born African American Womanist scholars and Allomothers who, in the spirit of voices from the margins, modeled by the original Hip-Hop artists—wish to speak our own radical critique. The designation "*allo*" comes from the Greek for "other than" and refers to any other care giver, male or female, who gives assistance to a mother in provisioning for a child.[5] As Allomothers, we protest the co-optation of Hip Hop into Gangsta' Rap Hip Hop. We feel as if we are watching the multi-generational effects of the Hip-Hop culture—which has become more intensely "gangsta" in form and consequences—push our children out to sea, while we stand helplessly on shore. As second-wave feminists who have been clinical practitioners with a focus on Black girls and women, we are particularly alarmed for this group. Since the early 1970s, this musical and lifestyle idiom has had a scarring effect on the identities of African American youth with a resounding traumatic force on Black girls and women. This is so traumatic that we would even say that Gangsta' Rap Hip Hop arrests the development of Black girls and ruptures their passage to full womanhood. Sadly, it continues to capture the hearts and minds of pre-teens and teens with ever increasing intensity. Unlike a fad, however, it shows few signs of abating, and instead is spilling over into the lifestyles of parenting adults and teens.

Needless to say, innocent children pay the ultimate price when parented by those whose mature development has been stifled.

Seeing these cycles unfold with ever increasing voracity, we have been questioning for some time now why it is that African American pregnant teens and nascent mothers subscribe to Hip Hop's Gangsta' Rap culture. Why do so many young mothers reject the gains of the Civil Rights era and the second-wave feminist progress that it ushered in? And yet we understand from those who have studied the evolution of feminism that the third wave has been characterized by generations invested in individualism, and wedded to technology as a means of expression. In addition to their technical savvy, these contemporary feminists are often insistent upon expressing sexualities as a significant demonstration of their agency and self-assertion. Astrid Henry's essay in Jo Reger's book *Different Wavelengths* describes third wavers as defining themselves in contrast to second wave politics. They are in disagreement with their mothers, yet they are ambivalent about the perceived clarity of "our" politics and the potential for solidarity among us. They were, by words of their own choosing, daughters critiquing us, rather than sisters critiquing how we might fashion a movement with each other.

Sadly, we see the deepest tensions, ruptures of trust, and ambivalences among daughters of the Gangsta' Rap Hip Hop generation. While all girls need to differentiate from the motherline by choosing which of its values to keep and how, the daughters of Gangsta' Rap rashly sever connection to motherline values altogether. This rupture leads them to an individualism that seeks expression in the act of motherhood. Yet it is a motherhood eerily devoid of the fullness of Black maternal capacities and wisdom. Why such a recalcitrant break with the African American mother-care ethic? When they discover themselves frustrated by a lifestyle that is inevitably disappointing for so many and is unable to deliver on its material or social promises—why do they refuse to turn to the Allomothering supports that we extend with aching arms outstretched?

As Black feminists and Womanists of the second wave, we see with increasing alarm and shame what has happened on our watch. To our lament, it seems that the Gangsta' Rap Hip Hop culture has colored this group's mothering ethic in ways that are antithetical to communal progress and healthy child rearing. At its most extreme, when Gangsta' Rap Hip Hop standards supplant all else, we see an aberrant form of mothering characterized by distance, harshness, and mother convenience over the needs of the child. The culture of Gangsta' Rap Hip Hop now socializes many of our youth. It is no longer the whole village raising the child, but the Gangsta' Rap Hip Hop wire-mesh monkey.[6] Furthermore, transfixed to larger-than-life portrayals of Gangsta' Rap Hip Hop royalty, large numbers of our girls aspire to its lewd audacity. Though in our experience the average viewers are under-educated, under-skilled, and impoverished, they fantasize that they too can attain all of the symbols and trophies of super bling-bling, limitless collections of ghetto-fab wear, Bentleys, mansions, and swimming pools. Unfortunately, in the Gangsta' life fantasy they themselves are among the tantalizing objects, occasionally chosen to gain the temporary and fleeting attentions of barely interested men. They are thus lured into an abyss of self abnegation and social, sexual, and economic or material exploitation.

Interestingly, the emergence of Hip Hop's co-optation into Gangsta' Rap coincides with the inventions of the McDonald's Happy Meal, 24-7 access to Black Entertainment Television music videos and the poor person's luxury drug, crack cocaine.[7] In addition to these societal changes, structural factors and institutionalized oppression of the 1980s and 1990s extended and reinforced its stronghold on those who were already most vulnerable. In Black inner city communities, these decades saw widespread and unchecked drug sale, inadequate gun control, and an overabundance of alcohol distributors. These same communities saw the proliferation of predatory financial institutions (e.g. subprime lending and home finance), the disappearance of jobs, and indeed, an entire manufacturing sector. With these changes came the reduction and elimination of employment for unskilled laborers due to technological advancements. Communities denuded of their stable working class saw Black middle-class and white flight, the re-segregation, under-funding and subsequent deterioration of public schools in inner city and/or poor communities, and many other converging factors.

In spite of the dogged strengths, resilience, talents, and resourcefulness of those who remained and who cared (see Wilson), communities could not effectively combat the simultaneity and intensity of these ravaging and multiplicative social ills. The vulnerability of generations growing up in these urban "war zones" found them creating their own mechanisms of power and protection in the form of gangs. A rising crime rate in contexts so ripe for it brought about rates of incarceration heretofore unseen—with Black women becoming the most recent population to be caught in this expanding net. Their crimes often reflect their falling prey to the values of Gangsta' Rap Hip Hop—accomplices to drug sales, gang related crime, stealing, conning and fast money schemes, and violence stemming from the abusive relationships that are further fueled by a culture of misogyny (see Girshick).

As Gangsta' Rap Hip Hop culture leveraged its stronghold alongside these structural conditions, another kind of global shift was taking place. The age range of adolescence lengthened in developed countries, particularly among the more affluent. Adolescence began to span the ages of twelve to thirty rather than twelve to nineteen. Both developmental psychologists and economists noted that the Western World's economies were no longer growing at a rate that would support early self-sufficiency. The old lock step sequence of graduating from high school, moving out on one's own, marrying, and parenting no longer occurred in a predictable sequence. Today, childbirth commonly occurs before high school graduation or long-term partnership. Many scholarly sources and government statistics point to the rise in single-mother child births, in child births for girls in the United States under 18 years of age (see Casper and Bianchi).[8] Moreover, many girls of the Gangsta' Rap Hip Hop generation even see child-bearing as a desirable way (albeit distorted in modern times) to mark maturity by announcing their readiness to participate in the world of consumerism for themselves and their child/ren. At the same time, they reject the rules of exchanging labor for consumer privileges, or sacrifice for adulthood gains. Thus our concern as Allomothers focuses on the way that all of these structural inequalities have triggered a downward spiral in Black mother care. Under these standards of quick-easy-self indulgent-outward appearance-external reference-about-who-I-am, motherhood becomes synonymous with non-contact and diminished family connections.

Overall, the inculcation of Gangsta' Rap Hip Hop in place of an African American communal lifestyle marks the demise of the Black woman and Black mother culture. What was once thought to be a generational interlude is now an inter-generational pox scarring future generations of Black children. This removal of high-grade physical and emotional sustenance from Black children has created emotionally stultified and socially disconnected individuals. This generation's disassociation from the cult of Black mother care has caused the so called "old school mothers" or "mothers of the old guard" to stand up in defense of children first. At the same time, they steadily battle against the waves to rescue the Gangsta' Rap Hip Hop mothers from the tide quickly carrying them away in a wash of identity and role confusion. Misconceptions about the fulfillment of their biological urges, a search for quick wealth and fame, and few cares about the future threaten to pull them under. But the undertow is what we fear most. For in the undertow innocent children are pulled in along with the compromised grandparent corps who must come to their aid.

Clearly not all girls of the Hip-Hop generation are guilty of bad parenting. Many girls and women of the Hip-Hop generation have forged mothering methods and models that raised healthy and emotionally whole child/ren. We applaud them without romanticization. We pay tribute, and remain available in the village of communal care for them and their offspring.

Moreover, it would be an oversimplification to say that all Gangsta' Rap Hip Hop identified mothers are guilty of bad parenting. Some, though far fewer in our view, have the capacity, skills, and social support to bring many strengths and viable love and care to their children in spite of Gangsta' Rap Hip Hop's potent influence. To be sure, the complicated interaction between the values of Gangsta' Rap Hip Hop and the mother's psyche will have consequences for the mother and child/ren. On the other hand, we have to remember that some will live in a context that buffers their wholesale absorption, and immersion. In our society—known to scapegoat and denigrate the "welfare mother" without remorse, particularly when she is also Black—it is imperative to keep in mind the complexity of the issues we address. It is important that our critique remain a humanizing dialogue. To do this it is necessary to speak boldly to the issues as we see them, while remaining mindful of those for whom the shoe does not fit. We would be gravely remiss if we did not attest to the many competent, compassionate, and wise young mothers who have survived against all odds. Many of the young mothers living amidst the Gangsta' Rap Hip Hop cultural milieu have worked diligently to recover from the racism, classism, and sexism in our society. These young women and young mothers have struggled valiantly to learn from the painful life experiences our society produces in their lives. They have learned to see the poison bait and leg iron traps of hegemony, and have taken detours.

In contrast—though not surprisingly, given the social and structural barriers to mental, emotional, and physical well-being that we discussed earlier—many young mothers subjected to the "leg iron traps" of Gangsta' Rap Hip Hop have veered left of center in terms of socially accepted standards of mothering. It is to, and for, the mothers that have fallen prey that we direct our discussion. For these mothers, their child-unfriendly approach to mothering has brought them into the purview of both caring family elders, and the child welfare system. In Gangsta' Rap Hip Hop land, mothers do not respect parental input on time-tested methods of pre- and post-natal care, well child care, child development, nutritional consistency, and the regularity of daily life that helps to cement a feeling of security. In passing on what they know, these mothers indoctrinate their children into de-structured and chaotic lifestyles, exposing them to content and interactions far better suited to adults, as well as exposing them to drugs, violence, rage, and vulgarity. Structurally, this radical departure from the African American "cult of black mothering" is making for a more rigid class divide and the disintegration of the African American family.

Politically, there is a danger in speaking about this segment of the population of young mothers and critiquing them. In her book entitled *Don't Call Us Out of Name*, Lisa Dodson poignantly depicts the view society holds of poor single mothers. Virulent and pernicious stereotypes construct them as bad, ignorant, lazy, immoral, a drain on the economic health of the country, and as a severely eroding factor within a civilized and progressive society. Ange-Marie Hancock refers to these negative attitudes and the accompanying policies that have such dire consequences on their lives as "the politics of disgust." The relationship between stereotypes and policies that do not advance the interests of Black single mothers is not new. During the 1960s the "matriarch" stereotype blamed African American women heads of households for the ills of the Black community because they were not in the normalized submissive family role.[9] This history casts a heavy shadow over us as we speak. Yet, we believe it is possible to avoid colluding in the othering of this segment of the young single mothers and their children in need of our care. To remain silent risks a greater danger—which is to lose the expectation that our daughters have the capacity for growth, restoration, and a depth of humanity for the task of mothering. Our silence would be the ultimate dehumanization of seeing these girls as a lost cause. And so we "speak anyhow." We speak to create a third space beyond the dichotomy of blaming the "victim" or virulently stereotyping them. In this third space, our feminist/womanist ethic demands that we break silences, create humanizing dialogue, and step boldly into the fray. We challenge any reader to withstand misusing our critique. Rather than calling our daughters "out their names,"[10] we call out and name the iron leg traps of hegemony in the form of Gangsta' Rap Hip Hop. Our daughters sink under the weight of these leg irons. We remind the community of Allomothers, in this case, all of us—of an old African adage that says: "When one of us is not well, none of us are well."

We needed to painstakingly create common historical and contextual understandings so that there is safe socio-political space from which to speak, critique, and begin our second wave to third wave mother/daughter work. Historically, strong Black feminine ideals have allowed African American women to nurture and support the development of Black children in even the direst of circumstances. Hill Collins has aptly theorized the ethic of care and ethic of personal accountability at the core of Black women's ethos of community. Katie Cannon, Delores Williams, Alice Walker, Audre Lorde, and many others cut to the core of this philosophy. They speak to its intentionality for creating conditions under which women can survive and thrive in spite of social, psychological, political, and economic oppression. They understand that whole and empowered women see to the wholeness of children, of men, of communities, and of nations. Foundational to this ethic of care is the shared maternal function that Black women have brought to bear in every major organizational space they have created or been permitted to enter—education, nursing, social work, child care, churches, and mosques, to name a few. Yet the Gangsta' Rap Hip Hop generations spurn this Womanist ethic and its values, and defy the motherline tutelage that serves as the primary means and rite of passage to mature womanhood and productive mothering.

Currently this sharp divergence from core cultural and Womanist values has led to this group's disproportional representation in the child welfare system. Today, these maternal and child separations are exclusively linked to child abuse and neglect as associated with poverty, drug addiction, periodic and sustained incarceration, domestic violence, social isolation, and disassociation from family networks. These situations almost always result in the loss of custodial parenting rights, and child placement in foster care, orphanages, kinship care placements, and the displacement and aging out of adolescent youths from the system. When the extended family steps in to care for the child/ren, many grandmothers are forced to become full-time caregivers who lose pace with the developmental staging of their own lives. In the intensified tensions between old school-new school mothers, motherlines to daughters are pulled taut and sometimes severed.

Danielle's story gives perspective to the vast heritage of Black mother culture as well as to the staggering devastation of the Gangsta' Rap Hip Hop culture's invasion into Black family life. Yet her story also points to the possibilities of recovery, the ability to regain capacities for self reflection, and for choosing values outside the realm of the "gangsta" life style. In her case these reflections span a decade:

> It took me losing my kids to understand what mothering is and is not. After the fact, I learned that there is a whole body of Black mothering knowledge that I knew nothing about. It's strange, but today I am a day care teacher. So I have had to read and get training in child development and mother wit. The SCAREB Program[11] assigned me a personal mother mentor; she took me way back and reminded me of myself and my regal heritage as a Black

Queen. And now I have a pretty good sense of the kind of consistency kids need to grow up healthy and stay on the right track. In my wild days and Hip Hop kinda' life style I thought I knew it all. As soon as I was sixteen I went from being a mama's girl to somebody my own family didn't even recognize. All my life before that I'd gotten' good grades, went to church with my family, I was a part of Lady C's Drill team and played basketball. Even though my mom worked we were always supervised by Gram and my Aunties. Ever since I could remember my mom drilled it into me that I was going to college and I could become whatever I wanted to be. Mama's dream really was my dream but I got all turned out on the music, the men, drugs, and a total disrespect of my feminine self.

When I think back on how my life got out of control, plain and simple it was hormones, sex. I was boy crazy and I wanted romance, a hot sizzling sexuality. I really thought that having sex made me a woman. So I started sneaking out at night, going to clubs, getting involved with my boyfriend and his crew in drive-bys. I changed my look, moved out and got pregnant. I smoked pot, blunts, took Ecstasy and all kinds of stuff as a part of my clubbin' days. By the time I was nineteen I had three kids. My first was born healthy and normal but the hospital busted me the second time. I had a positive tox screen and so the County set the wheels in motion to remove my daughter and the baby I was carrying. My mother stepped forth as their caregiver. And I just hit the streets and went wild. I did not want to admit to myself or anybody else that I was a terrible parent. There were some days when I just let my daughter cry, I was too lazy to feed her or change her. Sometimes I would leave her over at a friend's house for a day or two and just disappear. I'd let the wash pile up and I'd just buy us new stuff. But I'd show up for Sunday dinners every now and then and my baby and I would be lookin' good in our brand spankin' new duds. One time when my daughter was nine months old, I left my daughter with my mother for a couple of days. When I came back she did not even respond to me. Everyone was sitting around the table and Gram said, "Honey it's a bad sign. What little bitty baby doesn't respond to its own mother?" I'll never forget the sting of it, but it still did not stop me from being irresponsible.

All I can say now is Mama, Gram and Aunty, I'm sorry. And I am sorry for my kids too. They have never seen me function as a mother. Even worse is what I have put my mom through. She is 56 and still working hard on her job and she has raised my kids well with practically no help from me at all. What I did is not what a decent and responsible mother does.

In Danielle's story, time, personal growth, and education opened her field of vision, but at a horrible cost. The tragedies of a mother separated from her children, bonds broken and those never set, and a grandmother raising her grandchild at a latter stage of her life are legion. Her story and others like hers are a call to mothers and Allomothers to bring their supports to bear post haste.

Diving Deep and Surfacing

...where was I when the girls began to change like this? Was it grad school, my early career years when I was working myself to the bone, my early marriage years when I was helping put my husband through school? I'm looking in the face of girls who seem to hate me just for having the audacity to look at them and their babies ... and for wondering how they are. I mean wondering how are they REALLY? (African American woman, higher education administrator)

Clearly, we have now sounded the alarm and issued the clarion call. There are many of our generation pointing to the ills of Gangsta' Rap Hip Hop—such as bell hooks, Gwendolyn Pough, and Michelle Wallace. As Womanist scholars, we join this dialogue and its critique. We see a part of our Allomother dialogue among the village wise women to include diving deep and surfacing with clarity about the tides that carried our daughters so far, so fast. So hear this. While we address the problem in tough love fashion, without mincing our words, in no way do we blame the pregnant and nascent Gangsta' Rap culture Hip-Hop mothers for their circumstances. We no more blame these girls often raised by girls themselves, than we would blame a woman for being raped, or for the subsequent meta-rape by institutions of law enforcement. While we do, as humanists and feminists, hold individual women accountable for their choices, we submit to a compassionate view of their mistakes in choice making. After all, they are the targets of a well orchestrated plan to dismantle the Black family structures. After all, the dire consequences of their poor choices in contemporary times puts them out to sea before they have matured enough to recognize the impossibility of getting back to shore without a community of care and in spite of the diminished resources available in their communities.

Beyond the anger induced by Gangsta' Rap Hip Hop itself, this societal rejection and communal abandonment is a part of their rage. In Layli Phillips' *Womanist Reader,* she includes Womanist interpretations by authors in the various fields of Womanist praxis, such as psychology, social work, nursing, and education. Kim Marie Vaz writes about the psychological injury affecting Blacks in contemporary times. She speaks particularly to the narcissistic rage that is a product of psychic assault. Be it invalidation, instability of care and nurture, disconfirmation of agency and dignity, the result can be fragility of the emerging self accompanied by the need to see one's self in grandiose terms. Similarly, there is a rage at those who are perceived to disconfirm this image of the self as perfect. Sadly, Gangsta' Rap Hip Hop deluges this generation with images of what constitutes perfection.

At another level, however, their rage is not completely irrational. At some level, they know that the *whole* village that raises a child in a secure network of love is being/has been disassembled for all intents and purposes in their lives. Their rage is all the more dangerous because it lives beneath their ability to articulate it. In essence, they have been set afloat on the capitalist Titanic of Gangsta' Rap

Hip Hop's consumerism. They have been commodified, this time not as chattel slaves, but as chattel consumers. Enslaved not to King Cotton, but to King Commerce.

If we are to successfully battle the waves, we need to understand the current. We need to dive deep and surface with a critical consciousness about our present circumstances. We need to scrutinize how we as Allomothers were distracted and duped by the heady progress of second wave advances. Surely one can not blame us for rushing headlong through doors newly opened for women, ignoring the implied emphasis on *white*. Certainly, we should be lauded for slipping through the revolving doors of progress using sheer wit, gumption—the self-same "audaciousness and willful behavior" that made us "walk to Canada."[12] Clearly, we have gone down in history as a generation of pioneers, onlys, and firsts, albeit also as tokens and twofers[13] depending on who you asked. Overall, as second-wave feminists, Civil Rights beneficiaries, and post affirmative action girls and women, we thrived on the opportunities available to us, even as we paid the price in our marriages, families, and long-term intimate relationships.

With our children in particular, we found ourselves struggling with new tensions. At that time we ran head first into questions of: How do we allow our children to benefit from new levels of access and exposure to the dominant culture, while keeping them rooted in core cultural values? How do we support our children in reaping the benefits of immersion in white schools, neighborhoods, social clubs, and activities, while not letting them succumb to the habits, norms, and mores of white society that would be annihilative to their survival? And, in retrospect, did we really know which aspects of integration were deceptive decoys luring them from the cultural shores that could anchor them?

Here is where we, as second-wave Black feminists, lost clarity and with it valuable time. Yes. We may have been able to do direct battle with the children in our direct care. And yes—in many cases we figured out errors as we went, sometimes giving too much one way or too much another. Nevertheless, we went toe-to-toe with our own kids until, if we were fortunate, they came round. Whether it was the negative effects of TV, video games, Gangsta' Rap Hip Hop music, adult disrespect and back-talk, drug culture, addiction to materialism, the lure of gangs or a gang mentality for identity and belonging, participation in the peripheral economies of drug selling, involvement in quick scams for easy money, extreme needs for external validation versus the hard work of internalizing one's worth … we worked to find out where they hurt. When able, we paid the literal price for private boarding schools, extra tutoring, corrective and rehabilitative camps or counseling, frequent or extended travel down south, travel abroad for purposes of service learning or for capping their sense of entitlement by seeing how other folks live, or still other cleverly devised measures as needed. Not always, but often, we reclaimed our kids, and sometimes those of extended family members, and even a few kids in our communities or churches, social agencies or programs. Sadly, this was not enough. Our immersion in new third wave mothering challenges at home, and with others we had immediate and ongoing access to, made us miss the boat in gearing up for third-wave challenges beyond our immediate sphere. The sheer numbers of adolescent and teen mothers, who were not under our direct purview, or within reach of our communal involvements, went unattended. These were the girls floating and adrift. With each generation of mothers, a rising tide of babies having babies left us looking out to sea at a wall of water crashing down around them.

We have paid a dreadful price for our second-wave liberation. And that price was in not seeing the requisite needs for third wave Allomothering models in our lives, communities, and nationally that would meet the new currents of third-wave girls. On the one hand, equal access has afforded scores of African Americans opportunities to make tremendous contributions to the society. On the other, it has meant alienation from ourselves and our people. Now some forty years after Civil Rights we lament the diminished state of our children and families. Diving deep and surfacing is the first step we take in the reclaiming of our ancestral role as village mothers. While we never left the role, we failed to adapt it to the escalation of racism, classism, and sexism fueled by global capitalism. The clarion call is not just about our prodigal daughters. It is a call to examine how the second wave positioned us in colonized space, lured us from shore, distracted our vigilance, making insatiable demands on our time and energies with its shiny bright ideals of equality, educational and occupational attainment, and upward mobility.

Crafting Lifeboats, Building Ships: A Third Wave Allomothering Agenda in Progress

> ...even though I'm retired, I still have permission to run my girls' group. I know my group! If I let them go, I don't think they'll let anyone else in for a very long time. Maybe never. I really wish there was someone else who could start another one with some of these other girls coming along. (retired public school administrator, facilitator of a high school teen and teen mother program)

Adolescent Black girls of the last two decades may see us second wavers as disingenuous. Bogus. Overall, they feel that the gains from the second wave and Civil Rights robbed them of their mothers and Allomothers. Many feel that their mothers have worked too hard, traveled too much, and spent too little time with family; gotten passed over at work despite their exemplary efforts; and still struggle to make ends meet. In short, their mothers lived lifestyles that they did not find enviable or even balanced. At one level, girls of the Gangsta' Rap Hip Hop generation have read the glyphs of racism and sexism incredibly well. They believe that it is a fallacy to buy into women's lib and civil rights because these freedoms are not totally real. If one wants something, be it the power of the presidency, wealth or fame, one must boldly take it or scornfully reject it. For it will not be fairly offered based on a just meritocracy.

The Gangsta' Rap Hip Hop mother's entry into the counter culture is an attack on the ethic of Black mother care and its demand for responsibility, struggle, and putting up with marginality. Their attack rejects the nurture that was too little too late in terms of saving them from a Gangsta' Rap Hip Hop culture that is now their addiction. The culture of Gangsta' Rap Hip Hop is their referent point for self worth. At its worst, their internalization of other referents was missed in the developmental process. So their own Gangsta' Rap Hip Hop mothering is their expression of rage, abandonment, and internalized oppression. Once ensnared in its web, it is the Gangsta' Rap Hip Hop way to go for broke—to hurl oneself into the mad dash for rewards and to wildly confront any obstacles to those rewards. There is no turning back until the madness has fully taken hold and created casualties.

Recognizing the tide, we have begun to incorporate more and more of the communal Allomothering strategy into our works with African American girls, pregnant teens, nascent mothers, and other women at the margins. Since the mid 1990s, we have seen many of their life situations and challenges appear to be linked to the level of under-mothering they received and to the internalized oppression from their biological mothers. Now in this second millennium, more and more of our Allomothering talent is being drawn upon in both our public and private spheres. Today, the call is to provide therapeutic Allomothering for pregnant teen girls and the nascent mothers of the Gangsta' Rap Hip Hop generation.

> *I had known this girl since childhood when she would sneak out of the house at 14 to date older men. She married and had three kids in quick succession. The oldest, at four, always had her fists balled up in anger, the middle one was afraid of her own shadow, the baby was listless. I called social services who began to investigate. I had to do something. I know traumatized children when I see them.* (retired teacher and church worker)

Given that we see this group going down for the third time, we know that their fighting our attempts at rescue is the consequence of their desperation, and dare we say their desire to live. So our first point of rescue is to provide the buoy that will hold them afloat, be it the basics of survival and safety for them and their child/ren or tough love tactics geared to engage and support the mothers' recovery. We will be called upon to intervene in severe cases of neglect, abuse or endangerment of self and child. Whether through interpersonal connections or organizational affiliations, we will have to step up to the inadequacies of current day social services. Like the Black women's clubs of the nineteenth and twentieth centuries, who filled roles missing in society to feed, clothe, shelter, or establish settlement houses, we will have to set collective agendas trained on current millennial needs.

Teen and out-of-wedlock pregnancies are by no means new phenomena. Historically, African American children born to teens and unmarried young adult parents have been reared by their mothers and with the ongoing support of extended kin.

However, in this Gangsta' Rap Hip Hop generation, the emergence of a breed of African American pregnant teen girls and young mothers losing children to the child welfare systems reflects a major breakdown in the cooperative structure of the African American family. Previously larger numbers of African American family systems have been able to negotiate the entry of new life, teach and model parenting, provide living space and supplemental child care, and actuate a plan for the mothers' continuation of her educational and career training plans. Without the infrastructure of the past, and with awareness of the assaults on our most vulnerable, we will need to quickly assess situations of mother-child break down, isolation, hysteria, and anomie—for its consequences on mother-child health and safety. Rather than waiting for our daughters to seek assistance, we will often have to assess and act with alacrity, without thanks and in spite of rancor.

> *I let my niece move in with me during her pregnancy. Every little thing I did for her she threw back in my face as if I were the enemy and she was a prisoner of war. I cooked meals, bought clothes for her and the baby, helped her find a job at the phone company, drove her places because she thought she was too good to ride the bus, dealt with her emotional blow-ups, gave her feedback and tried to hold my ground. It was beyond a doubt one of the most trying situations I've ever experienced. The turbulence in my household was almost unbearable.* (mid-life professional woman)

Our second point of rescue, whether in community or therapeutic spheres, is to use ourselves, our love, time, and presence to supplement the biological mothering function. Once we intervene in the process of drowning, we must apply ourselves to resuscitation. As therapeutic Allomothers we have tended babies, dried tears, told stories, sat in appreciative amazement of young brilliant minds, encouraged, coached and led cheers, taught practical crafts, lent hands and shoulders after a fall, seeded imagination, plotted escapes from dangerous relationships, charted new courses, and helped to revise life and career road maps. In the last decade and a half we have watched ourselves shifting this highly personal and communal art to the world of work. In our professional lives as therapists and behavioral scientists we are again cast into the role of supporting the life experiences and life chances of girls and women living in the margins. We believe they have come to us out of a deep yearning to experience the progression of our tribal collective and our appointed role as elders in communal rites of passage. Such women, like Danielle in our earlier story, have found their way into recovery from the sweeping oppression of multi-layered assaults on their personhood. With honor and pride we assume our collective responsibility to be role models, supports, and friends along life's journey to our community's young girls and women.

> *I was just promoted to an administrative role in a social program for girl offenders. I get to develop programs that I think they need that will help them develop into responsible adults. I've never been so challenged in all my life.*

I've started dance groups, tutoring sessions, art projects, gotten jobs for them.
But this is an after school program. What they need is immersion big time.
My dream, since I'm still pretty young in this field, is to start my own school
one day, or to have my own agency. (young public sector professional)

Our third point of rescue is perhaps our most essential. Here our work requires that we craft ships and build ocean liners to sail the ocean depths. Because of the level of access we have earned through second-wave achievement, we are differentially positioned throughout the society to leverage some institutional gains for these most vulnerable girls. At the level of policy, social services, program development, education, media, and national/international conferences, we must translate their silences into our actions. Their issues must become as prominent and obvious as HIV/AIDS, as well understood as the teen drop-out issue, and as imperative for society to resolve as violent crime. Audre Lorde has cautioned us, however, that "the master's tools will never dismantle the master's house" (110). Therefore we must move beyond liberal feminisms and strategies that derive within existing structures. We must craft ocean liners that can locate and carry our daughters home. These will be the social programs and policies of the twenty-first century informed by our mother wit, our ancestral wisdom, and our newly vigilant gaze. These will be the programs formed in our own image, wrought from the immutability of age-old healing practices in new locales and venues spanning social services, mosques, churches, households, retreats, street ministries, and community centers. As we salvage the daughters of Gangsta' Rap Hip Hop culture, mother them back to health, hold steady in the heat of their rages, and stand in the crucible of tough love, we will come to know them again and they us.

Only with force comparable to that with which we took up second-wave progress can we steer back to shore against the wave of our daughters' spiritual wounding. Only with the force with which we faced down all that has gone before in this saga of a people under siege can we steer back to shore against the storms of colonization that defined all things African as merely the spoils of war. This is our clarion call—to put down the luxuries of second-wave success so that we might approach wounded girls and work with them to rebuild the self from within the context of relations. From within such relationships we can work with them to revise their own mother-child relations. Our work as therapeutic Allomothers to pregnant girls and mothers of the infamous Gangsta' Rap Hip Hop generation has poignantly challenged our consensual imagery of Black mother culture. The clash of these inter-generational perspectives on mothering are reflective of each group's differential valuing of herself, womankind, and the communal collective. Despite the critique we lay out, we don't have the answers. Ours is one of many perspectives, from the standpoint of our work with girls that society left adrift. If they go down for the third time, we go with them. If we reach them in time, and they reach for us … we believe that they can become the mothers they have been waiting for.

[1] Lyrics From India Arie's "Video," from the album "Acoustic Soul," released in 2001 on the Motown label. Produced by Carlos Broady. Writers: India Arie, Carlos Broady, Shannon Sanders.

[2] Throughout this essay we draw a distinction between Hip Hop as a grass roots political voice and Gangsta' Rap Hip Hop as a commodified version of Hip Hop. At the same time that we delineate a distinction, we do not advance a sharp dichotomy as there is a spectrum of Hip Hop expression that is dynamic, continuously evolving and may even mix elements of the two forms we refer to with other yet to be named aspects of this alive and organic phenomenon.

[3] Cheryl L. Keyes provides categories of identity prominent in the rap music performance of African American women and girls. Her categories include: Queen Mother, Fly Girl, Sista with Attitude and Lesbian.

[4] Marcyliena Morgan provides a historical context for African American women rap artists by connecting them to blues and jazz women of the early twentieth century. She creates a context for understanding contemporary women MCs whose performances resist denigrating representations of women and/or resist and critique hegemony. Among those she views in this way are: Queen Latifah, Sarah Jones, MC Lyte, and Missy Elliot.

[5] Anthropologist, Sarah Blaffer Hrdy credits British Ornithologist Edward O. Wilson with coining the term Allomother in 1975.

[6] The wire-mesh monkey refers to psychological experiments on bonding and attachment relations. In these experiments on populations of monkeys, a wire-mesh figure is substituted for the real relationship between a baby monkey and its mother.

[7] Crack cocaine is a mind-altering substance powerful enough to break the mother-child bond and corrupt the capacity to parent. Further, children born addicted and reared in such home environments are at a much greater risk for entry into the child welfare system.

[8] See also <http://www.coolnurse.com/teen_pregnancy_rates.htm>, <http://www.washingtonpost.com/wp-dyn/content/article/2007/12/05/AR2007120501208.html>, http://teenshelter.org/data.htm.

[9] The stereotype of the matriarch is originally attributed to the research spearheaded by Daniel Moynihan, 1965.

[10] In African American culture, calling someone out of their name is a serious insult. The power of the spoken word is a revered principle in African descended cultures (see Asante, 1987). Moreover, the power of a personal name is considered sacred and even intimate. Hence to misuse or deliberately distort a person's name is tantamount to undermining their human dignity. Among African American youth, this form of insult is provocation for a fight. When this happens, the youth characteristically justify their verbal or physical conflict behavior to authorities such as teachers, principals, etc. by saying that someone "called them out their name."

[11] This culturally competent African/Kemetic woman's development program draws its name from the Egyptian dung beetle or scareb which symbolizes eternal life.

[12]This phrasing is used by Alice Walker in her widely quoted article, "Definition of a Womanist." She refers here to the leadership role Black women have played beginning at early stages of their lives, and exemplified by such icons as Harriet Tubman who led scores of enslaved Blacks to find freedom in Canada.

[13]The term "twofer" emerged as a pejorative colloquialism during the 1960s when implementers of Affirmative Action sought to demonstrate compliance with hiring those from under represented groups. Some companies saw Black women as individuals who could be counted twice for both their race and their gender. Hence they were describe as being worth "two for one" or "twofers."

Works Cited

Asante, Moleti. *The Afrocentric Idea*. Philadelphia: Temple University Press, 1987.

Betsch Cole, Johnnetta, and Beverly Guy-Sheftall. "No-Respect: Gender Politics and Hip-Hop." *Gender Talk: The Struggle for Women's Equality in African American Communities*. New York: Ballantine, 2003.

Blaffer Hrdy, Sarah. *Mother Nature: A History of Mothers, Infants and Natural Selection*. New York: Pantheon, 1999.

Canon, Katie Geneva. "Metalogues and Dialogues: Teaching the Womanist Idea." *Katie's Canon: Womanism and the Soul of the Black Community*. New York: Continuum, 2003.

Casper, Lynne M. and Suzanne M. Bianchi. *Continuity and Change in the American Family*. Thousand Oaks, CA: Sage, 2001.

Dicker, Rory, and Alison Piepmeier, eds. *Catching a Wave: Reclaiming Feminism for the Twenty-First Century*. Boston: Northeastern University Press, 2003.

Dodson, Lisa. *Don't Call Us Out of Name: The Untold Lives of Women and Girls in Poor America*. Boston: Beacon, 1999.

Girshick, Lori B. *No Safe Haven: Stories of Women in Prison*. Boston: Northeastern University Press, 1999.

Hancock, Ange-Marie. *The Politics of Disgust: The Public Identity of the Welfare Queen*. New York: New York University Press, 2004.

Henry, Astrid. "Solitary Sisterhood: Individualism Meets Collectivity in Feminism's Third Wave." *Different Wavelengths: Studies in the Contemporary Women's Movement*. Ed. Jo Reger. New York: Routledge, 2005.

Higginbotham, A. Leon. *Shades of Freedom: Racial Politics and Perceptions of the American Legal Process*. New York: Oxford, 2003.

Hill Collins, Patricia. "The Social Construction of Black Feminist Thought." *Signs: Journal of Women in Culture and Society* 14.4 (1989): 745-773.

Keyes, Cheryl L. "Empowering Self, Making Choices, Creating Spaces: Black Female Identity via Rap Music Performance." *The Journal of American Folklore* 113.449 (Summer, 2000): 255-269.

Kitwana, Bakari. *The Hip Hop Generation: Young Blacks and the Crisis in African American Culture*. New York: Basic, 2002.

Lorde, Audre. "The Master's Tools Will Never Dismantle the Master's House." *Sister Outsider: Essays and Speeches.* Freedom, California: Crossing, 1984.

Morgan, Joan. *When Chickenheads Come Home to Roost: A Hip-Hop Feminist Breaks It Down.* New York: Simon, 2000.

Morgan, Marcyliena. "Hip-Hop Women Shredding the Veil: Race and Class in Popular Feminist Identity." *The South Atlantic Quarterly* 104: 3 (Summer 2005): 426-444.

Moynihan, Daniel. *The Negro Family: The Case for National Concern.* Washington, DC: Office of Policy Planning and Research, United States Department of Labor, March 1965.

Naples, Nancy. "Confronting the Future, Learning from the Past: Feminist Praxis in the Twenty-First Century." *Different Wavelengths: Studies of the Contemporary Women's Movement.* Ed. Jo Reger. New York: Routledge, 2005.

Phillips, Layli, ed. *The Womanist Reader.* New York: Routledge, 2006.

Pinkola Estés, Clarissa. *Women Who Run With the Wolves: Myths and Stories of the Wild Woman Archetype.* New York: Ballantine, 1992.

Pough, Gwendolyn. *Check It While I Wreck It: Black Womanhood, Hip-Hop Culture, and the Public Sphere.* Boston: Northeastern UP, 2004.

Townes, Emilie. *Womanist Ethics and The Cultural Production of Evil.* New York: Palgrave, 2006.

Vaz, Kim Marie. "Womanist Archetypal Psychology: A Model of Counseling for Black Women and Couples Based on Yoruba Mythology (2006/1995)." *The Womanist Reader.* Ed. Layli Phillips. New York: Routledge, 2006.

Walker, Alice. "Definition of a Womanist." *In Search of Our Mothers' Gardens: Womanist Prose.* New York: Harcourt, 1983.

Williams, Delores S. "Womanist Theology: Black Women's Voices," *Weaving the Visions: New Patterns in Feminist Spirituality.* Eds. Carol P. Christ and Judith Plaskow. New York: HarperCollins, 1987.

Wilson, William Julius. *When Work Disappears: The World of the New Urban Poor.* New York: Vintage, 1997.

16
Representing Motherhood
Reading the Maternal Body in Contemporary Art

RACHEL EPP BULLER

I sometimes find motherhood to be an intensely isolating experience. Certainly, this sense of isolation is not unique to mothering in the third wave, for my own mother, staying home with small children at the height of the second wave, felt judged at times by "working" mothers (some of whom said, condescendingly, "I don't know how you stay at home. I'm such a better mother to my children because I'm working"). The more nuanced examination of pluralities in the third wave has at least lent a greater validity to the range of women's choices, including the one to raise children full-time. Still, unlike my grandmothers, I do not live with an extended family of mothers, grandmothers, sisters, and aunts to whom I can turn daily for emotional support, adult conversation, or help with childcare. I often feel so caught up in life at home with small children that I have neither the time nor the energy to seek out maternal role models, other mothers to provide a lifeline of support and to resonate with my experiences. Particularly as a stay-at-home mother, it is all too easy to feel invisible, disconnected from the outside world and overlooked by "working" people.

As an art historian by training, I am always drawn to images of motherhood and the maternal body, seeking in them some communication of my own experience. For although women in contemporary society mother in widely varied cultural and economic circumstances, I idealistically believe that any two mothers might find some common experience through which to discourse. Mothering is such a highly charged relational context, where one can feel judged over private decisions about breastfeeding, diapering, childcare, discipline, sleeping arrangements, and so on, that it is incredibly validating to find something of my own experiences addressed in art. By interacting with images and texts that speak to both the euphoric episodes and the discouraging days of mothering, women might find common ground across boundaries of class and race and better understand our own experiences of motherhood as well.

Art and Mothering in the Second Wave

Generationally speaking, I am a third-wave feminist, but, having been raised by second-wave feminists, I was familiar with the second wave long before I'd ever heard of the third wave. During graduate school, I embraced the feminist art movement of the 1970s, glorious in its strident poses, rebellious rhetoric, even in its sometimes fumbling and awkward repossessions of the female body. These women challenged the patriarchal oppressor, reclaiming their bodily representations, uniting against the violence of abuse and harassment, throwing off the constricting roles of wife and mother, and finding their artistic agency as women. It is only in recent years, since becoming a mother myself, that I have wondered: Where was the art on feminist motherhood? In many cases, if motherhood was addressed at all, it was satirized as a traditional and confining role, a burden whose restrictions were best cast off by liberated women. Unfortunately, much of the feminist art movement, like the larger women's liberation movement, was plagued by narrow vision. Many have criticized the women's movement for being largely a white women's movement; the feminist art movement was no less so.[1] In their eagerness to overturn traditional roles for women, feminists and feminist artists alienated many potential allies by privileging, and subsequently attempting to subvert, only white experiences of motherhood, the ones critiqued in Betty Friedan's *The Feminine Mystique.* They sought to free women from the burden of being trapped in the home and economically dependent on a male provider, but these felt constraints were characteristic primarily of white families. Patricia Hill Collins argues that this vision was much less applicable to Black families and others outside of a white perspective, for racial oppression and economic inequity often made stay-at-home mothers and private, nuclear families unfeasible.

As white feminists threw off the burdens of motherhood, many also dismissed the experiences of motherhood as a basis for serious art making. As Myrel Chernick discusses, some women hid the very existence of their children, facing ambivalence at best and rejection at worst, from the art world. At the pioneering Feminist Studio Workshop, an alternative feminist art school, the infamous *Womanhouse* exhibition of 1972 sought to make visible women's lived experiences, from the cultural shame surrounding menstruation to the oppressive drudgery of housework. The roles of wife and mother were characterized as unacceptably limiting, and thus were not, perhaps could not be, celebrated. There were exceptions, however. A small group of artists from the Feminist Studio Workshop identified the denial of motherhood as a credible experience from which to make art. As Michelle Moravec explains, they organized themselves as Mother Art, producing art and curating exhibitions around themes of motherhood. British artist Mary Kelly similarly embraced her role as mother and employed it as a basis for her artistic production. Kelly's *Postpartum Document,* made over the course of several years and first exhibited in 1979, chronicles her relationship with her son in the extended postpartum period, from his birth until he entered school at age six. The *Postpartum Document* is a pseudo-scientific record consisting of 135 parts. Each part contains journal-like entries, documenting the child's behavior and Kelly's evolution as a mother. Kelly focuses on developmental milestones such as weaning, speaking, and writing, and includes physical documents from the child such as markings, clothing, and soiled diapers. While the entire record focuses on the mother-child relationship, Kelly studiously avoids visual representations of either mother or child. Kelly seems to have embraced the writing of second-wave feminist film theorist Laura Mulvey who believed that the image of the female body could not be reclaimed after centuries of objectification but could only continue to be co-opted by the male gaze, despite the artist's intentions. To this end, Kelly examines motherhood through text and her child's memorabilia rather than through visual images.

Mary Kelly, "Post-Partum Document: Documentation VI," detail, 1978.
Courtesy of the artist and Rosamund Felsen Gallery, Santa Monica, California.

Kelly's compendium is a compelling record of the all-consuming nature of motherhood. Through it, we learn of the child and of the mother-child relationship, but little of the mother herself. Whether or not Kelly intended it as such, I read it in relation to my own situation as a phenomenon of self-loss. For although I often stare in wonder at my children and at the amazing physical and developmental growth of early childhood, I have struggled to maintain some form of an individual identity apart from my role as mother. Like Kelly, I fastidiously document my children's milestones and try to journal regularly so as to remember the everyday minutiae as well. Yet in compiling albums of photographs and filling in growth charts, I function as the observer-recorder mother, conveying little of my own self. When my oldest child was born, we still lived in a college town where I fairly easily continued my research and maintained my identity as a graduate student. Soon, however, a new job took our family to a smaller town where I suddenly felt isolated from my academic community. The frustrations of writing a dissertation were magnified by feelings that I knew almost no one who could relate to my experiences, either as a graduate student or as one struggling to combine writing and mothering. At the same time, however, this balancing act felt strangely validating. I was not just a stay-at-home mom; I was also a student. At the time, that distinction felt particularly important for my personal and feminist identities, convincing myself that I had not sold out and become a homemaker but rather that I was able to be a wife and mother amidst my professional studies, a third-waver making conscious choices about the combinations of work and family.

With my completion of graduate school two and a half years later, I found myself confronting a new identity: being a stay-at-home mom, exclusively, without the cover of being a student as well. Second wave or third wave, it didn't matter: I was stuck with two very small people and no grown-ups in sight. I endured some of the most difficult months of my life that winter as I learned to manage the needs of a toddler and a newborn while feeling utterly trapped without adult contact, particularly on frigid days when we could not leave the house. My individual identity felt lost amid the high needs of a nursing infant, and I struggled with feelings of resentment against parents and in-laws unable to be of much help. While rationally I knew that there would be plenty of years for work and very few years of small children, the days and hours could drag so as to seem never-ending. I fought to keep from asking myself, "Why did I get a Ph.D. if I'm only going to stay at home?" Kelly's *Postpartum Document* takes hold of the utter absorption of the mother-child relationship, transforming it into a vehicle for her own personal expression. In this way, her work becomes inspirational for those of us struggling with the same questions of identity thirty years later. I applaud Kelly's boldness in embracing her role as mother at a time when few artists even acknowledged that position, even if she herself seems lost to me in the work. Perhaps she was lost to herself then, too.

While Kelly departed from the majority in the feminist art movement by foregrounding motherhood in her work, she wholeheartedly embraced the race-specific concerns of bodily (mis)representation. True enough, the white female body has a lengthy history of objectification in art and society. A blanket statement, however, that elides representation at all effectively silences those who were scarcely represented in the first place. Betye Saar's *The Liberation of Aunt Jemima*, of 1972, addresses both the maternal body and Black representation. Saar's construction is comprised of found objects, scavenged from junk shops around the world, that speak to historically stereotyped roles of African Americans in white society. Here Saar combines the repeated background image of "Aunt Jemima," of pancake mix and syrup fame, with two additional images of a Black Mammy. In all three instances, the woman pictured appears large and happy, her hair covered by a scarf to indicate her domestic servitude and her overeager grin a sign of devotion to the white family she serves.[2] Saar subverts the stereotype of the passive Black

189

servant through her addition of a pistol, a rifle, and a clenched fist. Michelle Cliff asserts that Saar combines "the myth [of Aunt Jemima] with the reality of Black women's historic opposition to their oppression" (288).

Betye Saar, "The Liberation of Aunt Jemima," 1972. University Art Museum, University of California at Berkeley. Courtesy of Michael Rosenfeld Gallery, New York.

Saar's construction is crucial to a discussion of 1970s feminist art and mother-hood, for her images are clearly maternal figures. They do not mother their own children, however, as the foreground figure clearly illustrates. The historic position of the Black Mammy was to mother white children, even as she was forced to leave her own. Even the kitsch items in Saar's construction, namely the large cookie jar, make reference to how Black women nourished others. Saar calls attention to the Black female body so often overlooked, and/or grossly misrepresented, in art and society by exploding cultural stereotypes. Her historical references assert that images of Black motherhood are, by definition, layered with historical and political implications.

Strangely enough, my engagement with Saar's work has felt like a validation of my own mothering, particularly of the decision to care for my own children while they are small. Although I have yearned for a working life outside the home (on some days more than others), I have never relished the idea of daycare and the thought of a nanny seems far too bourgeois, not to mention unaffordable. It was not until we lived for a time in New York City that I came to ponder some of the larger implications of this decision. My son was then two years old, so we spent many hours at playgrounds around the city. On one of our first outings to Central Park, I was stunned to realize that the children surrounding my son were all being cared for by women who were not their mothers. My first thought was that it seemed like some kind of strange throwback to *Gone With the Wind*, a racial hierarchy where the children, who were all white, were cared for by minority women who, in order to make a living, left their own children to care for those of wealthier means. I would like to believe that these women were well compensated and that they chose this work because they enjoy it. I have to wonder, though, if as in Saar's work, white patriarchy has not simply put distinct limitations upon the jobs available to certain segments of the population so that domestic work is inevitably that of women in non-privileged groups. Several contributors to the recent anthology, *Global Women: Nannies, Maids, and Sex Workers in the New Economy*, discuss this as a form of imperialism, where "care workers" are increasingly imported from the "First World" to the "Third World," women forced to leave their own children behind in the hopes of making a livable income. In leaving their children for work, they are not unlike their prospective employers. But in most other ways they are quite unlike them: negligible status and reduced power; minimal resources; and little if any opportunity to see their own children, attend to their needs, or feel assured of their safe-keeping. Observing the nannies in Central Park ultimately reinforced my decision to stay at home with my children, even as I realized that my position is one of privilege, what Bonnie Thornton Dill and Patricia Hill Collins each discuss as the Eurocentric "cult of true womanhood" to which not all women have access, or even the desire to pursue (543-55; 44)

Art and Mothering in the Third Wave

Nearly twenty years after Saar's *The Liberation of Aunt Jemima*, Carrie Mae Weems examined motherhood and issues of power in her photographs within a changed cultural landscape for feminism. Where the 1980s witnessed a backlash against feminism, the 1990s ushered in a new and more visibly diverse generation of women embracing feminist ideals, if not a feminist label. At least initially, many third-wavers sought to distance themselves from the second wave, as Astrid Henry explains in her book *Not My Mother's Sister: Generational Conflicts and Third-Wave*

Feminism. Rebecca Walker, one of the first to use the term "third wave," and other leading feminists of color argued for an understanding of the complex intersections of race and gender issues. Motherhood, particularly young motherhood, became a political, even defiant, position for some third-wave feminists, as seen in Ariel Gore and Bee Lavender's groundbreaking anthology, *Breeder*.

In her *Untitled (Kitchen Table Series)* of 1990, Carrie Mae Weems employed a combination of photographs and text to examine power dynamics within a Black woman's relationships, some of which speak directly to the role of motherhood. Each of the photographs foregrounds the kitchen table, a space of intimacy where family comes together, laughs, talks, and argues. Weems further pictures the kitchen table as a space where rituals are passed on. In *Untitled (Woman and Daughter with Makeup)*, the mother and daughter share a ritual of female beautification, the daughter mirroring her mother's actions.

Yet in the narrative text that parallels the photographic tableaux, Weems pays little attention to motherhood. The narrative posits the main character's motherhood as something accidental, unwanted, unnatural to her. She loves her child but finds no great pleasure in motherhood. Certainly, motherhood takes a back seat here to the woman's relationship with her partner, or as the character says of herself, motherhood "caused deflexion from her own immediate desires, which pissed her off." The text, then, adds another dimension to *Woman and Daughter with Makeup*, the photograph it accompanies. The intimate nature of the setting is not reflected by the figures' actions. They are mother and daughter, sharing a space and a ritual, but the moment is not particularly tender. Their body language subtly conveys this sentiment but Weems' narrative reinforces the self-imposed distance between mother and daughter.

Weems provides a significant contribution to the visual language of motherhood by daring to show it in an unidealized form. Images of mothering tend to be grounded in what Terry Kurgan refers to as "a Christian symbolic construct" through which a mother and her child are represented as "a cosy [sic], mutually fulfilled and fulfilling couple." In contrast to this "mythology," Kurgan continues, is "a taboo domain: the acknowledgment of ambivalence and the critical representation of the lived experience of the maternal" (1). As a mother myself I wonder, what mother has not felt ambivalent at times about her activity? I always knew that I wanted children, but nothing prepared me for the shock of new motherhood. As I stumbled, sleep-deprived and hormones raging, through those early weeks, I was stunned at how completely this tiny person had changed my life. Because of him, my critical thinking capacities seemed to have vanished. For months, the books and articles for my dissertation collected dust on the shelf; in my foggy mental state of new motherhood, all I could get read in the course of a day was the newspaper—if that. As he grew older, my ability to think gradually returned but my days of reading and writing all day were gone. I quickly learned about mental multitasking, savoring the precious minutes and hours of naptime as my own academic time. I compartmentalized my time and my thoughts to make the most of naptimes, abandoning any thoughts of caring for myself (or cleaning the house) to instead struggle to meet my goal of writing one page per day. And while, in hindsight, I would not change the choices I have made, I fully admit to days of ambivalence, questioning my commitment both to my profession and to motherhood. When my son suddenly quit napping at two-and-a-half, it certainly felt like there was hell to pay.

As Weems brings attention to her character's ambivalence, she posits an alternate understanding of feminist motherhood. A woman may not fully embrace her role as mother, but this also is a privilege of feminist consciousness, that feminism may have lessened the stigma for those who do not wholly invest themselves in motherhood. Johnnetta B. Cole asserts that the patriarchal system deems that "all women are to be mothers, a rule applied to Black women no less than to White women;" and this ideal persists despite the fact that not all women are biological mothers and many women do not wish to be (xiv-xv). Weems's dynamic Black female protagonist submits neither to motherhood nor to patriarchal assumptions regarding women's role. The mother's voice comes through the third-person autobiographical text, saying, "A woman's duty! Ha! A punishment for Eve's sin was more like it. Ha." She will accept her role as mother but refuses to see it as her obligation or even to claim it as her own.

As such, the mother in Weems's narrative addresses a widespread concern of feminist mothers: how to mother while simultaneously rejecting patriarchal oppression. In published interviews, Weems has expressed her hope that in her work "it might be possible to use black subjects to represent universal concerns." "Yet when I do that," she continues, "it's not understood in that way. Folks refuse to identify with the concerns black people express which take us beyond race" (76). Still, this is precisely the importance of her work: critically addressing issues such as motherhood that "take us beyond race." Certainly, some of the text panels that accompany the photographs make reference to specifics of race. But as the character loves/fights with/loses her partner through the course of the photographic narrative, she could be every feminist woman, attempting to negotiate the power dynamics of an adult relationship. Here it is that we find commonalities as feminist mothers, acknowledging our limitations and feelings of confinement.

Whereas the character in Weems's *Kitchen Table Series* presents her motherhood as only a small part of her larger identity, photographer Renée Cox more explicitly embraces the fullness of motherhood in her *Yo Mama* series, 1992-97. Using her own body as subject, she is identified as mother in each image, whether pregnant, breastfeeding, or holding her child. Cox imparts significance to the seemingly mundane actions of the mother through her large-scale photographs. The scale of the figures and the simple settings lend a heroic quality to images benignly titled *Yo Mama Feeding* or *Yo Mama at Home*. In the series, Cox positions herself in the tradition of Madonna and Child imagery, yet draws specific attention to her body as a source of nurturing for her child. Her rounded belly, in the images of pregnancy, as well as her full hips and breasts, testify to her motherhood. She displays her body not as the source of male pleasure but rather as the source of life. It is significant that Cox uses the Black female body to address universal concerns of pregnancy and motherhood. In doing so, she forges links between mothers across boundaries of race and class and sets up the Black female body as a universal signifier.

Renée Cox, "Yo Mama Feeding," 1993.
Courtesy of the artist and Robert Miller Gallery, New York.

Cox's historical position differs significantly from that of Mary Kelly and allows Cox access to the body as a feminist artist in ways not afforded her predecessor. Feminist artists of the 1970s, like feminists in general of that time, were concerned primarily with women's rights and women's liberation, freeing themselves and their sisters from patriarchal oppression. Artists and feminists of Cox's era, on the other hand, emerged from a political generation in which a feminist consciousness was already acknowledged, as Amber Kinser's work has noted. At the same time, such feminists of color as bell hooks, Cherríe Moraga, Gloria Anzaldúa, and Audre Lorde, among others, had so influenced the feminist movement in the interim that, by the 1990s, Cox and other artists were firmly positioned to address the complexities of bodily representation. So Cox drew obvious attention to the Black female body while Mary Kelly consciously avoided representation of the body, likely fearing its immediate objectification given the lengthy history of patriarchal misuse and abuse of the female body in art and society. What Cox's photographs acknowledge, however, is that this pattern of (mis)representation focused almost entirely on the white female body. Cox not only reclaims the female body from objectification, but also proclaims her skin color as a source of an alternate and equal definition of beauty. In media culture as well, standards of beauty continually privilege images of whiteness, so that Cox's over-life-sized imagery is forceful, unpredictable, and unexpected. Cox's photographs require a heightened awareness from the viewer: in her own words, the images "demand enlightenment through an equitable realignment of our race and gender politics" (qtd. in Millstein 85). As Freida Tesfagiorgis argues, by foregrounding the Black female body, Cox's photographs are an act of self-determination, helping to produce a new art historical discourse that privileges rather than negates that body (73-92).

Cox further employs her own body to give high visibility to motherhood. *Yo Mama Feeding* is a particularly potent image from a series that upholds the power and beauty of the Black maternal body. Seated on a chair outdoors, Cox nurses her son. This simple act is fraught with both historical significance and contemporary political tension, while Cox's visage itself speaks to the power of the gaze and the uncertainties of motherhood. Like Saar's Mammy figures that mother white children, Cox's photograph conjures a history in which Black women served white families as wet-nurses, suckling infants not their own. By nursing her own child, Cox reclaims an historically lost motherhood. Operating from within a more racially aware and diverse third wave, Cox moves beyond the cultural stereotypes exploited in Saar's work yet seeks subtle ways to continue the historical references. In *Yo Mama Feeding* and other images from the series, Cox levels a direct and powerful gaze at the viewer. This, too, is loaded with historical significance. By reclaiming the power to look, or what bell hooks terms the "oppositional gaze," Cox implicitly makes reference to a history in which Blacks were not allowed to look, were indeed punished for looking (*Black Looks,* 115-131). By combining tender subjects with assertive postures in her photographs, Cox firmly articulates a reclaimed gaze of Black motherhood.

The compelling *Yo Mama Feeding* speaks to contemporary history as well. Breastfeeding has a conflicted history in the 20th century, struggling for legitimacy at times in US society. In their book *Milk, Money, and Madness: The Culture and Politics of Breastfeeding,* Naomi Baumslag and Dia Michels have detailed how formula companies exerted a powerful influence over mothers and doctors, many of whom came to view breastfeeding as difficult and inconvenient. Further, as Cindy Stearns argues, feminism also contributed to decreased breastfeeding, as women were "liberated" from the high needs of a nursing infant. While the stigma has lessened, Stephanie Ondrack points out that the bottle is still the dominant cultural image when it comes to infant feeding. In recent years, with more and more mothers again choosing to nurse, breastfeeding is increasingly debated in terms of public "decency." Breasts are no longer functional, but exclusively sexual. Fiona Giles notes that images of lactating mothers show up even on soft porn websites (14-15). Nursing mothers have been evicted from health clubs, restaurants, airplanes, and other public spaces for feeding their children, made to feel that this simple, vital action is shameful and obscene (O'Mara; Hausman; Marcus). Breastfeeding is increasingly becoming a legislative issue, as La Leche

League and other organizations lobby to pass bills in state senates to protect the rights of nursing mothers. My home state of Kansas, for example, passed legislation in March 2006 affirming a woman's right to breastfeed in public (Kansas House Bill No. 2284). Cox's image of the breastfeeding mother exudes an assertive but matter-of-fact attitude: she gave her child life and will continue to meet his nutritional needs. End of discussion.

At the same time, Cox's facial expression in the photograph gives me pause. Bob Myers reads Cox's expression as appearing "disturbed, 'put off' by her situation" and yet, he notes, "in no case does she surrender to it" (13). Her visage seems conflicted, difficult to read. As a nursing mother, I value what I perceive as the layered meanings of this image for it speaks eloquently to my own years of nursing babies. While breastfeeding was for me a wonderfully bonding experience, at times I did it simply by rote or while trying to do too many other things. (How many times have I nursed a baby while getting snacks for the older kids/reading them books/cooking dinner?) During times of high-need nursing, I felt frustrated and suffocated, forced to give up any sense of personal space, not to mention sufficient sleep. Although I remain committed to nursing and am ever in awe that my rather limited endowment could fully nourish three babies, I also have resented the constant demands on my physical being. My youngest, now a year old, can drive me up the wall with her tendency to fondle my nipple on one side while nursing on the other. And yet, in spite of the frustrations and annoyances, I continue on this path. Like Cox, I am committed to my choices yet recognize the emotional complexities of my maternal position. While Cox's subject contains an array of charged historical references, I believe that her stolid expression also evokes the contradictory and conflicting emotions inherent in breastfeeding and motherhood.

In an interview with Bob Myers, Renée Cox revealed that the Yo Mama character evolved as a result of her own experiences, having received little validation for her choice to bear children and make art (32). Rather than try to hide the fact that she had children, Cox retaliated against the culture of silence regarding motherhood in the art world. By creating Yo Mama, she not only made visible but legitimized, even glorified, the role of motherhood amidst career ambitions. Cox's position marks the end of a trajectory begun by Mary Kelly and other feminist artists of the 1970s who dared to embrace motherhood in their work. Not simply increasing the visibility of motherhood, the artists discussed here picture the all-consuming nature, the historical injustices, as well as the ambivalent days of motherhood. These non-idealized representations of the maternal role provide a much-needed antidote to the near-silence on the subject in society and in art history. As I come to the end of an essay that has been written in 10- and 20-minute intervals—in between nursings, during naptimes, and after bedtimes—I find hope in the work of these women who, each in their own way, have found paths to personal and professional self-fulfillment that include and embrace the journey, the history, and the complexities of motherhood. What an incredible inspiration.

[1] See, for example, Alice Walker's critique of the way in which Judy Chicago included Sojourner Truth in *The Dinner Party* but focused only on her difference rather than her womanhood.

[2] bell hooks levels an incisive critique of how and why white society created the Mammy stereotype in *Ain't I A Woman* (84). Other literature on the Mammy stereotype includes K. Sue Jewell, *From Mammy to Miss America and Beyond: Cultural Images and the Shaping of U.S. Policy*; and Carol Duncan, "'Mammy' in the Erotic Imaginary of Anaïs Nin."

Works Cited

Baumslag, Naomi, and Dia L. Michels. *Milk, Money, and Madness: The Culture and Politics of Breastfeeding*. Westport: Bergin, 1995.

Chernick, Myrel. "Maternal Metaphors: Artists/Mothers/Artwork." *Journal of the Association for Research on Mothering* 5.1 (2003): 24-29.

Cliff, Michelle. "Object into Subject: Some Thoughts on the Work of Black Women Artists." *Heresies* 15 (1982). Rpt. in *Making Face, Making Soul / Haciendo Caras: Creative and Critical Perspectives by Women of Color*. Ed. Gloria Anzaldúa. San Francisco: Aunt Lute, 1990. 271-90.

Cole, Johnnetta B. Preface. *Double Stitch: Black Women Write About Mothers and Daughters*. Ed. Patricia Bell-Scott et al. New York: HarperCollins, 1991. xiii-xv.

Collins, Patricia Hill. "The Meaning of Motherhood in Black Culture and Black Mother-Daughter Relationships." *Double Stitch: Black Women Write About Mothers and Daughters*. Ed. Patricia Bell-Scott et al. New York: HarperCollins, 1991. 42-60.

Cox, Renée. *Yo Mama* series. Collection of the artist, New York.

Dill, Bonnie Thornton. "The Dialectics of Black Womanhood." *Signs: Journal of Women in Culture and Society* 4 (1979): 543-55.

Duncan, Carol. "'Mammy' in the Erotic Imaginary of Anaïs Nin." *Journal of the Association for Research on Mothering* 4.1 (2002): 146-55.

Ehrenreich, Barbara and Arlie Russell Hochschild, eds. *Global Women: Nannies, Maids, and Sex Workers in the New Economy*. New York: Metropolitan, 2002.

Friedan, Betty. *The Feminine Mystique*. New York: Norton, 1963.

Giles, Fiona. "Fountains of Love and Loveliness: In Praise of the Dripping Wet Breast." *Journal of the Association for Research on Mothering* 4.1 (2002): 7-18.

Gore, Ariel, and Bee Lavender, eds. *Breeder: Real-Life Stories from the New Generation of Mothers*. Emeryville, CA: Seal, 2001.

Hausman, Bernice L. *Mother's Milk: Breastfeeding Controversies in American Culture*. London; New York: Routledge, 2003.

Henry, Astrid. *Not My Mother's Sister: Generational Conflict and Third-Wave Feminism*. Bloomington: Indiana University Press, 2004.

hooks, bell. *Ain't I A Woman*. Boston: South End, 1981.

hooks, bell. *Black Looks: Race and Representation*. Boston: South End, 1992.

Jewell, K. Sue. *From Mammy to Miss America and Beyond: Cultural Images and the Shaping of U.S. Policy.* London; New York: Routledge, 1993.

Kansas House Bill. No. 2284. 2006.

Kelly, Mary. *Postpartum Document.* Rosamund Felsen Gallery, Santa Monica.

Kinser, Amber. "Negotiating Spaces For/Through Third-Wave Feminism." *NWSA Journal* 16.3 (2004): 124-153.

Kurgan, Terry. "Mothers and Others." *Bringing Up Baby: Artists Survey the Reproductive Body.* Cape Town: Bringing Up Baby Project, 1998. 1-3.

Marcus, Jake Aryeh. "Lactation and the Law." *Mothering* 143 (2007): 48-56.

Millstein, Barbara Head, ed. *Committed to the Image: Contemporary Black Photographers.* Brooklyn: Brooklyn Museum of Art; London: Merrell, 2001.

Moravec, Michelle. "Mother Art: Feminism, Art and Activism." *Journal of the Association for Research on Mothering* 5.1 (2003): 69-77.

Mulvey, Laura. "Visual Pleasure and Narrative Cinema." *Screen* 16 (1975): 6-18.

Myers, Bob. "What Is My Legacy? Transient Consciousness and the 'Fixed' Subject in the Photography of Renée Cox." *Gendered Visions: The Art of Contemporary Africana Women Artists.* Ed. Salah M. Hassan. Trenton: Africa World, 1997. 27-35.

O'Mara, Peggy. "Breastfeeding in Whose Public?" *Mothering* 132 (2005): 10-14.

Ondrack, Stephanie. "Taking Down the Almighty Bottle." *Mothering* 137 (2006): 48-57.

Saar, Betye. *The Liberation of Aunt Jemima.* University Art Museum, Berkeley.

Stearns, Cindy A. "Breastfeeding and the Good Maternal Body." *Gender and Society* 13 (1999): 308-325.

Tesfagiorgis, Freida High W. "In Search of a Discourse and Critique/s that Center the Art of Black Women Artists." *Gendered Visions: The Art of Contemporary Africana Women Artists.* Ed. Salah M. Hassan. Trenton: Africa World, 1997. 73-92.

Walker, Alice. "A Child of One's Own: A Meaningful Digression within the Work(s)—An Excerpt." *All the Women Are White, All the Blacks Are Men, But Some of Us Are Brave.* Eds. Gloria T. Hull, Patricia Bell Scott, and Barbara Smith. New York: Feminist Press, 1982. 37-44.

Walker, Rebecca. "Becoming the Third Wave." *Ms.* (Jan/Feb 1992): 39-41.

Weems, Carrie Mae, and bell hooks. "Talking Art with Carrie Mae Weems." *Art On My Mind.* New York: New, 1995. 74-93.

Weems, Carrie Mae. *Untitled (Kitchen Table Series).* Collection of the artist, New York.

17

Mothering in the Digital Age

Navigating the Personal and Political in the Virtual Sphere

JUDITH STADTMAN TUCKER

In early 1999, the technology press was abuzz with predictions that women would soon outnumber men among US internet users. That was also the year I launched my first self-published web site. Cybermommy.com—a primordial version of what is now known as a "weblog"—was designed as an information filter and guide for "newly wired" women, and offered advice on where to find quality woman-oriented web content and how to get the best result from search engines (this was BG—Before Google, back when the internet and World Wide Web were still described as "emerging technology"). The site's perky tag line—"It's Your World, It's Your Web"—reflected my belief that the internet is a pretty good tool for empowering women, and my delight at the prospect of women's mass infiltration of the male-dominated culture of cyberspace.[1] Trend analysts anticipated an explosion of commercial web content in "women-friendly" markets such as health and wellness, lifestyle and shopping—which is exactly what happened during the dot.com boom—but ignored the more exciting implications of women joining the online revolution. "We are not a gaggle of technophobic impulse-shoppers trolling for sure-fire weight-loss tips and the latest shade of lipstick," I wrote in my first online commentary (which, in a burst of confidence, I entitled "Girls Rule"). "We are busy, capable women who want to use this technology to simplify our lives and expand our opportunities."

In the same entry, I made several prognostications about how the assimilation of the internet into daily life would shape women's experiences, on- and off-line. "Even as an average member of the online community,[2] I appreciate the potential of the Internet to eventually transform life as we know it.... As the World Wide Web completes its evolution into a mass medium, it is likely to mimic the trends of the entertainment and broadcasting industries—in other words, what we now consider cutting edge will soften into popular culture, and a more progressive forum will develop outside the mainstream: a sort of 'indie-net.'" That, too, is exactly what happened—and third-wave mamas have been willing and active participants in the creation of a mother-centric alternative culture in the digital sphere.

The Mainstreaming of Online Life

According to the Pew Research Center, the full-scale commercialization of the internet "has reached into—and, in some cases, reshaped—just about every important realm of modern life." Once the sole province of research scientists and the technically inclined, the internet is now integral to the way public agencies, businesses, media conglomerates, and non-profit organizations deliver information and services. The Pew Internet and American Life Project reports that the "mainstreaming of online life" has had a profound influence on almost everything we do: "the way we inform ourselves, amuse ourselves, care for ourselves, educate ourselves, work, shop, bank, pray and stay in touch" (57). The internet has also altered our perception of time, distance, and privacy by rewiring our expectations of how much, and how quickly, information should be available to the public—and who produces it.

From its emergence as the first interactive mass medium, the penetration of the internet into everyday life has been acknowledged as a cultural phenomenon as well as a technological triumph. In 1996, psychologist Sherry Turkle characterized cyberspace as a daring new social frontier, the cutting-edge realm of connectivity and creative endeavor where fluid rules of conduct and self-representation permit users to transcend the stale boundaries of "real" life—including the boundaries of gender. Computers, Turkle wrote, "are not just changing our lives but changing our selves" ("Who Am We?").

The internet's virtual mystique quickly faded as the demographics of core users changed. Today, the vast majority of US adults who spend time online use the internet as they would any other communication device,[3] rather than as an extension of what philosopher Drucilla Cornell calls "the imaginary domain" of the self-invented self (8). Nonetheless, the popular culture of the digital sphere remains fixated on the exploits of risk-takers, trailblazers, and renegades.

North American mothers—particularly urban- or suburban-dwelling, college educated, middle-class mothers[4]—have not been insulated from these cultural and technological currents. In fact, mothers have been among the most avid adopters of the internet. According to Deborah Fallows of the Pew Internet and American Life Project, 80 percent of women with children under 18 spent time online in 2005, compared to 57 percent of their childless counterparts (3). The sheer volume of web resources pertaining to women, work, and family life—a quick Google search for resources on "moms," "work" and "family" yields nearly 2 million results—has undoubtedly influenced mothers' appraisal of their access to useful information, services, and support. With everything from ages-and-stages parenting tips to mom-specific discussion forums vying for our attention—not to mention the ubiquitous advice on how to lose weight, get a better job, find a reliable child care provider, and rekindle romance with your parenting partner—mothers increasingly view the internet as a place where they "belong." In keeping with this trend, over the last five years a growing number of women in their active child-bearing and child-rearing years have planted a stake in their own piece of virtual turf. Today, third-wave mothers use the World Wide Web to share their stories, increase their personal and collective visibility, record their grievances, construct online communities, and facilitate social activism. Whether this flurry of online activity will have a positive ripple effect on mothers as a whole is impossible to predict. But even as an emerging trend, mothers' excursion into the digital sphere raises enduring questions about the relationship between cultural and political activism.

A Cyberspace of One's Own

The development of affordable, user-friendly tools for personal web publishing in the late 1990s—combined with the option of anonymity and the internet's lingering reputation as an experimental environment—has helped to accelerate mothers' foray into the virtual sphere. Compared to the technical and editorial requirements of conventional publishing and broadcasting, creating online content is fast, easy, and remarkably cheap. Weblogs and self-published web sites have rapidly become the preferred alternative for journalists and creative writers who wish to supplement or circumvent traditional channels. Personal blogs and small-scale web publishing also offer absolute control over messaging and content—an advantage which is not lost on groups and individuals who feel their interests, experiences, and perspectives are poorly represented by mainstream media. Reader participation in message boards and comment-enabled blogs and news sites provides another popular outlet for self-expression. The ease of use, open culture, and potential to reach millions of viewers make the World Wide Web an ideal forum for anyone with a tale to tell, an axe to grind, or a yearning to be noticed. Uppity women who raise their voices online are still a minority, however—fewer than one out of every five US women who spend time online has ever produced user-generated content.[5]

Cultural momentum and feminist-informed attitudes also influence mothers' online activities. As Susan Douglas and Meredith Michaels note in their 2004 book, *The Mommy Myth*, mass-market media rarely provide accurate representations of mothers' problems and experiences (7). Mothers who create online content often construe their projects as corrective. In particular, blogging and web-publishing mamas tend to share the philosophy that women's voices and ideas matter, and the belief that mothers' stories—without the conventional sugarcoating—have the power to reveal important truths about the conflicts and complexity of women's social and emotional world. On a cultural level, recent trend stories in the *New York Times* (Jody Wilgoren, "At Center of a Clash, Rowdy Children in Coffee Shops") and *USA Today* (Olivia Barker, "Mommy Hottest;" Sharon Jayson, "Hip, Happy Housewives") suggest the present generation of mothers is reluctant to surrender the public visibility and cultural inclusion they enjoyed in their pre-maternal lives. Third-wave mothers may cultivate an online persona to restore their self-concept as cultural citizens and to relieve (or complain about) their sense of displacement. The internet's cachet as a realm of innovation and social adventure may prove especially attractive to mothers who wish to dispel the unflattering misconception that motherhood makes women passive, dull, and unreflective.

The expanding universe of mother-made web content is as varied as the women who create it. Today, mothers use the internet as a platform for self-expression; to make and sustain supportive connections with like-minded mothers; to earn money as content or service providers and through self-promotion; to protest and resist romanticized representations of motherhood and rigid gender roles; to defuse (or exacerbate) the perpetual "mommy wars;" to identify and discuss the unique opportunity costs, economic risks, and inequalities associated with mothering; to facilitate change-oriented consciousness raising and grass-roots organizing; and to leave a public record of the mundane details of their daily lives.

While revolutionary discourses and practices are not widespread among con-temporary mothers—either on- or off-line—two recent developments have a distinctly feminist flavor. The first is the emergence of an independent, alternative mothers' media, which has a strong online component and includes award-win-ning print publications. The second is the burgeoning number of frank personal weblogs written by and for mothers, and the online subculture created by the blogging mom movement.

The Rise of the Alternative Mothers' Media

Douglas and Michaels recount how feminist perspectives on marriage and mothering—which were reasonably well represented in mass-market women's magazines in the 1970s—had all but disappeared from mainstream literature by the early 1980s (36-50). Despite the World Wide Web's reputation as the unorthodox, "new" medium, commercial web sites catering to the interests of mothers typically replicated the formulaic style and focus of conventional fare—primarily because most woman-centric web content migrated from mass-market periodicals, and new profit-making ventures mimicked established content models. The resulting void of probative new writing on motherhood and mothering provided the impetus for the founding of the alternative moth-ers' media, which coincided with the emergence of web publishing as a viable market sector. As Camille Peri and Kate Moses write in the introduction to *Because I Said So,*

> Two conversation-starved and over-caffeinated mothers...started to talk about how underserved they felt by the standard motherhood books and recycled how-tos. They decided they would create an alternative—a website where mothers could read honest, unsentimental essays by women who were struggling with the same issues they were.... They would call their creation Mothers Who Think, in homage to Jane Smiley's essay "Can Mothers Think?" which ponders the question of whether mother-hood turns women's brains to mush. (i)

Mothers Who Think debuted in June, 1997 as a multi-featured content section of Salon, then a frontrunner among the narrow field of successful online magazines. Between its premier issue and May, 2000—when Peri and Moses relinquished editorial oversight and Mothers Who Think was quietly folded into Salon's lifestyle section—MWT published hundreds of thought-provoking essays, interviews, commentaries, and reviews by known and emerging writers on women in society, motherhood, marriage, family life, child rearing, reproductive issues, sexuality, and popular culture.

Hip Mama, produced and edited by Ariel Gore, was another pioneering project. Gore, a young, tattooed, and defiantly politicized single mother initially attracted attention by publishing *Hip Mama* as a small-run print 'zine. She launched HipMama.com, a companion web 'zine with topical message boards, in 1996. Bee Lavender joined the project as online editor in 1998 and introduced Girl-Mom.com, a content area and online community dedicated to the experiences and concerns of teen mothers. Originally conceptualized as a "forum for young mothers, single parents, and marginalized voices," Hip Mama currently attracts a broad readership but continues to project the raw energy and edgy attitude seen in the vibrant post-punk feminist 'zine scene in the 1990s. Lavender's content site, Mamaphonic, also launched in 1998 and continues to publish new writing on motherhood and creativity.

Although other mother-made websites appeared in the late 1990s, most focused on practical rather than social issues. Few, other than Mothers Who Think, attempted to reproduce the content range and editorial style of leading literary magazines. The landscape shifted again in early 2003, when a group of mother-writers organized by co-founders Andrea Buchanan and Amy Hudock launched Literary Mama ("a literary magazine for the maternally inclined"), and I published the first edition of The Mothers Movement Online, which I envisioned as a clearinghouse for "resources and reporting for mothers and others who think about social change." (Time pressures and changing interests led me to abandon Cybermommy in 2001, although I keep the site live out of a sense of nostalgia.) These launches were followed by the 2004 introduction of Mommy, Too!, the first full-feature online magazine for mothers of color (founded and edited by Jennifer James), and the arrival of mamazine in 2005, "a feminist publication for mamas and people who love them" (founded and edited by Amy Anderson and Sheri Reed).[6]

Each of these outlets has a unique style, focus and presentation, although there is considerable crossover in readership and contributing writers. Mamaphonic and Literary Mama offer prose, poetry, and mothering memoir, while mamazine also publishes commentary by regular columnists, creative non-fiction, and interviews. Hip Mama publishes short first-person essays and commentary, and aims to create a sense of community among marginalized mothers and mamas who self-identify as non-conformists. Mommy, Too!'s coverage of lifestyle, work/life and parenting issues for middle-class mothers of color is consistent with the founder's social justice perspective, and The Mothers Movement Online—which attracts a diverse readership but skews to an intellectual audience—offers feminist-informed analysis and is intended as a resource for the activist community.

The common features distinguishing these forums from conventional mother-centric web sites are an awareness that today's mothers are inadequately served by the usual repertoire of parenting, relationship, and lifestyle advice found in mainstream sources; the editorial perspective that mothers *do* think, and think deeply, about the personal and political complexities of motherhood and other matters of social import; and the belief that mothers' stories and opinions, conveyed in their own words, can be powerfully illuminating. Because the underlying agenda of these editors and publishers is to controvert stereotypes of who mothers are and what they like to read and think about, the alternative mothers' media is, by its very nature, activist media—even when the subject matter is not overtly political.

Although very much a product of third-wave culture and consciousness, the proliferation of the independent, web-based mothers' media since the end of the twentieth century owes much of its philosophy, if not its immediate inspiration, to the feminist publishing movement of the 1960s and 1970s. But rather than positioning our projects as a response to the systematic silencing of mothers' voices, we see our mission as exploring and challenging the social construction of motherhood; modeling an alternative discourse on women, work, and family; making a public space for maternal creativity; and documenting the diversity of maternal experience.

The Blogging Mom Rebellion

Weblogs, writes technology expert Rebecca Blood, are "the mavericks of the online world ... beholden to no one, weblogs point to, comment on and spread information according to their own quirky criteria." As the ultimate form of decentralized media, the weblog's greatest strength is its "uncensored, unmedi-ated, uncontrolled voice" (114). During the formative phase of the blogging era (1995-1999), maintaining a weblog required specialized software or considerable technical skill. Technology reporter Roger Yin estimates that prior to the end of 1999—when the first user-friendly blog authoring application was released—the massive information stream referred to as "the blogosphere" consisted of fewer than 100 hand-crafted web sites ("Blogging On"). In the US, public interest in personal and political blogging intensified during the 2000 elections, but several more years passed before the blogging revolution rolled out in earnest. (According to an analysis by Technorati's David Sifry, the blogosphere grew from 4 million blogs to over 57 million between October, 2004 and October, 2006.)[7] "Some observers have suggested that blogging is nothing more that the next step in a burgeoning culture of narcissism and exhibitionism," write Amanda Lenhart and Susannah Fox of the Internet and American Life Project. "But others contend that blogging promises a democratization of voices that can now bypass the institutional gatekeepers of mainstream media" and will reshape "the future of civic and political discourse" (1).

While no reliable estimates of the current number of motherhood blogs exist, a growing number of middle-class moms are setting up personal outposts in the blogosphere. While accessibility, ease of use, and affordability have definitely stimulated the blogging mom trend—which is to say, *we blog because we can*—Lenhart and Fox found that the majority of bloggers use their blogs as an outlet for creative self-expression and to share personal stories (8).

At first blush, mothers—who are known to take a dim view of public scrutiny of their parenting skills and personal habits—appear to be a poor fit for the wild and woolly culture of the blogosphere, where warts-and-all self-disclosure is celebrated as an art form. However, mothers may opt for anonymity—Lenhart and Fox report that more than half of all US bloggers use a pseudonym (10)—and the opportunity to create a distinctive online persona and relieve the social invisibility of motherhood may trump concerns about privacy. Mothers also use their blogs to sabotage the stodgy norms of maternal propriety, and an especially popular "clique" of mom bloggers has risen from this group. As technical writer and blogger Asha Dornfest remarks, "Mother-written weblogs are as diverse as the women who write them":

> Some offer a window into the writer's domestic life, reality TV-style. Others are more literary or philosophical, musing on current events and social trends as they apply to motherhood. Still others act as "release valves;" where mothers vent their frustrations in a public, but safely anonymous, forum…. Spend some time perusing the "A-list" mom blogs, however … and you'll begin to notice a surprisingly consistent tone. There's a certain prickliness, an attitude that says, "I'm a tough-talkin' mama. You got a problem with that?" ("The Blogging Mom Clique")

A casual survey of motherhood blogs suggests the average entry is rather prosaic. The typical mother blogger seems content to record the unexceptional events and observations she might share with trusted friends in the real world—a first-grader loses another tooth; a child is ill or uncooperative; toddlers cling and cry; the mother is moody or desperately sleep deprived; unwashed dishes and laundry multiply at exponential rates; another day did not go as planned. Although random reflections on the daily grind of mothering don't always amount to spellbinding reading, *Mother Shock* author Andrea Buchanan considers motherhood blogs a rich repository of maternal narrative:

> The word BLOG—it reminds of BLURT—and in fact, sometimes that's what these things turn out to be—snatches of conversation, quick transcripts of a person's day, a Bridget Jones-like tally of routine events, or even startlingly personal admissions— the kinds of revelations you might share with only very close friends. The real, gritty, funny, mundane, sometimes boring, sometimes riveting secret life of mothers is the one revealed in these mother's largely unfiltered voices…. These are

real mothers struggling to create a narrative out of the often disjointed, complex, and simultaneously occurring events of their lives. ("The Secret Lives of Mothers")

Others argue that mother bloggers' accounts of maternal experience are less sanitized and lie closer to the bone than the bland personal writing found in mainstream parenting fare. "Mother blogs are real, raw and authentic," writes Ann Douglas of The Mother of All Blogs. "Their content isn't sliced, diced, homogenized and filtered through the mainstream parenting media.... They reflect the reality—and the messiness—of real life, with kids. Hearing about the experiences of other parents can be tremendously affirming and empowering."

One of the defining functions of the weblog interface is the comment feature, which allows readers to add their observations, digs, or notes of support and appreciation in response to an entry, and for subsequent readers to review earlier comments and record their own reactions. On motherhood blogs, the comment function enables bloggers to identify and interact with readers, and readers to "see" who else is among the loyal fan base of a specific blog. The comment feature also serves as a de facto discussion forum where readers and bloggers engage in extended conversations or disagreements. Bloggers Cooper Munroe ("Mombloggers, Unite!") and Andrea Gordon ("Moms find a safety net") suggest opportunities for social networking and support are often key factors in mothers' commitment to blogging, and high-profile mama bloggers such as Ayelet Waldman ("Living out loud—online") and Heather Armstrong have credited blogging with saving their lives and sanity (David Hochman, "Mommy (and me)").

The sense of intimacy cultivated in the maternal blogosphere is somewhat illusory, however, since most mother bloggers are cognizant that their online disclosures have repercussions IRL ("in real life"). In addition to writing under a full or partial pseudonym, mothers protect their privacy by withholding personal information and muting self-revelations that might strain relationships with friends and family members. Maternal bloggers may boldly chronicle their real stories for the all the world to read, but they are not divulging the complete, unexpurgated story—only selective parts of it. As social researcher Danah Boyd explains, the key practice of online social networks "is that you have to write yourself into being." She describes the process of composing an online identity as "a performance.... And in that performance some things get magnified" (Kate Sheppard, "Networked").

Nor is the burgeoning "momosphere" free of status-seekers, professional jealousies, or opportunists who see blogging as a stepping stone to more lucrative pursuits. As Dornfest suggests, rather than being a great leveler, the blogosphere tends to breed cults of personality. While mothers may turn to weblogs to increase their sense of visibility, some blogging moms are more visible than others—and only a handful of motherhood blogs attract the high-volume traffic and minor celebrity bestowed on top-ranking bloggers in other categories. "Parents who are technologically savvy and who have time to stay on top of the latest blogging innovations are more likely to make their voices heard online," notes Ann Douglas. "The growing emphasis on blog traffic and blog links...has led to unhealthy competition amongst the very people who should be providing one another with support." In "Mothering in the Age of the Blog," Douglas concurs with Dornfest's observation that, "Highly controversial posts by high-profile bloggers" command the most traffic, drowning out the voices of new and little-known bloggers who may have something equally witty or thought-provoking to say. She adds that mother bloggers are not above "cyber-bullying" to discourage the competition:

> The blogging environment is ideally designed for "girl bully" techniques—relational exclusion. "I won't add your link to my blog." "You can't be part of my group blog...." "I have way more incoming links than you do." "I have more blog awards than you do." "Have you heard what people are really saying about you? Here's the link. I thought you should know...."

It's tempting to compare the emerging status dynamics of the maternal blogosphere to the internal tensions and infighting that disrupted women's liberation groups in the 1970s (which Susan Brownmiller describes in painful detail in her snarky memoir, *In Our Time*). Although the blogging mama community lacks the rigorous doctrine and radical fervor that nourished the confrontational culture of the women's liberation movement, an influential group of mother bloggers echo radical feminist idealism when they envision their project as a non-exclusive, non-hierarchical, woman-centered realm where all contributions have equal value, every voice is amplified, and power resides in the collective.

Like members of feminist consciousness-raising groups, denizens of the momosphere place a high value on authenticity and self-expression, and believe women's private experiences and recurring frustrations—no matter how ordinary—have special meaning and require attention. Unfortunately, this outlook tends to elide the critical link between privilege and visibility. While the rise of the blogosphere has opened new opportunities for information sharing, community building, and self-assertion for internet users, it has also spawned a new category of social exclusion for non-blogging, non-wired, and non-computer literate women.

As was true for liberation feminists, third-wave mother bloggers are a subgroup of a subset of women, and their interpretations of their experiences, feelings, and problems are rooted in their social location. But the most unexpected parallel between second-wave feminists and third-wave mother bloggers is the accusation that some women are exploiting the strengths and vulnerabilities of the collective project to increase their personal status.

Blurring the Personal and Political

The central question raised by the maternal blogging phenomenon—and one that is impossible to answer at this time—is whether blogging produces a closed-circuit of self-absorption among its practitioners, or whether it changes the way women think about the social and political context of their lives. Some mother bloggers are deeply aware of systemic factors that disproportionately disadvantage women who mother, and their comments and critiques are incisive and inspiring. But whether their words move readers to see their own situation in a new light or simply attract a like-minded audience is difficult to assess.

A far greater proportion of mother bloggers write eloquently about the daily pressures of mothering, particularly the weight of unrealistic expectations and the frustration of being invisible, overburdened, and unsupported in their caring roles. But most mom bloggers never take the crucial step of politicizing the personal. As author Faulkner Fox observes, consistently recording the disturbances and discontents of motherhood is not enough to transform society—even when done conspicuously, and en masse. Nor is it enough to be contrarian and provocative for the sake of style. As Andrea Buchanan remarks in her essay "The Escalation of Cool," "You'd think all this shocking talk of the 'real' face of motherhood would give us more options, but I posit that it hasn't."

For memoir writing to have social impact, Fox suggests—and memoir writing is what the majority of mother bloggers are engaged in, although in a highly ephemeral and serialized form—it must be artfully written, emotionally compelling, *and* raise questions that force readers to "think structurally." While the narrative texts of maternal blogs may serve a therapeutic purpose by normalizing maternal imperfection and shattering the myth of maternal bliss, bloggers who routinely address the structural context of motherhood are the exception rather than the rule.

"A Web Site is Not a Social Movement"

Rather than mounting a strategic assault on the patriarchal institution of motherhood, mother bloggers are staging a cultural rebellion by refusing to wear the repressive "mask of motherhood." According to sociologist Susan Maushart, the mask of motherhood "minimizes the enormity of women's work" and "keeps women silent about what they feel and suspicious of what they know" (2). Abandoning the mask of motherhood is not a trivial exercise, but it mainly benefits those who actively participate in it. Blog writers and blog readers remain a minority among women who use the internet, and a significant minority of mothers overall.[8]

From a communication standpoint, reliance on reciprocal linking (blogging mothers increase their readership and ranking by linking to other motherhood and parenting blogs) produces a self-referential circuit rather than a hub where information flows outward in all directions, undermining the capacity of motherhood blogs to function as a forum for "shouting out" or speaking truth to power. ("Power," generally speaking, is unlikely to sift through the cacophony of the maternal blogosphere to hear out its detractors.) Although the revolutionary implications of mothers claiming public space to share their secrets and stories should not be underestimated, in practice what happens in the momosphere stays in the momosphere.

Third-wave mothers are the first generation of mothering women to benefit from—and feel the pressures of—the mainstreaming of online life. Whether they are consumers and creators of internet content or members of excluded communities, the experiences, opportunities, and expectations of contemporary mothers are shaped by their level of immersion in online culture and their ability to access digital information on demand. Mothers, in turn, shape the internet with their online activities. While mothers claiming the right to online space has political overtones, in practice the majority of mothers who actively contribute to online culture—particularly those who inhabit the maternal blogosphere—do not stray far from conventional formulas of maternal self-representation. Although they may ruthlessly record their flaws and failures, blogging mamas write almost exclusively about their lives in relationship to their children, and rarely about their lives as women situated in a sexist culture. The alternative mothers' media is more sensitive to social context, but motivating readers to close the gap between ideas and action will almost certainly require breaking out of the digital mode. As one observer remarked dryly, "A web site is not a [social] movement" (Glaser, "The Future of Feminism").

In digital culture, there is a tendency to confuse revolutionary *forms* with revolutionary *acts*. Our optimism that new technologies will render old social arrangements obsolete in a generation or two is not substantiated by history, and mothers and others who think about social change must be cautious about putting too many eggs in the virtual basket. The rapid assimilation of the internet into everyday life has occurred precisely because it *did not* require a radical redistribution of power or the reorganization of social relations—which may explain why mothers in the digital age have resorted to similar strategies, and have encountered similar setbacks, as earlier generations of mothers who resisted the silencing of women's voices.

[1]In 1995, less than one-quarter of US adults were internet users and the online population was predominantly male. By early 2006, 74 percent of US men and 71 percent of US women were spending time online, up from 49 and 44 percent in 2000. Among American women who use the internet, three out of five go online at least once a day (Fallows 2-3).

[2]Of course, I was not then, and am not now, an "average" member of the online community. Although my general demographic profile is very much typical for women internet users, I'm considered both a "high frequency user" and an "early adopter" (see John Horrigan, *A Typology of Information and Communication Technology Users*, Pew Internet and American Life Project, 6 May 2007).

[3]Primary online behaviors are nearly identical across gender lines—predominant

activities include sending email, using search tools, and gathering information related to personal hobbies or travel destinations—but women are more likely than men to look for health and medical information or seek support for personal problems online (Fallows 11-12).

[4]Women's internet use increases with education and household income: 89 percent of women with a four-year or advanced degree spend time online, compared to 56 percent of women with only high school education. Ninety-five percent of women living in households with annual incomes over $75,000 are 'net-goers, compared to 76 percent of women with household incomes between $30,000 and $50,000. Married women are more likely to be internet users than non-married women (75 versus 56 percent) (Fallows 2-3).

[5]Just 14 percent of US women who use the internet have ever created content for the internet, such as "helping build a web site, creating an online diary, or posting your thoughts on an online bulletin board or other online community" (n.b.: this figure represents over ten million women). Only eight percent of women who spend time online have ever created a blog, and just ten percent participate in social networking sites such as Friendster and MySpace.com (Pew Internet and American Life Project, "Usage Over Time").

[6]Any discussion of the emergence of the progressive/alternative mothers' media would be incomplete without a reference to the award-winning quarterly, *Brain, Child: The Magazine for Thinking Mothers*, founded in 1999 by co-editors Jennifer Niesslein and Stephanie Wilkinson (first edition: March 2000). Although *Brain, Child* has a companion web site, it is first and foremost a print publication.

[7]Experts report that a high proportion of blogs (approximately 45 percent) have a life span of less than three months. Forty-seven percent of US bloggers post material to their blogs "every few weeks" or less often, and only 13 percent post daily or more frequently (Lenhart and Fox 12).

[8]In 2006, fewer than eight percent of women in the connected population had ever created a blog. However, blog readership among women is on the rise. In February 2006, 35 percent of female internet users reported that they had ever read a blog—up from 25 percent in October 2005. (Pew Internet and American Life Project, "Usage Over Time" [table]).

Works Cited

Barker, Olivia. "Mommy Hottest." 26 Jan. 2005. *USA Today* 19 Nov. 2006 <http://www.usatoday.com/life/lifestyle/2005-01-26-hotmoms_x.htm>.

Blood, Rebecca. "Weblogs Ethics." *The Weblog Handbook: Practical Advice on Creating and Maintaining Your Blog.* Cambridge, MA: Perseus, 2002.

Brownmiller, Susan. *In Our Time: Memoir of a Revolution.* New York: Dial, 1999.

Buchanan, Andrea. *Mother Shock: Loving Every (Other) Minute of It.* Emeryville, CA: Seal, 2003.

Buchanan, Andrea. "The Escalation of Cool" [blog entry]. 6 Nov. 2006.

Mother Shock Blog. 8 Nov. 2006 <http://www.mothershock.com/blog/archives/2006/11/the_escalation.html>.

Buchanan, Andrea. "The Secret Life of Mothers: Maternal Narrative, Momoirs, and the Rise of the Blog" [blog entry]. 16 June 2005. Mother Shock Blog. 7 Nov. 2006 <http://www.mothershock.com/blog/archives/2005/06/blogher_confere.html>.

Cornell, Drucilla. *Freedom, Sex, and Equality*. Princeton, New Jersey: Princeton University Press, 1998.

Dornfest, Asha. "The Blogging Mom Clique: Anyone Can Join." Mothersmovement.org. Feb. 2006. The Mothers Movement Online. 7 Nov. 2006 <http://www.mothersmovement.org/features/06/02/blogging_mom_clique.html>.

Douglas, Ann. "Mothering in the Age of the Blog" [blog entry]. 28 Oct. 2006. The Mother of All Blogs. 7 Nov. 2006 <http://www.parentinglibrary.com/articles/motheringintheageoftheblog.pdf>

Douglas, Susan and Meredith Michaels. *The Mommy Myth: The Idealization of Motherhood and How It Has Undermined Women*. New York: Free, 2004.

Fallows. Deborah. *How Men and Women Use the Internet*. Pewinternet.org. 28 Dec. 2005. Pew Internet and American Life Project. 3 Oct. 2006 <http://www.pewinternet.org/pdfs/PIP_Women_and_Men_online.pdf.>.

Fox, Faulkner. Keynote address: "Personal and Political—the Mothering Memoir as Example." Paper presented at the 10th Annual Conference of the Association for Research on Mothering, Toronto, Ontario. 29 Oct. 2006.

GirlMom. 6 Oct. 2006 <http://www.girl-mom.com>.

Glaser, Sarah. "The Future of Feminism." *Congressional Quarterly Researcher* 16 (14 April 2006): 313-335.

Gordon, Andrea. "Moms find a safety net." *Toronto Star* 17 Dec 2005: L1.

Hip Mama. 6 Oct. 2006 <http://www.hipmama.com>.

Hochman, David. "Mommy (and Me)." *The New York Times* 30 Jan 2005, Sunday Styles 1-6.

Jayson, Sharon. "Hip, Happy Housewives." *USA Today* 2 Feb. 2005: D8.

Lenhart, Amanda and Susannah Fox. *Bloggers: A portrait of the internet's new story tellers*. Pewinternet.org. 19 July 2006. Pew Internet and American Life Project. 7 Oct. 2006: <htcp://www.pewinternet.org/pdfs/PIP%20Bloggers%20Report%20July%2019%202006.pdf>.

Mamaphonic. 6 Oct. 2006 <http://www.mamaphonic.com>.

Mamazine. 6 Oct. 2006 <http://mamazine.com>.

Maushart, Susan. *The Mask of Motherhood*. New York: Penguin, 2000.

Mommy, Too! 6 Oct. 2006 <http://www.mommytoo.com>.

The Mothers Movement Online. 6 Oct. 2006 <http://www.mothersmovement.org>.

Mothers Who Think. 1997 Archive. Salon. 8 Oct. 2006 <http://www.salon.com/archives/1997/mwt_feature.html>.

Munroe, Cooper. "Mombloggers, Unite!." *Pittsburgh Post Gazette* 24 Jul. 2005. *Pittsburgh Post Gazette*. 22 Nov. 2006 < http://www.post-gazette.com/pg/05205/542392.stm>.

Peri, Camille and Kate Moses. *Because I Said So: 33 Mothers Write About Children, Sex, Men, Aging, Faith, Race and Themselves*. New York: Harper, 2005.

Pew Internet and American Life Project. "Usage Over Time" Mar-00 to Feb-Apr-06 [spreadsheet: UsageOverTime.xls]. 7 Oct. 2006 <http://www.pewinternet. org/trends.asp#usage>.

Pew Research Center. "The Mainstreaming of Online Life." *Trends 2005*. Washington, DC: Pew Research Center, Dec. 2005. 56-69. 3 Oct. 2006 <http://www. pewinternet.org/pdfs/Internet_Status_2005.pdf>.

Sheppard, Kate. "Networked." Wiretapmag.org. 11 Jan. 2007. *Wire Tap Magazine*. 3 Feb. 2007 <http://www.wiretapmag.org/stories/42930/>.

Sifry, David. "State of the Blogosphere, February 2006 Part 1: On Blogosphere growth." Technorati.com. 6 Feb. 2006. Technorati. 6 Nov. 2006 <http://technorati.com/weblog/2006/02/81.html>.

Sifry, David. "State of the Blogosphere, October, 2006." Technorati.com. 6 Oct. 2006. Technorati. 6 Nov. 2006 <http://technorati.com/weblog/2006/11/161. html>.

Stadtman Tucker, Judith. "Girls Rule." Cybermommy.com. Feb./Mar. 1999. Cybermommy. 9 Feb. 2007 <http://www.cybermommy.com/Commentary/ Commentary1.0/commentary1.0.html>.

Turkle, Sherry. "Who Am We." Wired.com. Jan. 1996. *Wired Magazine,* 4.01. 18 Oct. 06 <http://www.wired.com/wired/archive/4.01/turkle.html>.

Waldman, Ayelet. "Living out loud—online." Salon.com. 14 Mar. 2005. Salon. 7 Nov. 2006 <http://dir.salon.com/story/mwt/col/waldman/2005/03/14/blog/ index.html>.

Wilgoren, Jody, and Gretchen Ruethling. "At Center of a Clash, Rowdy Children in Coffee Shops." *New York Times* 9 Nov. 2005: A14.

Yim, Roger. "Blogging On: Web loggers bare their souls—and reading lists—to the Internet." *San Francisco Chronicle* 28 Feb. 2001: E1.

About the Contributors

Akosua Adomako Ampofo is an associate professor at the Institute of African Studies, and Head of the Centre for Gender Studies and Advocacy (CEGENSA) at the University of Ghana. She has written and published on both gender and mothering in Africa, and is an international consultant and an activist in Ghana. She writes as both a mother and daughter, and can be reached at <adomako@gmail.com> and <adomako@ug.edu.gh>.

Lorin Basden Arnold has experienced eating disorder for over two and a half decades, and feminism and motherhood for almost twenty years. She is a mother of six children, a feminist, a spouse, a family communication scholar, and a professor and department chair of Communication Studies at Rowan University. She can be reached at <arnold@rowan.edu>.

Anca N. Birzescu was born and raised in Bucharest, Romania. Her research areas include, among others, representation of women in South Eastern European media, and women intellectuals in the region. Her current doctoral research focuses on the Roma Diaspora's online identity, and the potential of European Union policy to enhance Roma rights. She can be reached at <a_birzescu@yahoo.com>.

Rachel Epp Buller is (in no particular order) a feminist-mother-art historian-printmaker-freelance writer-curator-editor who aims to balance child-rearing and creativity, and maintain a professional identity in the invisible world of the stay-at-home mom. The daily juggling act has gradually become more manageable and is, usually, rewarding. She can be reached at <rebuller@ddtr.net>.

Kelly A. Dorgan is an associate professor at East Tennessee State University. She was raised in central Appalachia, a region that has influenced much of her writing and research. She is a new—and thoroughly humbled—mother of one boy and a passionate researcher of communication issues as they intersect with health, sexuality, and cross-cultural interactions. She can be reached at <dorgan@etsu.edu>.

Susan Driver bridges queer and feminist frameworks in her work. She has just published a book titled *Queer Girls and Popular Culture* (Peter Lang 2007), and is editing a collection titled *Queer Youth Cultures* (SUNY Press). She is an assistant professor at York University. She also is a new parent along with her trans-butch partner, Carrie. She can be reached at <sdriver@rogers.com>.

Andrea Fechner knows intimately, from her own efforts to grow her family, the complexities of mothering intersecting with race, adoption, and special needs. She teaches Women's Studies, drawing from her background in sociology and gender studies. She can be reached at <andreafechner@hotmail.com>.

S. Alease Ferguson is an African American therapist. Dr. Ferguson is the Director of Family to Family Systems of Care Programming for the Cleveland Urban Minority Alcoholism and Drug Abuse Outreach Program (UMADAOP). Her daily practice is dedicated to family uplift, and improving the parental leadership and nurturing capacities of at-risk parents involved in the child welfare system. She can be reached at <kenferguson7@aol.com>.

Marlene Fine is a white lesbian woman who is married to her partner of 30 years, with whom she adopted and raised since infancy two African American boys, who are now 17 and 19 years old. She has published on feminism, gender, multiculturalism, and their intersections. She can be reached at <fine@simmons.edu>.

Heather Hewett is an essayist, literary critic, and mother who writes frequently about contemporary world literature, motherhood/mothering, and feminism. Her articles, essays, and reviews have been published in a wide range of mainstream, feminist, and academic publications. She is an assistant professor of English at SUNY-New Paltz, where she also coordinates the Women's Studies Program. She can be reached at <hewetth@newpaltz.edu>.

Toni King is an African American therapist who works with women to address the contemporary effects of race, class, and gender oppression. She is an associate professor of Black Studies and Women's Studies at Denison University. Her scholarship and service focus on women's leadership development—with particular attention to creating spaces, relationships, and methods for psychological healing. She can be reached at <kingt@denison.edu>.

Amber Kinser is a white, heterosexual, working-class-rooted, middle-class feminist who identifies as a mid-waver. She is a teacher, a partner and a mother who is raising her daughter and son in a blended family in the U.S. Mountain South. She writes largely about complexities and contradictions in feminist parenting, and also directs the Women's Studies Program at East Tennessee State University. She can be reached at <kinsera@etsu.edu>. She is the author of the upcoming book, *Motherhood and Feminism* (Seal Press).

Lara Lengel has mothered her children in Europe, Asia, and the US. She has volunteered on feminist advocacy projects ranging from increasing technology access for women in the Middle East and North Africa (MENA), to advising new mothers on breastfeeding at Chelsea Westminster Hospital in London, England where her children were born. Her publications focus on MENA women, gender and performance studies, and feminist ethnography. She can be reached at <lengell@bgsu.edu>.

Larissa M. Mercado-López the mother of three young daughters, a wife, a university instructor, and a Chicana doctoral candidate in the English/Latina literature program at the University of Texas at San Antonio. She is an advocate for mothers-of-color on campus and in the community, and is currently writing her dissertation on mystiza maternal bodies, epistemology, and maternal facultad. She can be reached at <lari2121@hotmail.com>.

Jennifer Minda writes from the perspective of a feminist domestic worker, drawing from her ten years' experience caring for children in the U.S. and Britain, and from her experience interacting with other caregivers during her time living and working abroad in London, England, and Shanghai, China. She is currently researching the development of a Domestic Worker Bill of Rights to recognize the efforts of domestic workers. She can be reached at <jenniferlminda@yahoo. com>.

Wendy Jones Nakanishi, an American, has been resident in Japan for the past 23 years after living and/or studying in the U.S., England, Scotland, France, and Holland. She teaches in the Department of Language and Culture at Shikoku Gakuin University. She is married to a farmer and has three sons. Her research interests and publications include eighteenth-century English literature, contemporary Japanese literature, and 'creative writing,' largely concerned with stories about her life in Japan. She can be reached at <wendy@sg-u.ac.jp>.

D. Lynn O'Brien Hallstein is an assistant professor of rhetoric at Boston University. She has published in U.S. academic forums, focusing on a variety of issues within feminist theory and more recently on past and contemporary feminist approaches to understanding motherhood and mothering. She draws on her own cross-cultural experiences mothering her two boys in Switzerland. She can be reached at <lhallst@bu.edu>.

Maura Ryan is a lesbian, a feminist, a teacher, an activist, and a future mother. Since coming out as a lesbian at 14 she has experienced various forms of community organizing from presiding as a rural GLBT community center president to being a lesbian avenger; she is an avid feminist and anti-racist pedagogue who has published in popular and academic forums. She can be reached at <mryan@ ufl.edu>.

Judith Stadtman Tucker is a writer, activist, and the founder and editor of the Mothers Movement Online (www.mothersmovement.org). Her essays on feminism, maternal activism, and public policy have appeared in academic anthologies, feminist periodicals, and various online publications. She can be reached at <editor@mothersmovement.org>.

Laura Camille Tuley is an instructor in English and Women's Studies at the University of New Orleans. She received her Ph.D. in Comparative Literature at SUNY-Binghamton in 1998. Tuley has written on feminist theory, aesthetics and culture, has a regular column on mothering in *Mamazine,* and is a co-editor of the forthcoming volume *Mother Knows Best: Talking Back to the Experts* by Demeter Press. She can be reached at <ltuley@uno.edu>.